Global Inequalities in World-Systems Perspective

During its 500-year history, the modern world-system has seen several shifts in hegemony. Yet, since the decline of the U.S. in the 1970s, no single core power has attained a hegemonic position in an increasingly polarized world. As income inequalities have become more pronounced in core countries, especially in the U.S. and the U.K., global inequalities emerged as a 'new' topic of social scientific scholarship, ignoring the constant move toward polarization that has been characteristic of the entire modern world-system. At the same time, the rise of new states (most notably, the BRICS) and the relative economic growth of particular regions (especially East Asia) have prompted speculations about the next hegemon that largely disregard both the longue durée of hegemonic shifts and the constraints that regional differentiations place on the concentration of capital and geopolitical power in one location. Authors in this book place the issue of rising inequalities at the center of their analyses. They explore the concept and reality of semiperipheries in the twenty-first century world-system, the role of the state and of transnational migration in current patterns of global stratification, types of catching-up development and new spatial configurations of inequality in Europe's Eastern periphery as well as the prospects for the Global Left in the new systemic order. The book links novel theoretical debates on the rise of global inequalities to methodologically innovative approaches to the urgent task of addressing them.

Manuela Boatcă is professor of sociology and head of the School of the Global Studies Programme at the Albert-Ludwigs University of Freiburg, Germany. Her work involves world-systems analysis, postcolonial and decolonial perspectives, gender in modernity/coloniality and the geopolitics of knowledge production in Eastern Europe and Latin America. She is author of *Global Inequalities beyond Occidentalism* (Routledge 2016) and co-editor (with Vilna Bashi Treitler) of 'Dynamics of Inequalities in a Global Perspective', *Current Sociology* monograph issue 64 (2), March 2016.

Andrea Komlosy is professor at the Institute for Economic and Social History, University of Vienna, Austria, where she is coordinating the Global History and Global Studies programs. She has published on labor, migration, borders and uneven development on a regional, a European and a global scale, recently: 'Centers and Peripheries revisited', *Review* Fernand Braudel Center Special Issue XXXVI, 3–4 (2013), ed. by Andrea Komlosy and Klemens Kaps; *Work: The Last 1000 Years* (Verso 2018).

Hans-Heinrich Nolte is professor emeritus for History of Eastern Europe at the University of Hannover. He published on religious and social history of Early Modern Eurasia, Internal peripheries in Europe, Second World War, esp. Holocaust and slave-labor in Eastern Europe, structure and development of Soviet socialism and on the place of Russia and Eurasia in the World-System.

Economic inequality is a leading contributor to today's escalating global tensions and uncertainty and thus the most urgent social issue of our time. This timely and pathbreaking collection offers a wealth of conceptual and methodological innovations to advance new understandings of inequality and the contemporary crises of global capitalism. Leading scholars from several countries offer diverse perspectives and insights that will advance our thinking about today's global predicament and how social science can help us both understand and act to address it.

—**Jackie Smith**, Professor of Sociology, University of Pittsburgh and editor Journal of World-Systems Research

How does one comprehend contemporary global inequalities? Using the modern world-system perspective this book brings together some innovative essays that explore the way inequalities are being structured in the semi-peripheries through state interventions and migration patterns. A must read for those interested in global stratification patterns.

—**Sujata Patel**, President of the Indian Sociological Society, and Professor of Sociology, University of Hyderabad.

This book contains valuable reviews of the research literature on topics that are central to the world-systems perspective as well as new contributions that extend the framework to issues that have emerged from recent developments in the story of the world. Global inequalities continue to generate both progressive and reactionary social movements and the trajectory of the 21st century could either become another "age of extremes" or it could see the birth of a collectively rational and democratic global commonwealth. The chapters in this book contribute to this second possibility.

—**Christopher Chase-Dunn**, Institute for Research on World-Systems, University of California-Riverside

Inequality is a burning problem of the early-21st century world that is fueling revolts and influencing the future. There are several contradictory regional trends today from decreasing to increasing inequalities, the catching-up of East Asia and some of the former European peripheral regions (Ireland, Finland, Spain) to the 'third-worldization' of Russia, Ukraine, Moldova and other Soviet successor states. Deep factual analysis and theoretical debates are needed for a good understanding. This volume is an important contribution for a better understanding.

—**Ivan Berend**, Professor Emeritus, University of California, Los Angeles (U.C.L.A)

GLOBAL INEQUALITIES IN WORLD-SYSTEMS PERSPECTIVE

THEORETICAL DEBATES AND METHODOLOGICAL INNOVATIONS

edited by
*Manuela Boatcă, Andrea Komlosy,
and Hans-Heinrich Nolte*

Political Economy of the World-System Annuals, Volume XXXIX
Immanuel Wallerstein, Series Editor

NEW YORK AND LONDON

First published 2018
by Routledge
711 Third Avenue, New York, NY 10017

and by Routledge
2 Park Square, Milton Park, Abingdon, Oxon, OX14 4RN

Routledge is an imprint of the Taylor & Francis Group, an informa business

© 2018 Taylor & Francis

The right of Manuela Boatcă, Andrea Komlosy, and Hans-Heinrich Nolte to be identified as the authors of the editorial material, and of the authors for their individual chapters, has been asserted in accordance with sections 77 and 78 of the Copyright, Designs and Patents Act 1988.

All rights reserved. No part of this book may be reprinted or reproduced or utilised in any form or by any electronic, mechanical, or other means, now known or hereafter invented, including photocopying and recording, or in any information storage or retrieval system, without permission in writing from the publishers.

Trademark notice: Product or corporate names may be trademarks or registered trademarks, and are used only for identification and explanation without intent to infringe.

Library of Congress Cataloging-in-Publication Data
A catalog record for this book has been requested

ISBN: 978-1-138-10677-2 (hbk)
ISBN: 978-1-138-10678-9 (pbk)
ISBN: 978-1-315-10139-2 (ebk)

Typeset in Adobe Garamond
by Apex CoVantage, LLC

This book had its origin in the 39th annual meeting of the *Political Economy of the World-System*, which was held in 2015 in Berlin.

CONTENTS

Introduction   *ix*
    Manuela Boatcă, Andrea Komlosy,
    Hans-Heinrich Nolte

PART I
Semiperipheries in the World-System   1

1   World-System Zones in the 21st Century:
        Beyond Core and Periphery, Who Fits Where?   3
    David A. Smith

2   World-Systems Analysis and Political Economy   18
    Hartmut Elsenhans

3   The Semiperipheral Abandonat and the Unmaking of
        the Capitalist Geoculture   33
    Antonio Gelis-Filho

PART II
Global Stratification and the State   47

4   Statehood at the End of the Rainbow? Agonistics of
        Potentiality in the World-System   49
    Juho T. Korhonen

5   Migration as a Response to Global Inequality   63
    Vilna Bashi Treitler

6   Long Waves and Changes in the Structure of the Capitalist
        World System   78
    Zenonas Norkus

viii *Contents*

7 "Creative Destruction" From a World-Systems Perspective:
   Billionaires and the Great Recession of 2008   94
   Scott Albrecht and Roberto Patricio Korzeniewicz

PART III
Developments on and From Europe's Eastern Periphery   **117**

8 1918–1945–1989: Political Shifts in Eastern Europe and
   Three Logics of Catch-up Development in Poland   119
   Dariusz Adamczyk

9 Debt-Ridden Development on Europe's Eastern Periphery   131
   Tamás Gerőcs and András Pinkasz

10 New Configurations of Inequality and Glam-Capitalism
   Structures   154
   Dmitry Ivanov

PART IV
Future Prospects   **173**

11 Prospects for the World Left   175
   Immanuel Wallerstein

Contributors   193

Political Economy of the World-System Annuals Series   197

Index   199

INTRODUCTION

In March 2015, we had the privilege of hosting the 39th Annual Conference on the Political Economy of the World-System of the American Sociological Association at the Institute for Latin American Studies of the Freie Universität Berlin. The conference addressed the theme of "Global Inequalities: Hegemonic Shifts and Regional Differentiations", drawing attention to how the *longue durée* shapes contemporary struggles for hegemony. More than 40 researchers from all five continents presented and discussed research on the conference theme. To help readers appreciate the context of the discussions that have shaped the following articles, we provide excerpts from the texts used as an organizing framework for the conference:

During its 500-year history, the modern world-system has seen several shifts in hegemony. Since the decline of the U.S. in the 1970s, however, no single core power has attained a hegemonic position, such that the twenty-first century world-system, while not dominated by one hegemon, has continued to move toward increasing polarization. As income inequalities have become more pronounced in core countries, especially the former hegemons, the U.S. and the U.K., global inequalities emerged as a "new" topic of social scientific scholarship, thus ignoring the constant move toward polarization that has been characteristic of the entire modern world-system. At the same time, the rise of new states (most notably, the BRICS) and the relative economic growth of particular regions (especially East Asia) have prompted speculations about the next hegemon that largely disregard both the *longue durée* of hegemonic shifts and the constraints that regional differentiations place on the concentration of capital and geopolitical power in one location.

As conference organizers, we sought to focus attention on the following questions related to historic and contemporary struggles and shifts in the world-system hegemony:

1. **Reconsidering Semi-peripheries: Evolutionary, Epistemic, or Anti-systemic Potential?** With the collapse of state socialism, the Eastern European and the former Soviet states have experienced a high degree of fragmentation and differentiation. Piecemeal integration into the

European Union for some states has been accompanied by "Third Worldization" (A.G. Frank). Does the building of the EU regional block play play an increasing role in peripheralizing new regions ("inner peripheries" of the European South, the Arab world)? Are the BRICS the new semiperipheries and, if so, is a new hegemonic shift to be expected from them?

2. **Latin America and Eastern Europe Facing the East Asian Challenge.** On the one hand, Latin America and Eastern Europe have been seen as the "first large-scale laboratories of underdevelopment" (H. Szlajfer) as well as to solutions for underdevelopment. On the other hand, Latin America and the Caribbean have long been the prime examples of "persistent inequality", frequently traced back to colonial rule, while Eastern Europe's inequality rates have risen considerably since the 1990s. In contrast, East Asia counts as a model for "growth with equity". How are such regional differentiations helpful in understanding overall system dynamics of inequality (re)production? Are these neat patterns blurred by the relative decline in inequality and poverty in parts of Latin America and Eastern Europe?

3. **Coloniality of power and the imperial difference.** Inequalities of race, ethnicity, gender, epistemic status and economic position put in place during colonial rule have largely translated into enduring inequalities in postcolonial times. While the corresponding term, "coloniality of power" (A. Quijano) has been coined in relation to colonized regions, especially Latin America, its workings are harder to pinpoint in the absence of former colonial rule in other parts of the world. Can we therefore speak of the "racialization" of Eastern Europe along the lines of a system-wide coloniality of power? Is "imperial difference" (W. Mignolo) in those regions never colonized by the Western core the counterpart of "colonial differences" put in place by European great powers' overseas colonialism? How do these different positions in the power hierarchies of the world-system translate into opportunities and disadvantages today?

4. **Migration as global social mobility.** Recent legal as well as world-systems scholarship has suggested that migration to wealthy regions is the most effective means of global social mobility for populations in most countries of the world, far surpassing the prospects awarded by a better education, a better job or one country's economic growth. Are there recognizable patterns for this reversal of the century-old trend of migration from the core to the periphery? Which sending and receiving regions are primarily involved? What are the main constraints on transnational migration as a form of social mobility?

Immanuel Wallerstein (Yale) led off discussions by reiterating his view that the imminent end of the world-system will offer the possibility of more freedom, equality and solidarity "in the spirit of Porto Alegre". In contrast, Salvatore Babones (Sydney) argued that the world is now governed and led by the American Empire. Andrea Komlosy (Vienna) highlighted the decline of U.S. hegemony, yet considered it probable that the system would be rejuvenated in the context of a stronger participation of the BRICS countries, which also might offer chances for more self-determination.[1]

Selected contributions to the conference are published in four different volumes.

The present volume 1 is dedicated to Global Inequalities in World-Systems Perspective and reunites the contributions which placed the issue of rising inequalities at the core of their analysis.

The first section is entitled "Semiperipheries in the World-System". In his chapter on world-system semiperipheries in the twenty-first century, David Smith (UC Irvine) inventories and critiques both attributional and relational measures of 40 years of research on world-system position. He argues that a network analytic approach is most satisfying, but only if it is theoretically informed, uses the most updated and complete data and employs state-of-the-art methodologies. Hartmut Elsenhans (Leipzig) instead contends that the concept of the semi-periphery is an ideological one, which basically defends Conservative Marxist mainstream growth theory and conservative mainstream modernization theory against the necessity of rising mass incomes as a condition for capitalist growth. Antonio Gelis-Filho (São Paulo) looks at semiperipheries through the lens of the abandonat, a loose semiperipheral social group that he views as an important representative of the core's geoculture in the semiperiphery, acting as "geocultural police". Gelis-Filho's thesis is that the abandonat's conservative stance, from a world-systemic point of view, has the potential of being an accelerating factor on the dismantling of the current world-system.

The second section is dedicated to "Global Stratification and the State". In it, Juho Korhonen (Providence) approaches the issue of statehood by means of his concept of agonistics of potentiality, that describes a particular tension of systemic crisis arising from a widening divide between world systematicity and state efficacy as well as from the knowledge(s) employed, successfully or unsuccessfully, to navigate that divide. Korhonen suggests that the concept helps us approach an on-going crisis as actuality rather than anomaly. The paper by Vilna Bashi Treitler (Santa Barbara) deals with migration as a response to global inequality. As such, it overviews findings from a transnational qualitative study of black Caribbean global migrant networks and subsequently offers an overview of network structures, processes and outcomes that directly attest to network members' quests to overcome their initial assignment in a racialized and economically unequal global hierarchy of peoples. The chapter by Zenonas Norkus (Vilnius) in turn argues that the number of intermediate (or semi-peripheral) structural positions in the capitalist world-economy grows with each new long economic cycle. Drawing upon the Weberian concepts of opportunity closure and usurpation as key mechanisms of class building, Norkus argues for the persistence of the divide between the core of the system and the "Rest", as well as for increasing internal differences within the "Rest". The paper by Roberto P. Korzeniewicz and Scott Albrecht (College Park) draws on an original source of data to argue that the rise and fall of billionaires allows us to identify and map key changes in the accumulation (and redistribution) of income and wealth across the world-economy, changes that have substantive implication for existing patterns of social stratification. Not only does data on billionaires provide a unique empirical basis for mapping sites of accumulation, but it also provides greater historical specificity to Joseph Schumpeter's concept of Creative Destruction.

The section dealing with "Developments on and from Europe's Eastern Periphery" starts with the paper by Dariusz Adamczyk (Hannover), which discusses three types of catch-up development in Poland, understood not only as determinants of world-system dynamics, but also as strategies characteristic in the respective specific historical phases. Adamczyk thereby shows how fundamental political shifts in the twentieth century impacted the strategies of catch-up development in Poland. The chapter by Tamás Geröcz and András Pinkas (Budapest) asks whether reindustrialization in Eastern Europe is a "catching up" model for Eastern European semi-peripheral states, and contends that the historical process of integration is highly determined by the access to technology and capital. The authors argue that analyzing Hungarian industrial and financial development demonstrates how the integration of this country into the international division of labor means a new version of dependency. The paper by Dmitry Ivanov (St. Petersburg) introduces the concept of glam capitalism in order to address how the spatial configuration of inequality is increasingly headed towards a transnational network of globality enclaves: the largest cities. Ivanov argues that the rising social significance of access to trendy goods creates a new configuration of inequality, as the traditional quantitative gap between "having more" and "having less" is combined with the temporal lag between "having now" and "having later".

The volume concludes with Immanuel Wallerstein's keynote address "Prospects for the World Left?" in which the longue durée of anti-systemic movements is subjected to detailed scrutiny. For Wallerstein, the net result of worldwide anti-systemic struggles is a divided Global Left. In the political struggle over the new systemic order it is trying to build, the Global Left is attempting to tilt the bifurcation in the direction of a relatively democratic, relatively egalitarian world-system (or world-systems).

Volume 2 is collecting research on World Regions, Migrations and Identities[2] and addresses the consequences of the rise in inequalities worldwide on the movement of people and on processes of identity-building.

Introduction xiii

In their opening article, Ramón Grosfoguel (University of California/ Berkeley) and Eric Mielants (Fairfield-University) start with the fact that, in the face of rapid changes in the world-economy, many people, especially people in the peripheries, resort to migration in order to make a living. In this context, in periods of economic upturn, racism is used to legitimate lower wages for racialized workers, while in periods of downturn, racism is used for expelling them from the labor force altogether. The authors discuss the differences between Europe and the U.S. and point to the relationship between racialization in the colonies and in Europe itself. In their conclusion, they call for a decolonization of enduring colonial structures of the core.

Christian Lekon (University of Lefke, Northern Cyprus) makes the point that the migrations of Hadhrami-people to many places around the Indian Ocean from Indonesia to Hyderabad and Hijaz to Tanzania may not be sufficiently explained in terms of World-System-Theory. He proposes to bring in categories developed by Anthony Giddens and offers a synthesis of Giddens and Wallerstein for further discussion.

Roberto Ortiz (University of Binghamton/NY) raises the question of what connection there was between the influx of oil rents into the capital market of semiperipheral countries and the crisis of "developmentalism" in Latin-America as well of the statist economy of the U.S.S.R. His comparisons of Mexico, Brazil and the U.S.S.R. are indeed pointing to desiderates in research on the role of semiperiphery in general or the BRICS-group in particular in the world-system.

Márton Hunyadi (Corvinus-University Budapest) presents interviews with Hungarian and Indonesian immigrants to the Netherlands, which he analyses using Mignolo's and Quijano's concept of "Coloniality of power". Especially telling are the hierarchies between different groups of immigrants.

Luigi Ferrara and Salvatore Villani (both University of Naples Federico II) present research on the economic impacts of migration on relations between regions and medium incomes. Their examples are Northern and Southern Italy. They offer data and cite research showing that immigration of skilled labor does reduce inequalities in the destination-countries, but also may contribute to the downturn of the sending ones. They put their findings into the frameworks of European and Italian law, but also into that of the developing citizenship assigned to regions.

Stanislav Holubec (Charles University Prague) offers an overview to the intellectual history of the former socialist states in Central and Eastern Europe concentrating on the question, which memories are fostered. One of his findings is, that mass crimes of western powers (for instance against indigenous populations in colonies) tend to be overlooked.

Volume 3 on Coloniality of Power and Hegemonic Shifts in the World-System[3] focuses on hegemonic shifts in the world-system, relating rise and

xiv *Introduction*

decline as well as attempting to catch up with the historical position of specific regions in the world-system.

The first pair of articles makes use of the concept of "Coloniality of power" in the context of Eastern Europe. Taking the example of the Habsburg province of Galicia in the eighteenth century, Klemens Kaps (University of Vienna) points to the double process of socio-economic peripheralization, going hand in hand with ascribing backwardness to the region and their inhabitants, as conceived by E. Said in "Orientalism". He argues that this legitimated the annexation and economic integration into an unequal division of labor. While Kaps focuses on Habsburg times, Agnes Gagyi (Working group for public sociology "Helyzet", Budapest) addresses post-socialist transformation in Hungary. There, the historical legacy of peripheralization has overshadowed debates about the appropriate way of catching up ever since. Today, Gagyi claims, both the liberal, Western-oriented factions and the conservative, national factions of the Hungarian political arena are caught in a vicious circle of a specific type of "Coloniality of power" that channels internal strategies of development into the external requirements of dependent accumulation.

The second pair of articles challenges the widespread assumption that the rise of the BRICS indicates a shift towards more global equality. Lindsay Jacobs and Ronan van Rossem (University of Ghent) present results of their network analysis, comparing BRICS states with the U.S. from 1965 to 2005. On the military level, the leading role of the U.S. is evident. On the economic level, the upward mobility of China comes at the expense of growing disparities between cores and peripheries world-wide. Their findings conform with the conclusions of Pedro Vieira and Helton Ricardo Ouriques (Santa Catarina University and USP Marília), who also stress the continuity of the global power system over structural change. Brazil's golden age under President Lula was based on the commodity boom, which allowed the government to finance social programs while satisfying the demands of the global monetary institutions. BRICS membership did not offer a way to overcome internal conflicts over distribution and external constraints imposed by global financial regimes.

The last articles in the issue share the observation that the stability of the world-system, and its capacity to overcome cyclical crisis, is likely to be over. They draw different conclusions, however. Leonardo Figuera Helland and Tom Lindgren (Westminster College Utah) present a radical critique of capitalist accumulation processes and the post-colonial elites who failed to reject the "Coloniality of power". Their article reflects indigenous and eco-feminist analyses and proposals of alternatives to the hegemonic model of growth. Andrea Komlosy (University of Vienna) is neither convinced of the inevitable collapse nor of the onset of a new imperial era under U.S. dominance. Today, we are witnessing both attempts by the U.S. to curb its demise and maintain the existing hegemonic regime and the rise of new hegemonic aspirants, including alliances from Europe to East Asia. Multiple crises and conflicts over succession might also generate chaos fueling the struggles of varied anti-systemic movements. In this respect, Komlosy discusses the options and probabilities of broad cooperation of different anti-systemic movements.

Volume 4,[4] Hans-Heinrich Noltes' Religions in World and Global History, has by further addenda grown too voluminous for the foregoing three collections and has been published separately. Nolte argues that religious history is underestimated. He proposes ten examples illustrating the role of religion in structuring the world-system, from the fight between the Pope and the Emperor of the "Holy Roman Empire" in the 12th century to the global expansion of the Orisha-Religion in our days.

All contributions to the four volumes emphasize the importance of historical legacies for understanding the present hegemonic shifts and regional differentiations. In spite of obvious signs of decline, the U.S. led Western alliance is defending its core position vis-à-vis ambitions of the semi-peripheral Global South for more participation: they rely on military supremacy, one (U.S. $) or two ($ and Euro) leading currencies, control of strategic companies and commodity chains as well as the (soft) and attractive power of the American/Western way of life. Coloniality of (U.S. and E.U.) power is overarching the entanglement and the acceleration of multiple crises and conflicts, giving way to a highly explosive, dangerous situation.

Nobody can predict the outcome of the present crisis: whether or not local military conflicts will develop into a global war, whether or not the environment will survive "green" restructuring and semiperipheral attempts at "catching up", whether or not we will face a new hegemon, an age of multipolarity or the rise of a more egalitarian post-growth society.

Manuela Boatcă (Freiburg), Andrea Komlosy (Vienna),
Hans-Heinrich Nolte (Hannover)

Notes

http://www.vgws.org/files/pews_tagungsbericht.pdf

1 For a report on the conference see www.vgws.org/Projekte/pews.tagungsbericht.pdf or http://geschichte-transnational.clio-online.net/tagungsberichte/id=5937

2 Nolte, Hans-Heinrich, Boatcă, Manuela and Andrea Komlosy, eds.: "World Regions, Migration and Identities", *Zur Kritik der Geschichtsschreibung*. Band 13, Gleichen: Musterschmidt-Verlag 2016.

3 Komlosy, Andrea, Boatcă, Manuela and Hans-Heinrich Nolte, eds.: "Coloniality of Power and Hegemonic Shifts in the World System", *Journal of World-System Research*, 22 (2), Special Issue, 2016. Online: http://jwsr.pitt.edu/

4 Nolte, Hans-Heinrich. 2015. *Religions in World- and Global History. A View from the German-language Discussion*, 69 S., Frankfurt usw. (Lang).

PART I

SEMIPERIPHERIES IN THE WORLD-SYSTEM

1

WORLD-SYSTEM ZONES IN THE 21ST CENTURY

BEYOND CORE AND PERIPHERY, WHO FITS WHERE?

David A. Smith

Understanding the world in terms of the rise and expansion of global capitalism over the past 500 or so years is, indubitably, the most important insight of world-system analysis (cf. Wallerstein 1974, 1979) and it led to a fundamental paradigm shift in the macro-sociology in the late twentieth century (away from developmentalist and modernization theory misconceptions of nation-centric social change). The political economy of the world-system (PEWS) perspective championed its own interpretation of crucial ideas like long historical cycles, incorporation of "external arenas," hegemonic succession, uneven development and unequal exchange, among others, and raised critical questions about the defining nature of capitalism, the rising power of transnational corporations, the role of states and warfare in a modern world-economy

4 *David A. Smith*

(Chase-Dunn 1989) and, whether what we now call "globalization" is new and novel or "in reality the swan song of our historical system" (Wallerstein 1998: 32).

One of the most familiar ideas from the world-system perspective is the notion of a core/semi-periphery/periphery hierarchy in the global division of labor that can help us understand the dynamics and contours of worldwide inequalities. Indeed, the idea of a "single ongoing division of labor . . . based on differential appropriation of surplus produced (such that) positions are hierarchically ordered, not just differentiated" (Evans 1979b: 15–16) is a key insight of world-system analysis. The argument is that the different "zones" of the world-system perform distinct functions in the international division of labor related to the degree of capital- versus labor-intensity of production process and/or the costs/remuneration for the commodities or goods produced in each area. Historically, core countries/regions pioneered the move into industrial production and remain primarily capital intensive, while peripheral countries/regions are primarily labor intensive and were incorporated into the world-economy as exporters of agricultural goods and raw materials. But, Wallerstein emphasizes, there is also a very distinctive stratum: the semiperiphery, which lies "between the core and periphery on a series of dimensions," but is more than just an in-between category since it "is a necessary structural element of the world-economy" (1974:349). Subsequent arguments claim that the semiperiphery is a both a particularly dynamic and volatile zone, a place where various sorts of innovation may occur (Boswell and Chase-Dunn 2000), where, we see the emergence of both potentially upwardly mobile "marcher states," but also the most potent "anti-systemic movements" (Chase-Dunn 2005), and, perhaps, even a place where future hegemonic power may gestate.

If semiperipheral status is so important, the challenge for social scientists becomes how to identify which countries or regions "fit." Presumably, those that are "in" will be likely to share common characteristics or follow similar dynamics of social change: Wallerstein tells us that "their internal politics and their social structure are distinctive" (1979: 97). In his encyclopedic historical volumes, explaining the history of the modern world-system, he often notes the emergence of semiperipheries (and their importance to overall global dynamics) (cf. Wallerstein 1974, 1980). This sort of logic, pushed back even further, characterizes efforts by Chase-Dunn and his colleagues to study the "upsweeps and collapses" of ancient empires over several thousand years (Inoue, Alvarez, Lawrence, Roberts, Anderson and Chase-Dunn 2012). But for those social scientists that are most interested in the contemporary period, we need some idea about how nations in the late twentieth century might be classified. In his essay in *The Capitalist World-Economy* on the topic, Wallerstein provides a list (presumably relevant in 1975 when the paper was written) that definitively includes Brazil, Mexico, Argentina, Venezuela, Algeria, Egypt, Saudi Arabia, Israel, Nigeria, Zaire, Turkey, Iran, India, Indonesia,

China, South Korea and Vietnam (as well as some countries in "the outer rim of Europe," "most of eastern Europe," and "the old white Commonwealth: Canada, Australia, South Africa") (1979: 100). There may be legitimate issues about the unit of analysis (for a critique of "state-centricism" and a discussion of focusing on regions at "scales" above and below the nation, see Brenner 1999). But Wallerstein and Chase-Dunn both link semiperipherality to states, and this essay is the usual "starting point" for later scholars who attempt to use various measures of "world-system position" in their own research.

The early conceptual discussions of the key role of the semiperiphery fascinated many comparative social scientists—and seemed to offer an enticing direction for both qualitative case studies and statistically cross-national research analysis examining global patterns. During the final two decades of the twentieth century there were quite a few examples of each sort of work grounded very strongly in the idea that something about semiperipheral development was important (Peter Evans' 1979b award-winning book, *Dependent Development* exemplified the case approach, a plethora of articles in the major sociology journals took the cross-national approach: for instance, Snyder and Kick 1979; Bollen 1983; Smith and White 1992). The studies were pretty consistent: the vast majority showed that the world-system notion of semiperipherality was useful and helped us to understand issues like democratization and development.

But it soon became clear that there was a major empirical problem, too. While Wallerstein's insight about the importance of this idea seemed right, his discussions—and even his mid-1970s list of the membership—offer scant guidance on how to "operationalize" world-system position or to precisely demarcate the boundaries of world-system zones. Specialists on world regions and particular countries sometimes took issues with the categorization of their favorite cases, claiming that they either should or should not be in the semiperiphery. It was also clear, just about at the time of this flowering of world-system scholarship, that a major transformation of the world-economy was underway. Prior to the 1960s or so, the international division of labor was relatively simple, and seemed very consistent with the world-system accounts of the emergence of global capitalism: Core countries specialized in produced manufacturing goods that were exported to world markets; the periphery was characterized by production of raw materials and agricultural products, often destined for core consumption (Mittelman 2000; Dicken 2015: chapter 2). This was the sort of initial advantage that Wallerstein (1974) saw in western Europe that led to the peripheralization of the East in the sixteenth century—and also the scenario described in classic descriptions of "unequal exchange" as a basic dynamic of global inequality underpinning historical world-system hierarchies (for a fuller discussion see Smith 2012). But by the late twentieth century we saw the emergence of a "new industrial division of labor" (Frobel, Heinrichs and Kreye 1980) and a "global assemblyline" (Fuentes and

6   *David A. Smith*

Ehrenreich 1984) that was fundamentally altering this pattern: now manufacturing increasingly locates in low-wage peripheral areas, while the core nations experience relentlessly "de-industrialization" (Bluestone and Harrison 1982). The world had changed! Minimally, this transformation suggests an urgent need to re-evaluate who is in and who is out of various world-system zones: so using classifications from the 1970s in the early twenty-first century seems dubious, at best.

Some people discuss this major shift as "globalization" and believe it pushes the world-economy into totally new territory making "old" world-system zones irrelevant. Some critics of PEWS use the change (and the recent "industrialization" and "development" of the periphery) as an argument against world-system analysis as a general framework (see Sanderson 2005 or Mann 2010, for an example). In fact, I would strongly argue that world-system position not only remains vitally important, generally, but a major *determinant* of national trajectories in the current international division of labor (and, indeed, for rather compelling evidence, see Mahutga and Smith 2011). However, the dynamism in the current world-economy means we must not only design good measures for world-system zone boundaries and measurements: it also requires those indexes to be capable of gauging changes in this hierarchy over time (and, of course, upward and downward mobility is built into PEWS views of this structure). Ideally, we should be able to construct "mobility tables" based on this information and capture regional and national ups and downs that correspond to wider debates (like the one about "the East Asian miracle" in the late 1990s or the recent controversies about the "rise of the BRICS"). Today we may want to explore issues like where China fits in the world-system hierarchy (and whether it is moving up) and where Greece does (and if it is moving in the opposite direction).

Alternative Approaches and Specific Measures

There are two broad approaches to classifying nations into world-system categories. One approach focuses on the attributes of nations or regions; the other takes a relational/network analytic perspective. I will discuss each critically, enumerating the advantages and disadvantages.

Attributional Measures

This approach uses measures of national (or any other unit) characteristics to define zone membership. There is some theoretical justification for this in the key conceptual discussions. For instance, Chase-Dunn (1989) (following

Wallerstein) defines "semiperipheral states as areas containing a relatively equal mix of core and peripheral types of production" (77) or "a predominance of activities which are at intermediate levels" *vis-à-vis* "the current world-system distribution of capital/labor intensive production" (212); elsewhere he suggests that average wage levels might differentiate core/semiperiphery/periphery (Chase-Dunn 1984).

The most well-known (and possibly most widely used—somewhat surprisingly, even today!) is a classification developed by Giovanni Arrighi and Jessica Drangel in *Review (Fernand Braudel Center)* in 1986. This paper is very long and may provide one of the most thorough and comprehensive theoretical discussions about "the semiperipheral zone" in the entire literature. But it also presented a five-fold classification system and a table showing where countries "fit" in two time periods, 1938–1950, 1960–1970 and 1975–1983—and many scholars used their measure as the "definitive" categories for world-system position. This is based on an extremely simple measure, arguing that "the command over the total benefits of the world division of labor must necessarily be reflected in commensurate differences in the GNP per cap of the states in question" (which, ironically, was the primary index of "national development" used by the old modernization theorists).

On its face, this claim is bold . . . but also *prima facie* ridiculous! Do we really believe that the "high" GNP/capita of rich oil states or tiny resource rich principalities make them the equivalent to core countries like the United States or Germany? How can a single number like this, capture the national "attribute" of the mix of production types—or even the relative wage levels of workers? Why would scholars interested in the world-system hierarchy essentially "rename" GNP per capita—a very standard variable used in a plethora of cross-national studies before and after the Arrighi and Drangel article—as a measure of core/semiperiphery/periphery?

On the other hand, of course, there is the advantage not only of the simplicity of a single variable measure, but also one that is very widely available on many nations, over a long period of time (albeit, with some variance in precision and degree of reliability). It does provide a population adjusted gauge of national economic size, which certainly has *something* to do with where nations fit into the global hierarchy that Wallerstein, Chase-Dunn and others discuss (but see Chase-Dunn 1989: 215–216 for a more detailed critique).

The classification tables Arrighi and Drangel provide are difficult to read. To simplify, below is a brief list of the countries in their five levels for the most recent (1975–1983) period:

>*Core*: Canada, Sweden, United States, Australia, Denmark, Germany, New Zealand, Norway, Switzerland, United Kingdom, Austria, Belgium, Finland, Italy, Japan, Netherlands, Libya, Saudi Arabia
>*Perimeter of Core*: Ireland, Hong Kong, Israel, Spain, Trinidad/Tobago

8   *David A. Smith*

> ***Semiperiphery***: South Africa, Algeria, Argentina, Brazil, Chile, Columbia, Congo, Costa Rica, Greece, Hungary, Iran, Jamaica, Malaysia, Mexico, Nicaragua, Panama, Romania, Syria, Turkey, Uruguay, USSR, Venezuela, Yugoslavia, Dominican Republic, Ecuador, Guatemala, Paraguay, Peru, South Korea
>
> ***Perimeter of Periphery***: Ivory Coast, Morocco, El Salvador, Papua New Guinea, Zambia, Zimbabwe, Nigeria, Philippines
>
> ***Periphery***: Ghana, Angola, Egypt, Honduras, Senegal, Afghanistan, Bolivia, Burma, Burundi, Cameroon, China, Central African Republic, Ethiopia, India, Indonesia, Kenya, Madagascar, Malawi, Mali, Mauritania, Mozambique, Nepal, Pakistan, Rwanda, Somalia, Sri Lanka, Sudan, Tanzania, Thailand, Togo, Uganda, Upper Volta

Unfortunately, while there are some "correct" classifications in the above (the US, Germany and the UK in the core, South Korea and Brazil in the semiperiphery, a periphery that includes many very poor African countries), there are also many very "odd" results: Libya in the core, Trinidad/Tobago in the "near core," China, India and Indonesia—all consensus semiperipheral countries even as early as the mid-1970s—in the low periphery, all ranked *below* Papua New Guinea. (Interestingly, Arrighi and Drangel were aware of network measures of world-system position. But—without explanation—they dismiss Snyder and Kick (1979) and Nemeth and Smith (1985) as "unhelpful in identifying the three zones of the world-economy (30).")

More recently, other scholars developed much better attributional measures. A widely known one is by comparative sociologist Kentor (2000, n.d.) that uses a composite score of three national statistics for each country at three points in time (1980, 1990 and 2000). There are two measures of economic power: (1) Gross Domestic Product to gauge national "productive capacity" and (2) GNP/capita as an index of "the capital-intensive quality of the economy"; the third variable is "coercive power" reflected in total military expenditures. These three scores are combined equally to yield a value, which produces a series of ranked scores on "overall position" (with classification into core, semiperiphery and periphery according to numeric cut-off points of uncertain origin). These results possess much higher "face validity" than those of Arrighi and Drangel. But there still are some anomalous results: for instance, the United Arab Emirates, Saudi Arabia and Kuwait are three of the top nine countries in 1980 and the "semiperiphery" for that year seems to include a very large number of nations that would probably seem "peripheral" to most of us; the 2000 results look considerably "better"—but because of its huge lead in military spending and very large gross domestic product, the United States is a distant "outlier" from all the other core countries (despite popular notions of some "hegemonic decline"); another potential "problem" with this measure is that data only "rank" 69 countries (Kentor, n.d.).

Relational Measures

The imagery of the world-system structure and hierarchy is deeply grounded in the idea of a global division of labor in which various sorts of "unequal exchange" link the constituent parts; international connections, roles and relationships are defining elements of this hierarchical formation and a key basis for various types of global inequality (see Tilly 1984 on the more general convergence between this sort of "structural approach" and many sociological theories). Formal network analytic methods are a fairly recent addition to the social science repertoire, with many new techniques refined in the past three or four decades (Wassersman and Faust 1994 provide an overview). They offer sophisticated mathematical approaches to rigorously determine formal properties of system structure, the clustering of units, the precise "positions" connected units hold in networks, etc.

Applying network analysis to PEWS themes is neither new nor novel. Indeed, the relational approaches to assessing world-system position actually came first! In 1979, the iconic Snyder and Kick analysis in the *American Journal of Sociology* was the initial attempt to sort out core/semiperiphery/periphery (that same year, Steiber published a less well-known, but equally interesting relational analysis of world trade using a three-fold classification—which I do not have space here to discuss). For many years, the Snyder/Kick measures were widely used in various statistical cross-national statistical analyses (that same year, Steiber (1979) published a less well-known, but equally interesting relational analysis of world trade using a three-fold classification—which I do not have space here to discuss). They used a technique called "blockmodeling" to examine four different types of relations (trade, military interventions, diplomatic exchanges and shared treaty membership) to sift and sort countries into several blocks based on the structural similarities of their ties to other countries. They found ten hierarchically ordered blocks that they argue reflect a core to periphery structure (with semiperipheral strata in the middle), and through a combination of data driven diagnostics and theoretically motivated logic argue that we can reduce this structure to core, semiperiphery and periphery; furthermore, when they used these network-derived results as a categorical independent variable in regression equations it was positively and significantly related to recent cross-national economic growth rates.

The Snyder and Kick (1979) study illustrated the utility of network analysis for probing world-system structure. But Evans (1979a) noted that it should only be considered a "first cut." They used the presence or absence of a tie on four equally weighted dimensions. But the sort of "unequal exchange" that results in global capitalism is actually grounded in "a territorial system of exchange of fundamental commodities" (Chase-Dunn and Rubinson 1977: 454). Given this assumption, adding in military interventions, diplomatic exchanges and treaty signatory status, and weighing those *equally* with a very

10 *David A. Smith*

simple measure of total trade between countries above a certain threshold, seems rather crude (and straying from the materialist basis of the original Wallersteinian model).

So Roger Nemeth and I set out to do better. We gathered trade data on a variety of specific commodities (from the United Nations) that provided the dollar value of the flows between countries. Using factor analysis, we derived five broad types of commodities that ranged from raw materials to finished products in matrices and used a similar blockmodeling procedure. Snyder and Kick's (1979) results were fairly congruent with world-system expectations (particularly given the limited data). But there were some inconsistencies: they placed Cyprus in the semiperiphery, while Brazil, Mexico and China were all labeled "periphery." Interestingly, our results (Nemeth and Smith 1985) put Brazil, Argentina, India, Iran, South Korea and Nigeria in a "semiperiphery" group with some countries from the "edges" of Europe like Greece, Spain, Finland and Norway. And our core cluster is smaller with the United States, Japan and six leading European countries. Unlike Snyder and Kick, we only examined the data for one point in time: 1970—so we are unable to gauge "mobility." But we did find that structural position not only impacted overall national economic growth in the subsequent decade, but also other key indicators like income inequality and child mortality, with membership in the periphery especially damaging and tending to lead to "the development of underdevelopment" in those countries.

The "next" step in moving the network analytic approach forward was to improve the methodology and add data at multiple time points (Smith and White 1992). In this study we shift from blockmodeling (using algorithms that capture "structural equivalence") to a newly developed technique to measure "relational equivalence." Eschewing technical details, relational equivalence more accurately captures the idea of "role." So in a family system there is a unique structural position of being a particular person's sister's (or brother's) son (or daughter), but in each case that child refers to the older adult as "uncle" (or "aunt"): relational equivalence captures that sort of position directly and more generally (all "nieces" or "nephews" of a specific generation)—and simplifies the representation of the results. While the older methods sorted units into discrete "categories"; by 1992 we were able to represent the network positions of each country in two dimensional space (using Multi-Dimensional Scaling or MDS). This removed the illusion of undifferentiated categories and reveals that each unit (in this case, a country) is a little different from each other in terms of network centrality and power. The results are, first, a two dimensional plot of points (in this case, with core nations on one end and peripheral countries on the other in a bent array pattern). The US, not surprisingly shows up spatially as the "most" core at each of the three temporal waves. Based on statistical inference rules we found five categories: a core, a first and second semiperiphery and a first and second periphery. The longitudinal nature of the data allows us to construct national mobility tables showing some intriguing results: several semiperipheral countries (including, Brazil and South Korea) "move up" between 1965–1980, while only Pakistan and India "move down" during that time span. Unfortunately, however, there are some remaining issues: there was a significant amount of missing data, including China, the USSR and many countries in Eastern Europe (which means that, in addition to not being able to classify these countries, we are also only capturing a partial image of the world commodity trade network).

The most recent study in this "progression" of articles is a recent one I co-authored with Matthew Mahutga. (There was also an earlier report of many of these findings in Mahutga's solo *Social Forces* article in 2006.) This analysis incorporates more data (including many of omitted countries from the Smith/White analysis) and includes data for 2000 (so we now can examine changes over a 35-year period, significantly longer). In Mahutga and Smith (2011) we find six strata (labeling them here core, core contenders, upper tier semiperiphery, strong periphery, weak periphery, weakest periphery). There is a great deal of structural stability over the 1965–2000 period, with some interesting mobility patterns (just a few examples: some downward movement by 2000 for Portugal, Pakistan, Egypt, Algeria and some sub-Saharan African countries; while China, Brazil, Saudi Arabia are all "rising"). Clearly, the bottom three categories are all peripheral, and the top one is the core, but we argue that "core contenders" (which by 2000 include some European countries, but also India, China and Brazil) and our "upper tier semiperiphery" (by 2000 this is comprised of Turkey, Indonesia, Israel, the Philippines, Greece, New Zealand and Hungary) can be combined to form a larger substantive semiperipheral category. Using the three (combined) categories, we also explore the predictive power of world-system position membership on development outcomes (once again, the big differences seem to involve countries in the peripheral categories, though we also get an interesting negative effect on economic growth for the "European semiperiphery" that includes Greece, Ireland, Portugal, Spain, plus Scandinavian and Eastern European nations).

Recently, various other scholars used network analysis to explore world-system positions (with varying degrees of success). Van Rossem (1996), despite appearing in the *American Sociological Review* (and using a relational equivalence measure), seems to unwittingly replicate many of the weaknesses of the earliest studies (his data are for a single point in time, his trade measure is "total trade" measured in a binary way—and, somewhat inexplicably, he analyzes both imports and exports—and he brings in two measures of "military" relations, as well as resurrecting the diplomatic ties data). Some results make sense (the US, France, Germany and the United Kingdom lead core group, India is in the semiperiphery, small/poor African and Caribbean countries cluster in his lowest "periphery 2"). But, again, there are some glaring anomalies: according to Table 6.2 for "1993" (his description of data suggests that it

12 David A. Smith

is from 1983 and the other tables do as well!) he finds Brazil and China in the core, while South Korea and several European countries (including Denmark, Norway and Finland!) are all in a periphery. Not surprisingly, a regression analysis shows that these network results don't predict much and the author (hyperbolically) proclaims "(t)he results presented here raise questions about the world-system model as a general theory of development." In fact, this badly flawed study does nothing of the sort!

Another, much stronger, study that deserves some comment is Clark and Beckfield (2009). This is a methodologically, statistically and conceptually sophisticated piece, frequently cited, with the classification used by other scholars in related studies. They focus exclusively on trade, but used aggregated data on "all trade flows" instead of commodity-specific ones (this is largely justified by a desire to "assign a world-system position for as many countries as possible" [11]). Using a "continuous coreness" algorithm from UCINET, they force a three-way division into core, semiperiphery and periphery adjusting the "cut points" based on intra-bloc density calculations. Using their results to do a multivariate regression on GDP per capita, they find that their classification "outperforms" the Snyder/Kick positions in predicting economic growth. Despite good theoretical grounding and methodological sophistication, there are some familiar drawbacks here: First, the data are temporally limited (essentially a single static network analysis, no ability to look at change/mobility) and "too simple" (only "total," undifferentiated, trade flows). There also is a technical issue with the continuous coreness measure they use, particularly for asymmetric matrices like the ones they analyzed (see Boyd, Fitzgerald, Mahutga and Smith 2010—but, note that Clark and Beckfield were almost certainly unaware of this issue when their article appeared in 2009). The various limitations on the data (and perhaps the methodological issue) once again lead to odd classifications: in this case, for example, not only China, but also countries like Pakistan, Romania and Morocco land in their "core."

There are some other rather recent attempts to network analyze world-system structure. Two of the latest are both in studies in which environmental pollution is the dependent variable (Prew 2010; Prell, Feng, Sun, Geores and Hubacek 2014). In each case (probably unwisely!) the authors decide to "create their own" measure of world-system position rather than use available classifications.

Prew's paper is strong on theory, but very weak methodologically (it uses aggregate country-to-country trade values and calculates "degree centrality" which is simply a variation on the sum of each country's total trade—the result is a continuous score, no attempt is made to distinguish world-system zones).

The Prell et al analysis cites the commodity trade driven analysis in Mahutga (2006) and Mahutga and Smith (2011) as providing the "guidelines" for their work, but for reasons that are not clear they decide to do their own analysis, using a single-year 2006 data set that they claim is "far more comprehensive" than other standard sources (5). They use five commodity trade bundles, plus an amorphous category of international "trade in services." Using relational equivalence, they derive a MDS plot. But, unlike the relative "clean" arrays in our studies, this graph is very random looking: it is hard to see any "pattern" and there is very little spatial differentiation. Network analysis is based on an assumption that we are looking at connections and flows between similar types of nodes (which is why all previous studies used countries at the "unit"), but this one includes conglomerates like "Rest of North Africa" and "Rest of Western Asiates" (it's particularly unclear what the latter one refers to; these residual categories are certainly not "nodes" of in and out trade flows). The commodity trade flows are well explained; but the "trade" in services is very ambiguous and never clearly defined (there is no hint at how this is measured). The scatterplot of results suggests that the clusters are rather "fuzzy," but they classify countries into four categories: core, semi-core, semi-periphery and periphery. Strata membership is never reported in lists, but from an online appendix, it is clear that there are several seeming "misclassifications": Morocco and Peru are in the semi-periphery, the semi-core includes Bangladesh and the "Caribbean" which outranks semi-peripheral "Rest of Europe," and both South Korea and China are in the core, with China very "close" to the United States. This latter "finding" becomes particularly important since in their substantive analysis of pollution, China is an "outlier" (most core nations have rather low emissions). But, in the article, the authors opt to "double down" and insist that China *is* currently a core country in the world-systemic sense (many would disagree). The reported study of commodity-linked air pollution in this article is very interesting—a contribution; their new world-system position measure is not.

World-System Hierarchies: Measurement, Some Issues, Why It Matters

The paper provides an inventory and critique of various measures of world-system position. Measurement may seem like a boring topic! But gauging who's "in" and who's "out" of the various strata is an important issue if, as world-system scholars assume, a country's role in the global division of labor is important for understanding the dynamics of social change. The PEWS central arguments about the polarization and tendency to "unequal exchange" between core and periphery, leading to global inequality and the singularly interesting idea of highly innovative, potentially upwardly mobile, but very volatile semiperipheries, make clear replicable classifications crucial.

My own view is that a network analytic technique to assign world-system positions is a particularly close match between a sophisticated methodology

14 David A. Smith

and an insightful theoretical framework. Wallerstein's world-system imagery is relational. That doesn't mean that we cannot operationalize it using various statistical attributes. But the best attributional measures, like those of various forms of investment or aid, already, in fact, capture at least simple two-way relationship (between two countries or between a country and the rest of the world). National attributes that are purely "internal" also may (and should) be highly correlated with the role a country plays in the global division of labor. In some cases, they may be helpful proxies for world-system position. If we had really good information on, say, cross-national wage levels in various economic sectors, we might be able to arrive at a classification system that reflected a world-system role. Or maybe we could find some combination of attributional variables (*ala* Kentor) that would approximate this. Certainly renaming GNP (or GDP) per capita as "world-system position" is ***not*** adequate: the highest scores on this measure don't necessarily reflect core positions, the ones in the middle are not always semiperipheral, etc.

That said, it is also important to note that existing network analytic definitions of the world-system hierarchy are also deficient in various ways. Like all methodologies, network analysis is no "silver bullet" that divulges global structure when international data is fed in to algorithms. Relational analysis of the world-system ***must*** start with strong conceptual grounding and a clear understanding of how the methodology can be used to assess theoretical ideas. But good information on many sorts of social connections, ties and flows is fairly limited—and this is a particularly vexing issue for international data (though it's even worse for some other interesting networks, like the relations between various cities around the world: see and Smith and Timberlake 2012). With powerful network techniques, there's a strong temptation to "plug in" data that is available, even if it's of tangential conceptual relevance (like diplomatic exchange *vis-à-vis* the world-system). Or to use information that is somewhat relevant (overall trade volume between all countries) and widely available—but cannot fully capture the nuances of a phenomenon like "unequal exchange." A major challenge, moving forward, is trying to turn up progressively "better" and more inclusive data. And this does not necessarily mean that we should "only" look at commodity trade patterns: it is quite conceivable that future analysts will provide compelling rationales to bring other "variables" into their world-system network constructs. But the "heavy lifting" of theory elaboration is a prior condition—the matrices that are examined in any multiple network analysis all need careful conceptual justification.

The idea of a world-system hierarchy that goes "beyond core and periphery" is useful and has opened up fruitful avenues of research. The utility of the idea rests on some rather clear answers to the question, "who fits where?" Social science requires measures of such things, so we know that we are all "talking about the same thing" to advance cumulative understanding. There is something enticing about a view of the world-economy where those "in the middle" or in an intermediary strata seem to be different from both those above and below; historically, it seems that the semiperiphery has been unique, a dynamic zone, in some cases a launch pad for world-system mobility and political challenges (see Boatcă 2006 for an interesting discussion of the "cultural-epistemological" angle on semiperipheral development). Perhaps this explains some of the current fascination with the BRICS nations.

But I must end with a brief coda: Because Wallerstein infused the semiperiphery with such importance, scholars attempting to measure world-system position may, perhaps, be a bit too focused on "three-ness." So Arrighi and Drangel (1986) believe that a "trimodel" classification is inherently important—and Clark and Beckfield (2009) purposefully construct a "trichotomous" categorization of world-system zones. But here I fully agree with Chris Chase-Dunn (in a statement, ironically, that is critiquing my early network analytic work!) who states that "(t)he vocabulary of zones is simply a shorthand. I don't see any advantage in spending a lot of time trying to define and empirically locate the boundaries between zones because I understand the core/periphery hierarchy as a complex continuum. Since there is downward mobility in the system there must be cases of countries or areas which are in between zones, at least temporarily. For me it doesn't matter whether there are 'really' three zones, four zones or twenty zones." In fact, the empirical evidence from relational analysis rather consistently suggests that there are more than three strata (but, of course, less than 20!). And newer techniques now allow us to see how various nations are distributed in graphs that represent, in effect, a "complex continuum" (in fact, we need at least two dimensional space to capture the complexity). So I would like to swear off strict "trinitarianism": in fact, there is nothing magical about three layers. Empirical research may show that there are good reasons to sift and sort countries into more strata, and those categories may help us unravel the complex dynamics of the world-economy. If so, that would be a refinement of world-system analysis, not a challenge to it.

References

Arrighi, Giovanni and Jessica Drangel. 1986. "The Stratification of the World-Economy: An Exploration of the Semiperipheral Zone." *Review (Fernand Braudel Center)* 10: 9–74.

Bluestone, Barry and Bennett Harrison. 1982. *The Deindustrialization of America*. New York: Basic Books.

Boatcă, Manuela. 2006. "Semiperipheries in the World-System: Reflecting Eastern European and Latin American experiences." *Journal of World-Systems Research* 12(1): 321–346.

Bollen, Kenneth. 1983. "World System Position, Dependency, and Democracy: The Cross-National Evidence." *American Sociological Review* 48(4): 468–479.

16 *David A. Smith*

Boswell, Terry and Christopher Chase-Dunn. 2000. *The Spiral of Capitalism and Socialism: Toward Global Democracy*. Boulder, CO: Lynne Rienner.

Brenner, Neil. 1999. "Beyond State-Centrism? Space, Territoriality, and Geographical Scale in Globalization Studies." *Theory & Society* 28(1): 39–78.

Chase-Dunn, Christopher. 1984. "The World-System since 1950: What Has Really Changed?" Pp. 75–104 in Charles Bergquist (ed.), *Labor in the World Economy*. Beverly Hills: Sage.

Chase-Dunn, Christopher. 1989. *Global Formation: Structures of the World-Economy*. Cambridge, MA: Basil Blackwell.

Chase-Dunn, Christopher. 2005. "Social Evolution and the Future of World Society." *Journal of World-Systems Research* 23(1): 171–192.

Chase-Dunn, Christopher and Richard Rubinson. 1977. "Toward a Structural Perspective on the World-System." *Politics and Society* 7(4): 453–476.

Clark, Rob and Jason Beckfield. 2009. "A New Trichotomous Measure of World-System Position Using the International Trade Network." *International Journal of Comparative Sociology* 50(1): 5–38.

Dicken, Peter. 2015. *Global Shift: Mapping the Changing Contours of the World Economy*. New York: Guilford Press.

Evans, Peter. 1979a. "Beyond Core and Periphery: A Comment on the Contribution of the World System Approach to the Study of Development." *Sociological Inquiry* 49(4): 15–20.

Evans, Peter. 1979b. *Dependent Development: The Alliance of Multinational, State and Local Capital in Brazil*. Princeton: Princeton University Press.

Frobel, Folker, Jurgen Heinrichs and Otto Kreye. 1980. *The New International Division of Labor*. Cambridge: Cambridge University Press.

Fuentes, Annette and Barbara Ehrenreich. 1984. *Women in the Global Factory*. Boston: South End Press.

Inoue, Hiroko, Alexis Alvarez, Kirk Lawrence, Anthony Roberts, Eugene N. Anderson and Christopher Chase-Dunn. 2012. "Polity Scale Shifts in the World-Systems since the Bronze Age: A Comparative Inventory of Upsweeps and Collapses." *International Journal of Comparative Sociology* 53(3): 210–229.

John Boyd, William Fitzgerald, Matthew Mahutga and David A. Smith. 2010. "Computing Continuous Core/Periphery Structures for Social Relations Data with MINRES SVD." *Social Networks* 32: 125–137.

Kentor, Jeffrey. 2000. *Capital and Coercion: The Economic and Military Processes That Have Shaped the World Economy, 1800–1990*. New York: Garland.

Kentor, Jeffrey. n.d. "The Divergence of Economic and Coercive Power in the World Economy 1960 to 2000: A Measure of Nation-State Position." Institute for Research on World-Systems, Working Paper #46. URL: http://irows.ucr.edu/papers/irows46/irows46.htm (Accessed March 15, 2015).

Mann, Michael. 2010. "Explaining the World as a System: Can It Be Done?" *British Journal of Sociology* 61(1): 177–182.

Mahutga, Matthew. 2006. "The Persistence of Structural Inequality? A Network Analysis of International Trade, 1965–1980." *Social Forces* 84(4): 1863–1889.

Mahutga, Matthew and David A. Smith. 2011. "Globalization, the Structure of the World Economy and Economic Development." *Social Science Research* 40(1): 257–272.

Mittelman, James. 2000. *The Globalization Syndrome*. Princeton, NJ: Princeton University Press.

Nemeth, Roger and David A. Smith. 1985. "International Trade and World-System Structure: A Multiple Network Approach." *Review (Fernand Braudel Center)* 8(4): 517–560.

Prell, Christine, Kuishuang Feng, Laixiang Sun, Martha Geores and Klaus Hubacek. 2014. "The Economic Gains and Environmental Losses of US Consumption: A World-Systems and Input-Output Approach." *Social Forces* 93(1): 405–428.

Prew, Paul. 2010. "World-Economy Centrality and Carbon Dioxide Emissions: A New Look at the Position in the Capitalist World-System and Environmental Pollution." *Journal of World-Systems Research* 16(2): 162–191.

Sanderson, Stephen. 2005. "World-Systems Analysis after Thirty Years: Should It Rest in Peace?" *International Journal of Comparative Sociology* 46(3): 179–213.

Smith, David A. 2012. "Trade, Unequal Exchange, Global Commodity Chains: World-System Structure and Economic Development." Pp. 239–246 in Salvatore Babones and Christopher Chase-Dunn (eds.), *Handbook of World-Systems Analysis*. New York: Routledge.

Smith, David A. and Michael Timberlake. 2012. "Global Cities and World City Systems." Pp. 247–255 in Salvatore Babones and Christopher Chase-Dunn (eds.), *Handbook of World-Systems Analysis*. New York: Routledge.

Smith, David A. and Douglas White. 1992. "Structures and Dynamics of the Global Economy: Network Analysis of International Trade, 1965–1980." *Social Forces* 83(1): 857–893.

Snyder, David and Edward Kick. 1979. "Structural Position in the World System and Economic Growth, 1955–1970: A Multiple Network Analysis of Transnational Interactions." *American Journal of Sociology* 84(5): 1096–1126.

Steiber, Steven. 1979. "The World System and World Trade: An Empirical Exploration of Conceptual Conflicts." *The Sociological Quarterly* 20: 23–36.

Tilly, Charles. 1984. *Big Structures, Large Processes, Huge Comparisons*. New York: Russell Sage Foundation.

Van Rossem, R. 1996. "The world system paradigm as general theory of development: A cross-national test." *American Sociological Review* 61(3): 508–527.

Wallerstein, Immanuel. 1974. *The Modern World-System I: Capitalist Agriculture and the Origins of the European World-Economy in the Sixteenth Century*. New York: Academic Press.

Wallerstein, Immanuel. 1979. *The Capitalist World-Economy*. New York: Cambridge University Press.

Wallerstein, Immanuel. 1980. *The Modern World-System II: Mercantilism and the Consolidation of the European World-Economy, 1600–1750*. New York: Academic Press.

Wallerstein, Immanuel. 1998. *Utopistics: Or, Historical Choices of the Twenty-First Century*. New York: The New Press.

Wassersman, Stanley and Katherine Faust. 1994. *Social Network Analysis: Methods and Applications*. New York: Cambridge University Press.

2

WORLD-SYSTEMS ANALYSIS AND POLITICAL ECONOMY

Hartmut Elsenhans

World-Systems Analysis (WSA) is in its 40th year if we disregard its antecedents, with the early twentieth century classical theory of imperialism undoubtedly belonging to one of those forerunners. WSA has a predominant explanation of the dynamics of the modern world system but insulates itself from criticism by claiming it aspires only to be a research perspective. Although there are often ad-hoc explanations, there is considerable agreement among WSA authors that capitalism drives the world-system through the need of the centre to draw additional resources through the exploitation of a periphery. Such exploitation is achieved by means of a semi-periphery, which in an analogy to Robinson's (1972: 138f) collaborative elites, are less exploited through their coalescence. The semi-periphery is perceived as the supporting element for the exploitation of the much larger periphery by the centre.

The foremost author of WSA,[1] Immanuel Wallerstein, has been less dogmatic about the inevitable unequalising tendencies of capitalism than other authors in WSA, for example Andrew Gunder Frank. Wallerstein accepts that there were not only processes of polarisation in the world system since the sixteenth century but there were the rise and decline of hegemony between the competing powers. Wallerstein introduced the concept of a semi-periphery in order to integrate catching up processes into a basically hierarchical model.

However, I will show these explanations are unsatisfactory and disconnected from all walks of modern economics. The aim of the present contribution is to show that taking note of recent contributions and having a more critical view towards the 1960s rediscovery of Marxian political economy will help WSA as a central reference point for explaining the rise of the modern world system. In order to account for complex processes of catching up and polarisation, post-Marxist approaches of growth theory have to be considered, especially with respect to delinking growth from capital accumulation. Such a delinking implies the transfer of value from exploited backward societies to the imperialist "centre" does not necessarily contribute to the growth of the exploiting society.

Political economy theories rarely developed models of growth which accounted for internal power relations as a condition of growth. Keynesians early on opposed the classical, neoclassical and Marxist belief the growth process was linked to the accumulation of surplus. Keynesians correctly argued that the capital-output ratio did not increase at times of growth. This discovery was not taken note of in WSA. WSA ignored this fundamental absence of increasing amounts of capital per output produced by referring to Marx's claim that the organic composition of capital has to rise in capitalism. The position of different countries in the world economy could not be seen as dependent on their capacity of using capital efficiently as a result of their internal class struggles. Even class struggles were considered by WSA to be entirely determined by the position of the respective societies in the international hierarchy of unequal division of labour and differential possibilities of appropriating surplus in economic and political power relations.

I start therefore by presenting the theoretical consequences of accepting the delinking between the accumulation of capital and growth. The tendency of the world system towards convergence in levels of development appears as dominant. There are areas, however, where stability of hierarchies can be diagnosed, however such stability depends on the leading economy not attempting to appropriate the economic value of its innovation from technically less advanced economies with which it exchanges. In addition, if the catching up economy becomes capable of appropriating rent[2] by imposing a transfer of financial resources away from the more advanced centres of the system, strong pressures arise which only intensify backwardness, even if those rents are then invested for technical innovation. Even if the members of the surplus appropriating ruling class are collectively interested in such innovation, the micro-economic framework of the incentives discourages such behaviour:

20   *Hartmut Elsenhans*

those that control the rents do not compete on anonymous markets but negotiate between each other on how to distribute available resources, this excludes economically more efficient members from implementing other investments on account of their earning capacity on the market.

Capitalism Is Not Characterised by Capital Accumulation

If one follows the interpretations of bankers or Marxists, capitalism is characterised by capital accumulation. They observe that the capitalist process of development is characterised by increasing values of capital in the production process, such that modern factories appear as being equipped by increasingly costly machinery. However, this observation is the consequence of an optical illusion. Investment goods which are produced by more expensive labour have to be more costly than investment goods which are produced by cheap labour. If real wages increase with capitalist growth, new investment goods incorporating an identical amount of labour time than when earlier investment goods were produced have to be more expensive because nominal wages have increased. If the share of investment goods in total national income is relatively stable, then a constant relationship between national income and stock of capital indicates an absence of capital accumulation in terms of the labour value of the capital stock.

The relationship between the value of the capital stock and national income is the capital-output ratio. The capital-output ratio has been stable since it has been observed, over more than the last 120 years (Kendrick 1961: 166; Helmstädter 1969: 54–60). If there is any discernible tendency, it is rather a steady fall of the capital-output ratio, especially since the microelectronic revolution of production methods (Gordon 1999: 8; Amin 2004: 19).

The stability of the capital-output ratio is not an accident or aberration. Critics of Marx's law of the tendency of the rate of profit to fall (Bortkiewicz 1907: 456; Okishio 1961) argue that capitalists to the difference of socialist planners can invest only in technologies which, at constant wages, reduce unit costs. More capital-intensive technologies characterised by increases in the cost of investment goods higher than increases in productivity require increasing real wages, not only for maintaining an equilibrium between production and consumption (Elsenhans 2014: 12), but also in order to satisfy the criterion of reducing unit costs in relation to a less capital-intensive technology. Capital-intensive technologies generally reduce the amount of labour used in their operation, which in the case of rising real wages can render older technologies uncompetitive because they use too much (newly expensive) labour.

Technical progress is therefore not the result of the accumulation of physical capital, but the result of increases in labour productivity through better skilled labour acquired in more or less science-based technical discovery processes. Historically and up to the modern day, learning-by-doing plays a central role. New technologies can be employed if quantities of products produced with a given technology increase. Wide-scale application of a limited range of technologies in order to discover new technological frontiers requires increasing mass incomes.

That bankers share the error of Marxist thinking does not remove the delusional argument that capitalist accumulation is required to become a technically leading economy.

The Tendency to Remove Unequal Technical Capabilities Within a Multi-Nation Capitalist System

For most WSA authors, the central thrust is criticising the fundamentally inequitable dynamics in the world economy. Undeniable changes occurring in the position of countries in the international hierarchy of specialisation are theoretically integrated in the WSA model via the concept of the semi-periphery—a category of countries identified ex-post as being able to catch up. This area of the theory is close to the theory of hegemonic cycles from diplomatic history (Dehio 1948). The theoretical value of the semi-periphery emerges only if WSA would be able to demonstrate that in these countries, efforts to catch up had been undertaken before they were ordained a semi-peripheral country while such attempts were not undertaken in those countries which did not upgrade to the status of the semi-periphery. I am not aware of any attempt in WSA to identify such a mechanism.

Stable hierarchies also provide an opportunity to conceive of shifts in status as dangerous situations, in WSA called hegemonic crises. WSA here follows closely the political theory of realism in international relations (inter-state, great power) as formulated in a long tradition of diplomatic history. Technically backward countries cannot keep up in the international struggle for dominance because military power is a major application of technical performance; however, it is difficult to trace the rise of Britain against the Netherlands or France in the seventeenth and eighteenth centuries from a lag of these economies in technical performance. Britain's overtaking of France was due to its specialisation in low-cost, low quality products, whereas France specialised on high-quality products (Komlos 1996: 17). The same principles apply to the rise of north-western Europe against Italy in the sixteenth century (Chorley 2003: 509).

Britain's overtaking by Germany did not lead to a hegemonic crisis, although two generations of German leadership hoped to trigger a change in hegemony (which implied a crisis) in two world wars. Germany's economic overtaking of Britain was the result of Germany specialising in productions with high learning opportunities, which initially came about because Germany was inferior in the leading production branches of the last quarter of the nineteenth century (Howard 1907: 91; Bairoch 1989: 243–248). The technical advance of Germany in relation to Britain was maintained through to the end of the twentieth century despite two catastrophic military defeats for Germany, also because Britain in contrast to Germany opted for exploiting first its colonial empire and then the rest of the world by specialising in a technically barren and ultimately parasitical activity—international finance.

The basic model of authors who claim hierarchies in the international division of labour are stable is based on technical advances providing leading economies with learning and resources upon which advances in newly emerging technologies and branches of production can be based. I do not deny that leading economies are more advanced than others in such new technologies and branches. I maintain, however, that this advance is not sufficient for providing them with comparative advantage in such new branches and technologies. Specialisation according to comparative advantage is not a characteristic of capitalism alone. It is a quite simplistic mechanism which any family applies for minimising effort: if the husband is more efficient than his wife in cleaning the floors but at the same time the floors have to be cleaned and trees have to be cut, wherever the husband is more efficient than his wife he will specialise—the wife will clean the floors and the husband cut the trees. Economies do not specialise in those products which they can produce better than others, but in those products where they are relatively better in comparison to the ones they are not (Elsenhans 2001: 55–61, 2004).

All major inventions of the so-called 1880s second industrial revolution (chemistry, machinery, electricity) were made in Britain and Germany at approximately the same time (Milward/Saul 1973: 229; Broadberry 1997: 165). Britain was, however, earning well from its textiles and other consumer products because of its lead in quality of production in comparison to the shoddy German products. The label, "Made in Germany", was introduced in 1876 as a signature of disrepute, not dissimilar to the warnings today against Chinese products. By not selling textiles on the world market, Germany had to opt for initially less remunerative products, and these happened to be the products of the second industrial revolution—chemical and electrical products.

If productivity growth depends on learning-by-doing, given it does not depend on accumulation of physical capital, then the leading economy has more learning-by-doing in established leading branches. Some, but not all, of this learning-by-doing can be used in newly emerging technologies and branches. In these new and emerging technology branches, the advance of an established leading economy in relation to economies which had no learning-by-doing effects in either old or new leading branches will be less than its advance in the old leading branches. The old leading economy will be forced to specialise in old leading branches if it does not enact non-market interventions in order to support the new champions on the world market. Germany is suffering already under this configuration, as its high efficiency in car production and machine building keeps it from developing a comparative advantage in the technologies of the future.[3]

The mechanism of new leading technologies being hindered in old leading economies to the benefit of newly industrialising countries is the exchange rate of the leading economies. The exchange rate reflects productivity differences between mixes of production and is therefore high in economies which are highly efficient in old technologies given they sell such products efficiently. The old leading economy has an exchange rate too high for diversifying into the new promising technologies of the future.

To overcome the leading economies of the past, neither state power nor state intervention in the catching up economy was necessary. Note there is little evidence for the narratives of American modernisation theory surrounding nineteenth century Germany and Japan or a particular role of the state in the catching up and eventual overtaking of old leading economies (Pierenkämper 2004: 70f.; Ma 2004: 374f.).

Clearly, improvements in infrastructure and skills help in catching up processes. They allow the transformation of comparative advantage into cost competitiveness. I cannot see, however, how such factors played a role in the upgrading of exports in somewhere like Singapore after 1945 or the performance of Mauritius, let alone the export offensives in the last three decades in Bangladesh on the basis of female workers of rural origin with very little schooling. Comparative advantage in new industries may help development but it is not necessary for it. Rather, the decisive mechanism is the acquisition of skills gained by producing for mass needs, and by choosing export productions which will increase employment and as a consequence strengthen the negotiating of the power of labour.

My historical reading does not say polarisation processes are excluded. Catching up is possible if comparative advantage can be transformed into competitive advantage, that is cost competitiveness by the reduction of the international prices of local factors of production. If local wage goods production is inflexible and cannot react to additional incomes of new export workers, devaluation peters off into inflation. If infrastructure cannot be provided at cheap prices, a similar blockage may occur. Economies may have made increases in productivity in new branches but are kept from transforming these new productivities into comparative advantage, for example because there are still other branches with comparative advantage such as in raw material production with high rents. It is not an accident that the first countries of the periphery which were catching up with industrial countries in the 1970s had exhausted raw material branches which provided them with differential and consumer rents.

24   *Hartmut Elsenhans*

There is no necessity of polarising specialisation and catching up is not bound to be protected by state power or the capacity to extract surplus from other economies. The newly industrialising countries are succeeding by mobilising an internal surplus from a not yet capitalist economy—a rent—such that their success results from their own initial exploitation (e.g., China today).

Stable Hierarchies Due to the Absence of Exploitation

The branch closest to the model of stable hierarchies in unequal specialisation is machine production. The share of the leading countries USA, Japan, Germany and Switzerland in machine tool exports (UNCTAD product categories 731, 733, 735) was 52% of world exports in 2013, in comparison with the share of these four countries in world exports of 63% back in 1995. Despite the tremendous rise of East Asia, it fell only slightly more than in the four above mentioned countries' share of total world exports (36% in 1995, 21% in 2013).[4] The share of these countries was probably still higher in highly sophisticated machine tools on which separate data does not exist.

Such a dominant position is associated with restraint in pricing these products. Any innovation in production is ultimately realised in machine building. Any invention in sciences can be applied in production processes only if a machine producer designs a machine which uses the invention in its operations for increasing productivity of the user of the machine (Elsenhans 2014: 156, fn. 49). Any invention of a consumption goods producer can be a means of cost reduction or quality improvement if it leads to a change in the operation of the machinery, either realised by the consumption goods producer himself or by his machinery supplier, to whom the consumption good producers have to hand their new insights in order that the machine producer can shape the machinery accordingly. Productivity in machine production is measured not by quantity of machinery but by its performance. Performance increases in consumption goods production are due to better machines and result in higher quantities and/or better qualities of goods per input (labour time, raw materials). If the machine producer fixes the price of his new product in relation to previous machines at a level where all these improvements of the machine-using consumption goods industry accrue to the machinery producer in the form of higher prices, he will not only have difficulties in increasing sales but many other machine producers will try to imitate him. Reverse engineering is a mechanism of learning available for technically less advanced economies since the start of the industrial revolution in Britain and continues to be widely used by competitors at home and abroad.

Under perfect competition, the machine producer will have to lower his price to the level where his costs, including wage costs at average wage rates for skilled workers of the respective economy plus his development costs of the future generation of machines, are covered. No competing machine building enterprise can survive without earning from sales the cost of development of new machinery, the obsolescence of which is already under way as all competitors invest in research for innovation in the respective technologies. Increasing performance of the machine is hence transferred to the user of the machine by introducing the new machine: the user of the new machine realises a productivity increase without any major learning on their part. If the machine can be operated in the periphery with the same technical productivity (as high productivities in capital intensive production lines in the South demonstrate, already Boatler 1975: 506), the periphery acquires a productivity increase. For users of the machine in economies where there is no machine production and no capacity for improving the technology, productivity in machine-using increases whereas there is no increase in productivity in machine building.

Performance increases are the measure of productivity increases in machine production in relation to the costs of production of the new machinery. Performance increases are at the same time the increases in the production in machinery-using branches which, for measuring productivity increases, have to be related to the total costs in the machinery-using chain of production. Performance increases in relation to cost increases are higher in machine production than productivity increases in the respective machine-using branch as the same increases in performance have to be related to higher costs (the cost of the machinery being only one element of the total costs in the machinery-using branch). Productivity increases in machinery production are therefore higher than productivity increases in machine-using. The economy where machine building has not occurred will inevitably specialise in productions which use machinery but not on machine production, as long as machines are supplied under competitive conditions where machine building enterprises cannot appropriate the advantages from improved performance by monopolistic prices for their products.

The technically less advanced country will specialise in machinery-using productions, as long as the imported machinery is part of the production chain on which it specialises. The machinery using country will opt for local production of machinery only when prices decline for the products manufactured with imported machinery to an extent that productivity measured in earnings (and not as an increase in physical output) declines massively—the shift of South Korea to a local textile machine production in the 1970s is an example of such a configuration (Haggard 1983: 83; Mytelka 1986: 258). Massively declining terms of trade of the machinery-using economy make local machinery production competitive despite large differences in physical productivity between the leading and backward economies.

The Futile Hope of Relying Exclusively on the State for Catching Up

Political modernisation theory which prevailed in the early 1960s, the time of academic socialisation for WSA's most prominent author Wallerstein, was an era which invested tremendous hope in the state. Wallerstein criticises on the basis of his African experiences the moral qualities of those in control of the state in most Third World countries, which explains his insistence on the coherent state as crucial in climbing the ladder of international hierarchies. The semi-periphery is characterised in Wallerstein's modelling (1974: 349) by the capacity of the state to organise available resources for improving technical performance. In his view the centre is characterised by a strong state. With respect to the quality of the state in contemporary underdeveloped countries, I have two arguments (Elsenhans 1994): first, there are rent-based state classes torn between the necessity to acquire legitimacy and their interest in preserving their privileges, and second, the failure of the rent-based development state in most of the raw material exporting countries which were able to appropriate rents.

Politically socialised often in the struggle for national liberation, idealistically minded young cadres developed coherent programs for economic change in order to create new productive structures which could be appropriate for organising technical learning and satisfying local mass needs. They hoped to realise this perspective by appropriating rents from the imperialist centres.

Rents emerge in technically backward countries whenever productivity differences in relation to the leading economies differ. They are not only associated with raw material production, as relatively simplistic models contend (Talahite 2015; Karl 1997). Rents are discussed most often with respect to oil states but not when discussing the typical structures of not-yet-capitalist countries, that is the underdeveloped periphery (Contributions in Beblawi/Luciani 1987, and cf. Sid Ahmed 1989 for a much more sophisticated position). Prices on the world market are very often (but not always, cf. textiles) determined by the leading economies (Amin 1973: 186). The less advanced economy sells products at prices which also have to cover its labour costs which are linked to the low average productivity of the economy. At low average wages the wages for the more productive branches despite their higher productivity are also relatively low. If the advance of leading economies is less in some products, the backward economy may sell these products where its productivity is less behind at prices higher than required for covering the costs of production, including an average profit rate. If higher prices do not lead to comparatively lower quantities sold, total foreign-exchange income increases. If Saudi Arabia does not increase its oil production to the level where it recoups just its labour and capital costs, then it increases its take from oil exports so this additional income constitutes a rent. If coffee countries hold back part of their production, coffee prices may go up more than exported quantities fall, therefore coffee countries receive a consumer rent. If Korea taxes its textile exports, quantities will go down less than prices go up. In all three cases I just mentioned, the only economic condition for rent appropriation is a price inelastic demand curve, which is the case for oldest products.

Rent is an income which is not required for paying the factors of production. It can be used for a wide variety of purposes, including waste. Rents can be used for alternative strategies of development if investment decisions are not taken on the basis of actually existing profitability. The "disarticulation" of underdeveloped economies, described as structural heterogeneity (Nohlen/Sturm 1982: 99), makes investment undertaken for change dependent on profitability in complementary investment: complementary investment creates markets for the products of particular projects. New demands emerge through backward linkages, initially isolated projects become markets for suppliers within the chain of production. The profitability of all these projects emerges when they are all simultaneously on stream creating incomes for workers and articulating demand for each other.

When profitability is not the criteria, the blind forces of the market cannot be used to discipline those in control of the investable surplus. Priorities and investment become the result of a negotiating process between different elements of these state classes, "segments" as I call them. As in any political process of coordination, compromises are achieved through alliances. Any segment which wants to push its project will try to find allies in the most diverse areas of the state apparatus in order to repel opposing coalitions. The difficulties found in the field of investment lead to inefficiencies in realising the scheduled production targets. Non-compliance with stated targets is a major reason for loss of prestige of a segment within these negotiation processes. All decision makers in the rent-based economy try to block information about their failure and manipulate perceptions so information is controlled and becomes oblique. Secretiveness is a universally followed rule of behaviour in rent-based societies and a major goal of the different segments of state classes. It results in even the centre of decision making being uninformed about the state of the economy. Following the centrally stated targets of the investment plan may be in contradiction with the need to appear as efficient: whenever it becomes clear that stated targets in the supply of semi-finished products for one's own plant are not realised, the plant director has either to accept further underperformance in achieving his own stated targets or look for supplies elsewhere. Unplanned imports, as well as other unplanned imbalances, undermine further the coherence of the planned development process. As in other cases of unregulated and unplanned scarcities, the relevant actors resort to power games and corruption in order to be able to meet as closely as possible the centrally stated targets. The moral deviations criticised in the behaviour of

28   Hartmut Elsenhans

the rent-based state classes may have a variety of causes, including rent-based cultural norms, but the decay occurs regardless of whether these other factors play a role or if they are simply absent.

Any acceleration of the catch-up process beyond the convergence by a new changing comparative advantage consists in the mobilisation of rents for proceeding to investments which are not yet profitable, but which under certain conditions may increase profitability. The already mentioned decision of South Korea to enter machinery production was taken when prices for Korean textiles fell in the world market without rapidly increasing quantities of sales. Blocking the import of textile machinery meant increasing the price of Korean textiles in Korean currency. The Korean textile producer had to address Korean machine producers, normally his suppliers of spare parts, transfer his knowledge about the specifications required for his machinery, and order textile machinery from his previous supplier of spare parts. The higher prices channelled a rent to the textile machinery producers by controlling the local market for initially expensive textile machines. Any process of state-promoted catching up is a process of intelligently using rents, as Korea has shown.

A comparison between the export-oriented East Asian cases of channelling rents and the oil countries, as well as the comparison between the pre-export orientation industrialisation efforts in South Korea, Taiwan and the People's Republic of China and their phases of export orientation, shows the channelling of rents is most efficient if the relation to the prices of the world market is not totally removed but modified only with limited state intervention. The extraordinary performance of these East Asian economies in relation to the initially technically more advanced economies, such as Mexico or Brazil, shows that export-oriented industrialisation is most successful when it is combined with expanding mass incomes. Independently of their ideological orientations, South Korea, Taiwan, the People's Republic of China, Vietnam and, for other reasons, Thailand, have achieved the removal of marginality of unskilled labour by egalitarian distribution of land. It afforded marginalised households acceptable levels of income for previously marginalised and unused labour on their family farms. The redistribution of land worked as a minimum wage which could be applied without permanent administrative intervention, as well as circumventing the inefficiencies such interventions involve.

Concluding Remarks

Diagnoses of the world system which characterise an increasing inequality should look beyond the international connections of economies to the internal structures created by rents. Internal structures which emerge in the process of internationalisation and the inability of the ruling classes to sterilise rents are determining factors. Solutions can be found in using those rents for supporting the catch-up processes through a changing pattern of the international division of labour. The three examples I presented: (1) catching up on the basis of new comparative advantage, (2) stable hierarchies in case that the respective branch is part of the chain of production and (3) state financed investment, show that any theory of the dynamics of the world system has to take into account the interaction between the two opposing tendencies of market-guided catch-up and rent-based destruction of social structures. The capitalist structure comes into being mostly in the leading economies, where rising mass incomes trigger investment goods production and leads to scarcity of labour.[5] Productivity increases lead to increases of real wages across the respective national economy as labour becomes scarce, even in branches where productivity is not increasing. There are technically less advanced economies where the same mechanisms exist, bringing about high levels of employment and an absence of marginality of labour, therefore wages increase when productivity increasing investment occurs. Such economies can form a benign model of international development, as was the case in the late nineteenth century between the capitalist countries.

There are, however, many societies where there is marginal labour. Marginal labour is that part of the labour force which produces less than it needs for survival (Elsenhans 1994: 394–401). It is kept alive by redistributive mechanisms of pre-capitalist societies. When capitalism penetrates marginality-suffering societies, it normally does not articulate enough demand for labour to integrate the marginalised labour into the capitalist sector. The exchange rate in the less advanced countries is too high given differential rents, often because there is raw material production. The capitalist mechanism is not transferred, and due to comparative advantage in some raw materials, existing local structures of production are destroyed.

Overcoming the simultaneous surplus of labour and surplus of financial resources from raw materials is not possible through the expansion of internal mass demand, as the respective economies are inflexible and do not react easily to increasing mass incomes. In some cases, the local production of wage goods allows them to benefit from the mechanism of devaluation for transforming newly emerging comparative advantage into cost competitiveness. However, in other cases, devaluation is not sufficient therefore planning for efficient rent utilisation may be desirable.

With regard to the differences with Wallerstein's model, in this process financial resources may be helpful, provided that the efficient use of rents can be achieved. A balance between being exploited and appropriating rents has to be found.

The position in the international hierarchy with respect to the capability of appropriating resources and the coherence of the state are legacies of modernisation theory. World-Systems Analysis suffers from this legacy, as well

30   *Hartmut Elsenhans*

as the legacy of archaic growth theory drawn from the 1960s which laid claim to "progressive" economics in a simplistic Marxian vision. As long as WSA binds itself to these legacies, its contributions will confine themselves either on descriptions of the inequalities at the global level or on appeals to start the revolution. WSA has already condemned capitalism as beyond redemption and therefore it should be overthrown, however remains silent on what should replace it and does not explore the possibility that what should replace capitalism can be developed by reforming capitalism.

Notes

1 Many critics and even followers speak of there being a World System Theory but Wallerstein declares that he does not develop a World System Theory. Despite contention over whether he does or not, I follow his definition of his endeavour.

2 I distinguish rent and profit as two different forms of surplus. Profit is appropriated on perfect markets, because there was net investment spending which creates mass income in excess of costs incurred in consumption goods production. Rent is appropriated by political means sustained from politically maintained market imperfections, Elsenhans (2014: 7–10).

3 Before exchange rates were floating, adjustments in price levels between different economies were realised through movements of precious metals between different economies, Ricardo (1951: 135–150).

4 From my own calculations on the basis of UNCTAD Database.

5 Two articles which focussed on this aspect have been rejected as not suitable for publication in *Review,* but were published without major changes in respectable journals, Elsenhans (2005, 2011).

References

Amin, Samir. *Le développement inégal. Essai sur les formations sociales du capitalisme périphérique* (Paris: Editions de Minuit, 1973).

Amin, Samir. "La révolution technologique au coeur des contradictions du capitalisme vieillissant", in: *Labour, Capital, and Society,* 37, 1/2 (2004); pp. 6–27.

Bairoch, Paul. "The Paradoxes of Economic History: Economic Laws and History", in: *European Economic Review,* 33, 2 (March 1989); pp. 225–249.

Beblawi, Hazem; Luciani, Giacomo. *The Rentier State* (London: Croom Helm, 1987).

Boatler, Robert W. "Trade Theory Predictions and the Growth of Mexico's Manufactured Exports", in: *Economic Development and Cultural Change,* 23, 4 (July 1975); pp. 491–506.

Bortkiewicz, Ladislaus von. "Wertrechnung und Preisrechnung im Marxschen System (3)", in: *Archiv für Sozialwissenschaft und Sozialpolitik,* 25, 2 (1907); pp. 445–489.

Broadberry, Stephen N. *The Productivity Race: British Manufacturing in International Perspective, 1850–1990* (Cambridge: Cambridge University Press, 1997).

Chorley, Patrick. "Rascie and the Florentine Cloth Industry during the Sixteenth Century", in: *Journal of European Economic History,* 32, 3 (Winter 2003); pp. 487–527.

Dehio, Ludwig. *Gleichgewicht oder Hegemonie. Betrachtungen über ein Grundproblem der neueren Staatengeschichte* (Krefeld: Scherpe, 1948).

Elsenhans, Hartmut. "Rent, State and the Market: The Political Economy of the Transition to Self-Sustained Capitalism", in: *Pakistan Development Review*, 33, 4 (December 1994); pp. 393–428.

Elsenhans, Hartmut. *Das Internationale System zwischen Zivilgesellschaft und Rente* (Münster: Lit, 2001).

Elsenhans, Hartmut. "Globalisation, Devaluation and Development", in: *Rajasthan Economic Journal*, 27, 1 (October 2004); pp. 1–14.

Elsenhans, Hartmut. "The Empowerment of Labor and the Transition to Capitalism", in: *Comparativ. Leipziger Beiträge zur Universalgeschichte und vergleichenden Gesellschaftsforschung*, 15, 5/6 (2005); pp. 50–79.

Elsenhans, Hartmut. "World System Theory and Keynesian Macroeconomics: Towards an Alternative Explanation of the Rise and Fall of the Capitalist World System", in: *Cahiers du CREAD*, 97 (2011); pp. 5–61.

Elsenhans, Hartmut. *Saving Capitalism from the Capitalists: A Contribution to Global and Historical Keynesianism* (Beverly Hills, CA; London; New Delhi: Sage, 2014).

Gordon, Robert J. *U.S. Economic Growth since 1870: One Big Wave? Revised Version of Forthcoming Paper in American Economic Review, May 1999* (Evanston, IL: MS, 1999).

Haggard, Stephan Mark. *Pathways from the Periphery: The Newly Industrializing Countries in the International System* (Berkeley, CA: Dissertation, 1983).

Helmstädter, Ernst. *Der Kapitalkoeffizient. Eine kapitaltheoretische Untersuchung* (Stuttgart: Gustav Fischer, 1969).

Howard, Earl Dean. *The Cause and Extent of the Recent Industrial Progress of Germany* (Cambridge, MA: Houghton Mifflin, 1907).

Karl, Terry Lynn. *The Paradox of Plenty: Oil Booms and Petro-States* (Berkeley, CA et al.: University of California Press, 1997).

Kendrick, John W. *Productivity Trends in the United States: A Study by the National Bureau of Economic Research* (Princeton, NJ: Princeton University Press, 1961).

Komlos, John: "Le développement de l'économie européenne dans la longue durée: Ce que l'on peut retenir du cas de l'Autriche", in: *Economies et Sociétés*, AF 22 (1996); pp. 11–51.

Ma, Debin. "Why Japan, Not China, Was the First to Develop in East Asia: Lessons from Sericulture, 1850–1937", in: *Economic Development and Cultural Change* 52(2) (2004); pp. 369–394.

Milward, Alan; Saul, S.B.: *The Economic Development of Continental Europe* (London: Allen & Unwin, 1973)

Mytelka, Lynn Krieger. "The Transfer of Technology: Myth or Reality?", in: Cosgrove, Carol; Jamar, Joseph. (eds.) *The European Community's Development Policy: The Strategies Ahead: Conference Organised at the College of Europe, Bruges, 4–6 July 1985* (Brugge: De Tempel, 1986); pp. 243–281.

Nohlen, Dieter; Sturm, Roland. "Über das Konzept der strukturellen Heterogenität", in: Nohlen, Dieter; Nuscheler, Franz (eds.): *Handbuch der Dritten Welt (1): Unterentwicklung und Entwicklung—Theorien, Strategien, Indikatoren* (Hamburg: Hoffmann & Campe, 1982); pp. 92–116.

32 Hartmut Elsenhans

Okishio, Nobuo. "Technical Change and the Rate of Profit", in: *Kobe University Economic Review*, 7 (1961); pp. 85–99.

Pierenkämper, Toni; Tilly, Richard. *German Economy during the Nineteenth Century* (New York: Berghahn Books, 2004).

Ricardo, David. *On the Principles of Political Economy and Taxation [1817]: The Works and Correspondence of David Ricardo (1)* (Cambridge et al.: Cambridge University Press, 1951).

Robinson, Ronald. "Non-European Foundations of European Imperialism: Sketch for a Theory of Collaboration", in: Owen, Roger; Sutcliffe, Bob (eds.): *Studies in the Theory of Imperialism* (London: Longman, 1972); pp. 117–140.

Sid Ahmed, Abdelkader. *Économie de l'industrialisation à partir de ressources naturelles (I.B.R.). (2) Le cas des hydrocarbures* (Paris: Publisud, 1989).

Talahite, Fatiha. "Le paradigme de l'Etat rentier dans la région MENA", in: *Economia* (June 2015); pp. 33–37.

Wallerstein, Immanuel Maurice. *The Modern World-System (1). Capitalist Agriculture and the Origins of the European World-Economy in the Sixteenth Century* (New York; Orlando, FL: Academic Press, 1974).

3

THE SEMIPERIPHERAL ABANDONAT AND THE UNMAKING OF THE CAPITALIST GEOCULTURE

Antonio Gelis-Filho

Introduction

The abandonat is a loose semiperipheral social group characterized by its strong support and identification with values that can be traced to the core of the world-system, by a lack of identification with the masses of their own countries, by its mostly middle-class roots, by its pseudo-revolutionary behavior during the recent political springs and by its opposition to popular movements in their countries.

The expression "middle-classes" in this text, as well as the expressions "elite" and "low classes", refer less to a purely quantitative classification than to a distribution of economic agents in categories inspired by those that Fernand Braudel utilized to describe capitalism (Braudel, 1992). "Elite" refers to the "big predators", the true capitalists that chase oligopoly by their close relation with governments. The "middle class" concept here roughly corresponds to the economic agents that live inside the "market sphere" of capitalism, where real competition takes place. Even when working to government agencies, they largely inhabit those positions in society where a free fall downwards is never too far away, at least not in the semiperiphery. Finally the expression "low classes" roughly corresponds to the inhabitants of the sphere of ordinary life where small trade takes place, usually involving one's own labor power. Without pretending that Braudel's categories can be perfectly transported to the reality of XXI century semiperiphery, that classification is nonetheless useful for the purposes of this work.

The abandonat's origins can be traced back to their social and economic reality. The semiperipheral middle classes face a much less stable situation in their countries than the situation faced by the middle classes in the core, even if it can be argued that the latter is changing for the worse. Lacking the economic power derived from vast wealth and political connections when compared to the local elites, always threatened to fall down back into the suffering lower classes, one of their main psychological and social defense mechanisms is to be strongly committed to what is often described by their members as being the superior values of the core. That connection is often fed by racial myths of belonging to an imaginary "White" or "European" brotherly race or at least of having adopted Western values that would somehow make the abandonat culturally superior to those people connected to local cultural values, values they usually consider to be of an inferior nature. It is important to notice that the abandonat acts in the world-system by absorbing the whole sociopolitical agenda from the core, by importing alien (at first) concepts like the original partition of the geoculture in centrist liberalism, conservatism and leftist radicalism. After importing ideologies, importing products and services is just a natural consequence.

Being the psychological expression of an economic reality, that connection is vulnerable to all sorts of stimuli that can shake such an unconscious framework. After the shocking event of the attack to the World Trade Center and the derived perception of the core vulnerability, after the unsuccessful Western wars in the Middle East and the dramatic ascent of ISIL, after the crash of 2008 and the unconvincing recovery that followed it, and in face of the growing importance of China, a country that has risen from the periphery to the condition of world-power and even of aspiring core, doubts abound in the semiperiphery concerning the current core's ability to keep its current dominant position. Above all, those doubts by the abandonat feed on a decisive factor: the perception that the elites are now less dependent on the traditional core, and more dependent on new players like China, towards which the semiperipheral middle classes can't connect as easily as to the Western core, at least for now. Of course, to the conscience of a typical member of the abandonat those perceptions are triggered not by an analysis of the world-system, but instead by a confusing state of affairs characterized by the perception of the ascent of new social actors, like the so-called "new middle class" in Brazil or the growing importance of the Islamic vote in Turkey, whose voice can no longer be silenced, and externally by a confusing world that no longer "works as it should", in the sense that core countries no longer can easily and constantly demonstrate their economic, cultural and military superiority over non-core states like China and Russia.

It is the pseudo-revolutionary component of its action that differentiates the abandonat from previous conservative (re)actions by peripheral middle classes. By pseudo-revolutionary activity, I mean a collective action that follows the behavioral patterns usually associated with revolutions (going to the streets, screaming political slogans, etc.) without its real content: a subversion in the structures of power and in the way that wealth and power is (or isn't) distributed among the different members of a society. In one extreme case, even *The Economist* (2014; Balza and Neves, 2014) couldn't avoid mocking what it called "the cashmere revolution": a demonstration in one of the wealthiest parts of São Paulo, just before the second round of the 2014 presidential election. On that demonstration, top executives, upper middle class and upper class young people, wealth professionals and "barons and financiers", as the British magazine has defined them, went to Faria Lima Avenue to protest against the then already probable victory of the incumbent leftist government of PT. In fact, the composition of the demonstration was predominantly one of middle class people, as a gathering of the abandonat. A little bit later, during the first months of 2015, many cities in Brazil were taken by huge demonstrations against the government, with some banners even asking, in English, "Armed Forces Please Help Us, Military Intervention Now".

That kind of demonstration shows, at least partially, the drifting apart between semiperipheral middle classes and the local elite's interests. Perceiving its most cherished connection threatened, facing growing pressure from new movements in their societies (like those above mentioned above concerning Brazil and Turkey) and also facing what is for them an astonishing indifference from the elite concerning such social developments, part of the semiperipheral middle class goes to the streets as a pro-West pseudo-revolutionary movement. Unlike what is often said, the goal of the abandonat by tagging along popular movements on the streets is not to change things, but to guarantee they'll remain the same. But the more they act, the more their powerlessness becomes obvious. Extracting what little power they can get from their real or imaginary connections to the world-system's core, the relative decline of the latter creates the condition for a repeated pattern of ineffective social action. The abandonat turns then into a street-marching group of growingly desperate people. From São Paulo to Moscow, from Istanbul to Cairo, the pattern repeats itself,

36   *Antonio Gelis-Filho*

making it clear that the structural crisis of the Capitalist World-System has arrived in the semiperiphery.

Why Study the Abandonat?

The importance of studying the *abandonat* lies in at least four reasons. First, it makes clear the importance of unconscious mechanisms in the spreading of the Capitalist World-System (CWS). Second, it stresses the economic and social precariousness of semiperipheral middle classes, by making the hypothesis that the lack of a middle class in China was perhaps central to its ascendancy to the condition of quasi-core. Third, it raises the question concerning the nature of anti-modern movements as "extra-systemic" and not just as typical conservative or counter-systemic movements, in the sense that they do not inscribe themselves in the fabric of the tripartition of geoculture during the XIX century described by Wallerstein (2011). Finally, it also makes it clear how the abandonat works as a spontaneous world-system police force, always alert to any possibility of a counter-systemic movement starting something new and potentially dangerous to the CWS.

I use the neologism "abandonat" as a way to stress the novelty of the concept. Originally created and discussed in Portuguese (abandonato), it describes the psychological process described in this paper, a process characterized by the geocultural connection between a set of people in the semiperiphery and the values of the core countries. That connection results in a disconnection from the local sociological reality, something that can be described as a feeling of being "abandoned" in the semiperiphery by the societies that belong in the core.

This article proceeds in the following way: in "world-system and geoculture" I explore the concept of geoculture, stressing its psychological elements. In "the abandonat" I describe the main characteristics and dynamics of the abandonat and its current nature as a true "desesperat", an expression of a deep crisis in the current arrangement of the CWS. In "Scenarios for the Evolution of the Abandonat" I present possible mechanisms involved in the unfolding of the current crisis for the abandonat.

World-System and Geoculture

Wallerstein defined geoculture as "a set of ideas, values, and norms that were widely accepted throughout the system and that constrained social action thereafter" (2011, xvi). He stated that centrist liberalism emerged as the triumphant ideology of the world-system during the "long century XIX" (2004, 2006, 2011, 277). Wallerstein also proposed the expression "era of

European universalism" as a description of the era whose end we witness (2006, 84).

The importance of social phenomena to the workings of capitalism was noticed by Marx in one of the most important concepts in his work: commodity fetishism:

> A commodity is therefore a mysterious thing, simply because in it the social character of men's labour appears to them as an objective character stamped upon the product of that labour; because the relation of the producers to the sum total of their own labour is presented to them as a social relation, existing not between themselves, but between the products of their labour.
>
> (Marx, 2000, 52)

Marx is definitely talking about a psychological phenomenon with an unconscious component. It is no wonder that he failed to mention its psychological nature: at the time of the writing, psychology was still firmly inside philosophy, and it wasn't until late in the XIX century that Wilhelm Wundt would establish the first psychological laboratory in the world (Heil, 1995, 728). Psychoanalysis would have to wait even more, until Freud published his *Interpretation of Dreams* in 1899. But perhaps no other author has captured such phenomenon as precisely as Lev Trotsky (2015). Describing a witness' sight of an unusual encounter between an anti-Czar demonstrator and a mounted Cossack, he defined the "molecular moment of revolution", the point in time and space when economic reality, incorporated into the psychological structure of ordinary people, turns into the kind of political action that materializes a change that had been accumulating for a long time:

> That street encounter of the workers with the Cossacks, which a lawyer observed from his window and which he communicated by telephone to the deputy, was to them both an episode in an impersonal process: a factory locust stumbled against a locust from the barracks. But it did not seem that way to the Cossack who had dared to wink to the worker, nor to the worker who instantly decided that the Cossack had "winked in a friendly manner." The molecular interpenetration of the army with the people was going on continuously. The workers watched the temperature of the army and instantly sensed its approach to the critical mark. Exactly this was what gave such unconquerable force to the assault of the masses, confident of victory.
>
> (Trotsky, 2015)

Undoubtedly, as illustrated by such a case, psychological phenomena are an essential component of a human system, and later the Freudo-marxist approaches would make it abundantly clear. World-systems are no exception to it at all. The structuration of a world-system needs a mechanism of friction

38 Antonio Gelis-Filho

reduction between core and non-core areas, so the dynamics of exploitation are less costly and more efficient. Armies, bribes and police can and are utilized as such, but psychological elements that make the dynamics of exploitation a natural, and therefore more easily acceptable occurrence are a very good, low-maintenance and, up to a point, self-replicating friction-reducer.

The elite, the true capitalists in the Braudelian sense of the word, is connected to the core by their deep interest in profiting from furthering the unequal exchanges that define the world-system. The low-classes, usually excluded from the economy except for its more basic components, rarely can articulate any real threat to the order of things.

The much smaller middle classes, however, aim to achieve more than the low classes. Inhabiting the small sphere of the market economy in semiperipheral countries, its habitat is always under the threat of being encroached by the elite or the desperate needs of the low classes. The lack of an institutional apparatus as the one that exists (yet) in the core, one that rewards professional excellence with social ascension and that protects middle class citizens from falling too deep in the case of life's accidents, shapes the semiperipheral middle class' behavior. Resenting the lack of fair opportunities and the precariousness of its standing, their members absorb the core's geoculture much beyond the mere adoption of its political spectrum, something that is dutifully accomplished. A cultural myth of local inferiority in the face of the core is created by the abandonat, an imaginary inferiority from which it tries to dissociate itself by turning into a "soul of the core trapped inside a semiperipheral passport". Even some instances of resistance may be modified from the core's own institutions (Cohn, 2013).

That psychological mechanism, once incorporated as part of what it means to be and to act normally, is a powerful resource for behavior manipulation, as described by the Turkish writer Orhan Pamuk in his book *The Silent House*:

> At that point Mehmet said that Mary wanted to go across to the island and at once everyone felt that sense of inferiority, the need to please the European, and so we piled into the boats.
>
> (Pamuk, 2002, 89)

In Brazil, some components of that phenomenon are known as *mongrel complex*, defined by Nelson Rodrigues in the late 1950s as "the voluntary relation of inferiority that Brazilians put themselves in when facing the rest of the world" (1993, 51–52). By "rest of the world" he was most probably talking about countries perceived as being in a better socioeconomic condition than Brazil. Originally described in relation to the then extremely important culture of football, it has been applied to other fields as well. Pamuk and Rodrigues, thousands of kilometers and decades apart, were talking about the same semiperipheral phenomenon. Such a feeling of inferiority is the other side of the idealization of the core by semiperipheral abandonat. That idealization was seen both as a potential way out of the precarious condition of being part of the semiperipheral middle class and also as a way of increasing its bargaining position when dealing with local elites, as if such connection would qualify the middle classes as being in a civilizational mission of bringing a little bit of the core to the semiperipheral "social wilderness". It has also a small but not negligible exchange value in dealing with elites: "either you give us better conditions or we'll leave to the core, carrying our skills and our cultural refinement with us". In that way it helped the core to tame semiperipheral elites, an ability that becomes all the more important during the decades after the fall of the Soviet bloc, whose real or imaginary support for worldwide socialist revolution used to represent a permanent threat and source of uneasiness to semiperipheral capitalist elites.

Those middle classes act like unpaid and unrecognized ambassadors of the world-system geoculture. Always avid in absorbing the core's cultural, social, political or consumerist agenda, it diminishes costs and manages to provide the core with yet another strategic resource: tamed consumers. After all, desiring foreign products and behaviors is usually the most natural connection with the core for many people in the semiperiphery.

But the whole building depended on a subtle and only marginally controllable play of socioeconomic and psychological factors. The geopolitical and economic mistakes committed by the core countries in the last couple of decades by unconvincing geopolitical actions, economic mismanagement, producing a continuous fall from the previously very high living standards for their own middle classes (a major psychological magnet for semiperipheral people) and the ascent of a non-submissive semiperipheral country that until recently was essentially irrelevant from an economic standpoint—China— may have contributed to a crisis on the previously invulnerable social and psychological connection between semiperipheral middle classes and the core.

From "Abandoned" to "Desperate" Middle Classes: The Case of Brazil

Fernand Braudel described three spheres of social and economic life in the modern world: the sphere of ordinary life, the sphere of the market and the sphere of the capitalism (Braudel, 1982, 229–230). Ordinary life includes the small deals people are involved in their daily lives, with no major repercussions to the order of things. The sphere of (real) capitalism is the sphere where money and power are connected and exchanged, where oligopolies are created and guaranteed, where the "too big to fail" companies operate. The market sphere is the one where people and companies do compete for economic and social success, where no one is "too big to fail". The abandonat inhabit the market sphere but can't access the sphere of the real capitalists. They are the professionals, the middle managers, the public officials, the small and medium businesspeople, a group that in the semiperiphery lives under almost continuous stress from the less organized local form of capitalism, and that must also deal with all the cost related to less developed institutions. They're characterized not by how much money they earn, something that can vary widely from person to person, but by the fact that they are excluded from the top positions, from the capitalist or political elite that thrives inside the sphere of real capitalism. Frustrated by the lack of the kind of bourgeois success that their skills were supposed to deliver and that they cherish so much, always fearing the not unusual slippage downwards through the social pyramid, the abandonat is the natural *locus* for the semiperipheral reproduction of a geoculture developed in the core.

The absorption of the ideological geoculture was just the first instance of the incorporation of the core's social agenda by semiperipheral societies. From then on, the abandonat would essentially reproduce the sociocultural agenda from the core. By doing that, its members aim at two goals. First, they manage to control a pseudo-civilizational place in the society: their inclination to occupy the relatively less profitable positions in the academia, in the arts, in the public service and in the professions than the power positions reserved to the elite in the world of "big business" keep them in direct contact with the core's agenda, creating value that can be exchanged with the elite for better, or at least less unsafe, social positions. Second, it serves as a vague threat against that same elite: "treat us better or we'll leave to the core".

But as the fall of the Berlin Wall severely reduced the negotiating power of the masses in the semiperiphery, where inequality has been barely dented during almost two decades of accelerated semiperipheral growth post-1989, the weakening of the current core severely weakens the negotiating power of the semiperipheral middle classes. During the period of frantic expansion of financial capitalism their consumption compulsion made them valuable as debt-makers. The realization of the consequences of the core's weakening was postponed a bit; but as the debt-driven model found its global limits in 2008, their usefulness has started to run out and the abandonat started to face the pain of the demise of the current world.

Semiperiphery in Turmoil: Brazil and Beyond

The complexity of the huge demonstrations that surprised Brazil in June 2013 has already being noticed by many analysts. Saad-Filho (2013) talks about "left neoliberalism"; Alves (2013) saw a "revolt of the precariat". Singer (2013) noticed that the demonstrations contained both a "traditional middle class, dissatisfied with aspects of the social reality" and the "new proletariat", which can be perhaps defined by the word "precariat", as used by Alves (2013) and Viana (2013) has noticed the media attempt to split the demonstrators in two groups: "law-abiding" and "hooligans".

Brazil's demonstrations are not alone in that peculiar composition. Concerning Turkey's recent demonstrations, Yörük and Yüksel (2014, 123) noticed that:

> At face value, the Gezi protests might seem to fit the third category, especially given the trigger—anger at government-backed commercial construction encroaching on a rare fragment of public green space—and the seeming youth of the protest leaders. But although Gezi shares some characteristics of this category, at least in terms of demands voiced by the protesters, we contend that it fits better into the second category: anti-authoritarian and pro-democracy protests. The alliance of "new proletarians"—typically, graduates working in telemarketing—with inflation-hit middle classes, which André Singer has defined as a central feature of the 2013 Brazilian protests, [does not capture the extent to which "old proletarians" participated in the Turkish events. Again, economic issues—including soaring prices in privatized public goods, such as transport—were crucial in Brazil, whereas in Turkey, the main triggers were political.

The same diversity was detected on Russia's demonstrations by Wood (2012, 5–6):

> The recent wave of protests has been seen, both in Russia and in the West, as evidence of a new awakening of Russian "civil society", roused from its long post-Soviet slumber by the corruption of Putin and his associates, and their brazen contempt for the popular will. The mobilizations displayed a striking ideological breadth, running the gamut from Orthodox chauvinists to neoliberals, socialists to environmental activists, anti-corruption campaigners to anarchists; attendance also spanned the generations, from pensioners to teenagers. But, as the Western press noted approvingly, the most vocal and visible component of the oppositional marches was "a sophisticated urban middle class", with consumption habits and expectations not unlike those of their Western counterparts.

It is clear from those examples that something unusual is going on in the semiperiphery. The abandonat goes to the streets, where it assumes a pseudo-revolutionary position. It aims to keep connections with the Western core intact, as they used to be in the "good times". Why does that happen now? Exactly because that very core—on which so much depends to the abandonat—shows signs of having its hegemony changing to mere domination, power

42 *Antonio Gelis-Filho*

without moral leadership, as noticed by Arrighi (2010, 29) on a Gramscian basis. But what is "moral leadership" by a hegemonic core but being able to impose geocultural submission?

Reinforcing the idea that Brazil is passing through its own manifestation of the crisis of the abandonat, the anti-government demonstrations that took to the streets of the country during the beginning of 2015 faded away as spectacularly as they had appeared. Lacking a real agenda but wanting to travel to the past and waiting for external help that is no longer available, the abandonat looks at the mirror in the streets, doesn't like what it sees and goes back home.

Conclusion: Scenarios for the Evolution of the Abandonat

At first, one could think that there are many possible future paths to the abandonat. But in fact its expression as a pseudo-revolutionary "desesperat" is just a temporary expression of a phenomenon connected to the crisis of the geocultural structure of the Capitalist World-System in the semiperiphery, in spite of different local colors and flavors in its expression.

The future of the abandonat lies on two factors. First, will the Capitalist World-System survive? Many authors have been writing for some time already about the current crisis of capitalism and its structural nature, with different diagnoses concerning its causes and perhaps even more varying prognoses concerning its future (e.g., Arrighi, 2009; Calhoun and Derluguian, 2011; Calhoun et al., 2013; Chase-Dunn, 2012; Collins, 2013; Mann, 2013; Streeck, 2011, 2014; Wallerstein, 2010). If the Capitalist World-System somehow manages to muddle through the current crisis, even then the second factor will need to be addressed: will the abandonat still be useful for a world-system that will perhaps bear little resemblance to the current one, even if still centered in the geopolitical West?

But not many authors among those quoted above seem to suggest that the odds for a "business as usual" scenario are significant. The abandonat's decision of going to the streets it has so solemnly ignored in the past becomes then more understandable: it is fighting for survival. In Brazil, in Russia, in Turkey, in Egypt and, most probably, soon in other places as well, some of which are probably inside the incorporated semiperipheries of Mexico and Eastern European Union, the future is feared by the abandonat-desesperat, and is feared for a good world-systemic reason.

If Egypt, Turkey and Russia are examples which may be generalized of what the future looks like, that might be constituted by an alliance between the local elites and popular movements, resulting in a serious weakening of the traditional abandonat. The common language for such a connection between elites and lower classes will vary. In Russia it was nationalism; in Turkey,

The Semiperipheral Abandonat   43

moderate Islamism; in Egypt, where a possibly temporary *status quo* blurs the big picture, it was a more radical form of Islamism. In Brazil, the coming years will possibly make it clearer who will be the intermediaries that will sign the pact between oligopolies and the masses, if the pattern repeats itself there. Lacking any other perspectives, after the futile resistance is over, the abandonat can only try to find a position, however precarious, inside the new order, strengthening it by doing that.

Whether the cases of Russia and Turkey allow a first glimpse of a new kind of world-system or just another feature of the current systemic bifurcation remains to be seen. What is more certain, however, is that the loss of the abandonat would most probably seal the fate of the Capitalist World-System as we know it, since such loss would unleash the positive historical feedback loops that would turn stagnation into rapid decline.

During the period of *Pax Occidentalis*, ideology, worldwide, would mostly be located inside a spectrum of the Western capitalist geoculture, as defined by Wallerstein: centrist liberalism, revolutionary leftism (at first Marxist, after 1968 increasingly pro-minorities) and conservatism (now essentially neoliberal/neoconservative). As the sun is setting for Western hegemony—at least as a perception, something quite relevant for psychological phenomena—the whole Western geoculture turns into just one pole in a whole new spectrum, while the opposite pole is located in a yet ill-defined set of extra-systemic ideologies. That set of extra-systemic ideologies will perhaps someday turn into a whole new and self-sufficient geocultural spectrum, in which case we'll have a completely different world-system.

References

Alves, Giovanni. 2013. "A Revolta do Precariado no Brasil". *Blog da Boitempo*, 24 June 2013. URL http://blogdaboitempo.com.br/2013/06/24/a-revolta-do-precariado-no-brasil/ (accessed 14 February, 2015)

Arrighi, Giovanni. 2009. "The Winding Paths of Capital" *New Left Review*, 56: 61–94.

Arrighi, Giovanni. 2010. *The Long Twentieth Century*. New and Updated Edition. London: Verso.

Balza, Guilherme and Márcio Neves. 2014. "Com Ronaldo e FHC, ato pró-Aécio tem 'viva a PM' e 'Dilma terrorista'". *UOL Eleições 2014*. 22nd October 2014. URL http://eleicoes.uol.com.br/2014/noticias/2014/10/22/em-ato-pro-aecio-militantes-xingam-dilma-e-gritam-viva-a-pm.htm (accessed 17 February, 2015)

Braudel, Fernand. 1982. *The Wheels of Commerce*. New York: Harper & Row. [Civilisation matérielle, économie et capitalisme, XVe–XVIIIe siècle: vol. 2: Les jeux de l'échange (1979)]

Braudel, Fernand. 1992. *The Structure of Everyday Life*. New York: Harper & Row. [Civilisation matérielle, économie et capitalisme, XVe–XVIIIe siècle: vol. 1: Les Structures du quotidien (1979)]

44 *Antonio Gelis-Filho*

Calhoun, Craig, Randall Collins, Georgi Derluguian, Michael Mann and Immanuel Wallerstein. 2013. "Collective Introduction: The Next Big Turn". In Wallerstein, Immanuel, Randall Collins and Michael Mann (eds.). *Does Capitalism Have a Future?* London: Oxford University Press, 1–8.

Calhoun, Craig and Georgi Derluguian (eds.). 2011. *Business as Usual: The Roots of the Global Financial Meltdown.* New York: New York University Press.

Chase-Dunn, Christopher. 2012. "Terminal Crisis or a New Systemic Cycle of Accumulation?" In Babones, Salvatore and Christopher Chase-Dunn (eds.). *Routledge Handbook of World-System Analysis.* London: Routledge, 125–126.

Cohn, Samuel. 2013. "O'Connorian Models of Peripheral Development—or How Third World States Resist World-Systemic Pressures by Cloning the Policies of States in the Core". In Babones, Salvatore and Christopher Chase-Dunn (eds.). *Routledge Handbook of World-System Analysis.* London: Routledge, 336–344.

Collins, Randall. 2013. "The End of Middle Class Work: No More Escapes". In Wallerstein, Immanuel, Randall Collins and Michael Mann (eds.). *Does Capitalism Have a Future?* London: Oxford University Press, 37–70.

The Economist. 2014. "The Cashmere Revolution". *Americas Blog.* 23 October 2014. URL www.economist.com/blogs/americasview/2014/10/brazils-presidential-election-0?fsrc=rss&utm_medium=twitter (accessed 18 February, 2015)

Heil, John. 1995. "Philosophical Relevance of Psychology". In Honderich, Ted (org.). *The Oxford Companion to Philosophy.* Oxford: Oxford University Press, 728–729.

Mann, Michael. 2013. The End May Be Nigh, But for Whom of Middle Class Work: No More Escapes". In Wallerstein, Immanuel, Randall Collins and Michael Mann (eds.). *Does Capitalism Have a Future?* London: Oxford University Press, 37–70.

Marx, Karl. 2000. *Das Capital: A Critique of Political Economy.* Edited by Friedrich Engels. Washington, DC: Regnery Gateway.

Pamuk, Orhan. 2002. *The Silent House.* London: Penguin.

Rodrigues, Nelson. 1993. "O Complexo de Vira-latas". In Ruy Castro *sombra das chuteiras imortais.* São Paulo: Cia. das Letras, 51–52.

Saad-Filho, Alfredo. 2013. "Mass Protests under 'Left Neoliberalism': Brazil, June–July 2013". *Critical Sociology*, 39(5): 657–669.

Singer, André. 2013. "Brasil, Junho de 2013: Classes e Ideologias Cruzadas". *Novos Estudos—CEBRAP*, 97: 23–40.

Streeck, Wolfgang. 2011. "The Crises of Democratic Capitalism". *New Left Review*, 71: 5–29.

Streeck, Wolfgang. 2014. "How Will Capitalism End?". *New Left Review*, 87: 35–64.

Trotsky, Lev. 2015. "Who Led the February Revolution?" In *The History of the Russian Revolution*, vol. 1. [First published in 1930, transl. by Max Eastman, 1932]. URL www.marxists.org/archive/trotsky/1930/hrr/ch08.htm (accessed 20 January, 2015) [История русской революции, 1930]

Viana, Silvia. 2013. "Será que formulamos mal a pergunta?" In Harvey, David and others (eds.). *Cidades Rebeldes: Passe livre e as manifestações que tomaram as ruas do Brasil.* São Paulo: Boitempo.

Wallerstein, Immanuel. 2004. *World-Systems Analysis: An Introduction.* Durham, NC: Duke University Press.

Wallerstein, Immanuel. 2006. *European Universalism: The Rhetoric of Power*. New York: The New Press.
Wallerstein, Immanuel. 2010. "Structural Crises". *New Left Review*, 62: 133–142.
Wallerstein, Immanuel. 2011. *The Modern World-System IV: Centrist Liberalism Triumphant, 1789–1914*. Berkeley: University of California Press.
Wood, Tony. 2012. "Collapse as Crucible: The Reforging of Russian Society". *New Left Review* 74: 5–38.
Yörük, Erdem and Murat Yüksel. 2014. "Class and Politics in Turkey's Gezi Protests". *New Left Review*, 89: 103–123.

PART II

GLOBAL STRATIFICATION AND THE STATE

4

STATEHOOD AT THE END OF THE RAINBOW?

AGONISTICS OF POTENTIALITY IN THE WORLD-SYSTEM

Juho T. Korhonen

Introduction

Charles Lemert has argued that the increasing disequilibrium and bifurcation of the world-system calls for a more robust understanding of the complexity, arbitrariness and fluidity of the changing relations of time and space, or what Lemert calls "uncertain worlds" (Wallerstein et al., 2013). Lemert's notion is based on Immanuel Wallerstein's work on transformational TimeSpace, a concept that seeks to capture "the struggle within the world of knowledge, which determines whether we can clarify the historical alternatives that we face, make more lucid our choices, both criticize and empower those who are engaged in the political struggle (from which of course the world of knowledge is unable to dissociate itself)" (Wallerstein et al., 2013, 181).

By starting a comparative research project on social sciences and academic knowledge production in post-socialist states worldwide I unknowingly took on Lemert's call to find a more robust way of analyzing this "struggle within the world of knowledge". Following preliminary research in 2011–2014 I realized that I should take a couple of steps back and develop a frame with which I could begin to capture the underlying condition within the world-system that has affected the trajectory of social science knowledge in post-socialist states since the global collapse of their system of legitimization in 1989 and 1991; a frame that would give me a little more analytical distance from today's dominant political struggles and their association with the world of knowledge—captured by Wallerstein in the concept of transformational TimeSpace—since it is the effects of the association that I wish to approach, not the association itself. In the following I propose one new way of having a wider lens to capture these uncertain worlds.

This project began as a comparative study that, inspired by arguments of the world-systemic reach and importance of knowledge production (e.g., Bergesen, 2000), sought to understand how post-socialist states, with state-building premised and dependent on the socialist alternative during the twentieth century, interacted with the world-system from the perspective of knowledge production following the collapse of their alternative legitimacy.

Georgia and Kyrgyzstan were chosen to represent peripheral, that is more dependent, Soviet states, whose statehood was largely a product of the socialist project and who did not lapse fully into authoritarianism but attempted to realign themselves with the liberal democratic capitalist model. Tanzania represents a similar case of reliance on socialism in state-building and knowledge production (Blommaert, 1997). Similarly, Tanzania has made efforts to realign with the capitalist world-economy through structural readjustment policies of the World Bank since the mid-80s. However, Tanzania provides comparative divergence as it was situated in the global rather than Soviet periphery of socialist states and championed the non-aligned movement. The inclusion of Tanzania also follows an argument of the wider role of socialism for the twentieth century states-system in general and for Africa in particular (e.g., Pitcher et al., 2006).

Thus, my three cases are joined by three conditions: Their location at the peripheries of the socialist alternative, the extent to which state-building was premised on the socialist project, and the existence of genuine efforts by the states to realign themselves with the dominant liberal democratic and capitalist model. Within these three conditions all the three cases, however, diverge slightly, thus offering parallel and contrast-oriented cases that can help develop an analytical framework for further study (see e.g. Skocpol et al., 1980). I therefore aim for an ideal type description to facilitate further empirical research, rather than an exclusionary model. Because of this, it was important for these initial cases that socialism had functioned as a primary initiator of state-building. More hybrid cases, such as eastern European post-socialist states, present a more complex picture and may be included in later steps.

Research in all cases consisted of meetings with interlocutors and participant observations in academic activities, conferences and discussions.

Towards an Agonistics of Potentiality

Wallerstein's transformational TimeSpace offers an analytic lens for locating a break or a shift in the relation of epistemology and politics when it comes to disjunctions between the core and peripheries of the world-system (Wallerstein et al., 2013). In a nutshell, it seeks to locate ways in which knowledge associates with politics to maintain contestation and hierarchy within the world-system. In the capitalist world-economy this is an integral way of reproducing global stratification amongst states.

However, I found this inadequate for my need to understand the situation in states that had been part of a semiperipheral alternative promising national liberation, an alternative that had lost its potential and promise almost overnight. Some of those states, such as the Baltic republics, were able to realign with the intellectual communities of the core. However, particularly such states that were located at the peripheries of the socialist semipheripheral alternative and whose statehood began as socialist state-building, have failed to realign and therefore lack the initial connections that would recognize their condition as a break or a shift, as transformational TimeSpace would have it, from a shared past or an imaginable future. Rather, these states have been in transition for a quarter of a century now. Therefore, instead of beginning my research project through either the lens of the problems that the past has bestowed upon them or the possibilities that the future may or may not promise for them, I wanted to be able to situate them and my research into a world-systems perspective through the lens of their current condition; the actuality of an on-going transition. I believe, that from this never-ending transition a condition of in-betweenness has arisen, neither aligning with nor contesting knowledge(s) in the world-system.

To continue with my research project and to begin analyzing this condition, I argue that the concepts agonistics and potentiality—borrowed from a growing literature of anthropology and political theory that is concerned with understanding the simultaneously growing prevalence of politics of plurality, of fundamentalism and of globalization (Wenman, 2013)—can be employed to situate this post-socialist predicament into an increasingly bifurcating world-system. Specifically, in a manner that avoids "the nonexplicit premises of the specific configuration put forward today by our global 'episteme' of cognitive expropriation of the world" (Wallerstein et al., 2013, xxxi), and thereby avoids reifying the dynamics of an unending transition as a temporary break or anomaly, and yet is not premised on providing a counter-hegemonic alternative, that is redemption, as Wenman characterizes the dominant political philosophies of modernity in contrast to agonistics.

Agonistics can be generally defined as modes of contestation (see Singh, 2015). Differing from a political theory formulation of contestation as an opposite of redemption (cf Wenman, 2013), I draw my general understanding of the origins of contestation from a structural longue durée view of world-systemic politics. For example, social theorist Peter Wagner (2012) has pointed out how modernity was historically conceived as containing universal commitments. Politically the most profound of these commitments has been the predominant construction of nation-states. Wagner continues that changes have come about over the past decades, which speak of a plurality of socio-political organizations and the existence of modernity in a variety of forms that serve to undermine the idea of general, linear and universal progress (Wagner, 2012, 150–153). A more flexible analytic lens therefore points to modes of organization demanding constant and increasingly contested production of continuities (real, imagined, rediscovered and reproduced) with the past as well as the future.

Historian Reinhart Koselleck suggests that the crucial element of modernity is the distancing of the horizon of political expectations from the space of experience (Wagner, 2012, 150–153). I suggest that when this distancing meets increased plurality and contestation, we can detect one new modality of modern socio-political organization that stretches beyond experience and expectation to encompass capacity and agency, or lack thereof, in dealing with the joint distancing of experience and expectations and the plurality of politics, with which societies respond to it. I call that modality *the agonistics of potentiality*.

I argue that this modality can be detected in its incapacitating form in parts of the post-socialist sphere, especially in what I would call the post-periphery, that is the peripheries of the so-called second world that existed roughly from the 1920s until the late 1980s. This is then an attempt to understand as a whole the discrepancy between the promises of statehood—especially the unreachability and incompatibility of the political horizon presented through the universal notion of a sovereign nation-state—and the demands of the world-economy, both residing in an ever more interconnected yet crises-ridden world-system.

In the core and peripheries of the world-system during the past two decades the response has been an increased pluralization of varieties of liberalism connected to a variety of retreats to the nation and the community; an interplay that actively seeks new political solutions between the two, often described as the two faces of globalization. However, I argue that in the post-peripheries this interplay fails to create alternatives or new configurations, new attempts at a social compact. Rather the move in the post-peripheries from

Lenin to liberty to the nation has failed without delivering any of the potentials that new forms of liberalism or nationalism/community conjure. In the post-periphery this interplay has created a limbo, an in-betweenness, where the prefix 'post' also signals how, as a consequence of the collapse of the second world, this periphery is no longer the hierarchically lesser or proto form of the core or the semiperiphery, as dependency in the world-system has become uncertain.

In effect, I hope to understand the condition of uncertainty when one systemic logic falters and new ones are yet to take shape. A process—not of discontinuity between two stages of equilibria, since the old has not been discarded or the future discovered—but of disorganization in which, crudely put, the whole is less than the sum of its parts. This is why I propose that modes of political organization of the past, such as sovereign statehood, now may hide in their promise of potentiality an actuality of agonistics[1] since they are unable to contribute productively to the organization of a whole.

At the same time, through fragmentation and institutionalization of knowledge production, the very rights to define what is correct knowledge are more strictly controlled. One of the main tools for this control is a short-term orientation to problem solving in which the future appears as a mere extrapolation of the present (Levitas, 2013, xvi). The core, representing the present, in order to maintain its hold on knowledge production, therefore favors forms of knowledge that are highly specialized and wherever reasonable critique is mounted against this model an ever eager pool of financially and symbolically hungry academic workers is deployed to reorient the alternative model of reality and reproduce the promise of universal potential and the space of agonistic striving to which the core has invested an increasing amount of resources to maintain a degree of sovereignty.

The post-socialist states provide an interesting approach to this condition. Following the collapse of the second world the post-socialist peripheries fell outside this tension. I hope my discussion below will give some sense of how they are now unable to join that race; the increased demands for capacity mean that they cannot both stretch the tightrope and walk on it at once, whereas in a previous less turbulent world-system they could first do one and then focus on the other.

Post-Socialist Predicament

The socialist project in its twentieth century incarnation was founded on seeking acknowledgement for an alternative form of knowledge divorced from its competing dominant bourgeois manifestation. But what becomes of a project founded on such a search for divergence that then collapses and loses its legitimation? When thrown back into the world, from which it attempted to diverge, specific challenges are apparent, especially when that dominant form of knowledge is itself undergoing drastic reconfiguration related to the function and legitimation of knowledge production grounded in the nation-state. Then, the question of local knowledge in the face of the global transformations of the past two decades is something to focus on.

While crisis always represents the possibility of alternatives in the sense of renegotiation it also presents the possibility of alternativelesness. Alternatives require capacity for knowledge production, what Wallerstein has called utopistics, that is "the serious assessment of historical alternatives, the exercise of our judgment as to the substantive rationality of alternative possible historical systems" (Wallerstein, 1998, 1). What the post-socialist states experienced was a delegitimization and crisis of their substantive rationality at a time when the world-system itself was entering an ever deepening crisis. Sarah Amsler has described this double crisis tellingly: "Within the post-Soviet academy all that was once solid had indeed melted into air and the future seemed both wide open and frighteningly impossible" and, she continues, "while there was ostensibly expanded space for intellectual experimentation, imagining what this might entail was difficult" (Amsler, 2007, ix).

Following the collapse of the Soviet Union not only social compacts founded upon or emulating the Soviet and the socialist model were delegitimized, similarly social inquiry and social science academia in its varied forms from social sciences to historical studies and Marxist theory in those regions became delegitimized. This was and continues to be a particularly difficult predicament especially where the state and the social sciences were wholly constructed during the Soviet or socialist eras, where no legacies, traditions and memories of those institutions predating socialism survived.

Especially so since the main goal of modernization in its socialist as well capitalist versions was to make the uncertain controllable and to produce predictability. Such activity is centered on a mutually re-enforcing relationship between theory and action or, in other words, between knowledge and political organization. With the current world-systemic crisis, however, this goal itself, the potential of modernity, has been subjected to competition for the sake of competition, agonistics.

The first problem then, that was encountered by post-socialist societies, was to come to terms with how their past—that all of a sudden lost its legitimacy as a modernizing project and social compact—had been built upon the premise of it being an incommensurable alternative to the capitalist mode of modernity that was now the option on offer. Following this first predicament the second one encountered especially by post-socialist knowledge producers and social science academics was the fact that the only critical perspective within the capitalist mode of modernity was nevertheless a variant or multiple variants of the very Marxism that they had just abandoned. These predicaments exacerbate each other as world-systemic disequilibrium drives onwards the deepening reconfiguration of the compact between liberalism and nationalism.

A multitude of adaptations arose. In Kyrgyzstan, for example, I encountered a fragmentation of the academic fields. Different universities and different departments hold onto different traditions that I would roughly categorize as Soviet, Western, National and Turkic/Islamic. According to interlocutors very little if any exchange of ideas or communication exists between these camps. The effects of such fragmentation, I believe, are dire to a society that is struggling to somehow anchor its identity and self-image as a sovereign state. This struggle is symbolically visible in the way in which the statue on the main square of the Kyrgyz capital Bishkek has been switched from Lenin to Lady Liberty (Erkindik) to Manas, the hero of the country's national epic, as one knowledge after another has failed to fulfill its potential. While the latest symbol, that of the nation, has been equally unsuccessful, no alternatives to replace it have emerged. I would suggest that, to accurately symbolize their predicament, they leave the pedestal empty.

In Georgia I encountered less of a fragmentation but more of a dichotomy and displacement. While the Western or Anglo-Saxon mode of academic knowledge is widely appropriated there, at least two cleavages emerged as patterns from my discussions. The first one is a practical one. This Anglo-Saxon academia in Georgia is still purely an imported good. Scholars who were trained in the West bring it to the country. What one then finds is that academic arguments over definitions or theories often happen in somewhat of a profane manner, in which the truthfulness of an argument is displaced outside an autonomous Georgian field of knowledge production. Rather, validity is sought in reference to connections to Anglo-Saxon academia in the West. This undermines the usefulness of any such debates for a society in orienting itself as well as in creating predictability.

The second cleavage that emerged from my discussion and observations in Georgia was the re-appearance and re-interpretation of Marxism, especially by young scholars, through Georgia's brief stint as an independent social democracy in the 1920s. While this is a possibly promising alternative, these scholars however expressed their frustration of how this perspective gives them little or no reference to the dominant Anglo-Saxon one that currently serves to reward, organize and orient social inquiry.

The situation in Tanzania spoke of similar displacement. At a conference in Dar Es Salaam a young scholar spoke widely of the need for a new "grand vision". He explained that it should not be another piece of paper, but a goal shared by all citizens of the country. This, however, immediately aroused strong criticism from the audience. The critique was based on the impossibility of sharing a vision as long the economy does not work and people remain poor. This is exemplary of the post-socialist predicament, especially in Tanzania with more than 120 ethnic groups and in contrast to the former Tanzanian leader Julius Nyerere's particular vision of socialism as joining people and transforming the society first in order to then transform the economy and lift people from poverty (see Nyerere, 1967, 1974). Nyerere's socialist model (first learning to walk on a tightrope and then stretching one) was abandoned in favor of an opposite logic of structural adjustment that believed in transforming the economy in order to then residually change the society too. The point is, however, that, while such reforms have successfully anchored other states to the world-economy, Tanzanian statehood and knowledge production, hand in hand, draws from Nyerere's opposite vision while, in addition, the world-system is increasingly demanding states to achieve both at once, leaving the state torn in between.

The relative lack of ethnic conflicts in the history of Tanzania is and continues to be an example of Nyerere's marching order. His logic however, was not consistent with the idea of Tanzania that was offered to it by the world-economy in the 80s and 90s. Market access was denied to Tanzania due to its mode of knowledge production that attempted to challenge the prevailing ideas of statehood. Once Tanzania let this mode go and accepted a position in the world-economy legitimized from elsewhere, only then were the potential economic benefits promised as a reward for being part of the family of nation-states. But now those economic relations were made such that should befit the new model's subordinated role, a role in which Tanzania is not a knowledge economy and does not self-legitimize its potential, and therefore its knowledge production is denied the access and protection of its peers in the core. Therefore the Tanzanian economy is supposed not to possess the ideational resources that arise from social welfare, equality and legal protection, but it had to succumb to economic activity conducive to exploitation and high income differences.

This game of one or the other is an integral component of global stratification that is offered to states in order for the world-economy to maintain its self-image. Alternate utopistics are perceived to hide in them a danger for this order and that self-image. Globally this contradiction arises from how "the recognition of knowledge reflects not just its intrinsic value but also the power and privilege organizing the systems in which that recognition functions" (Kennedy, 2014, xiii). The paradox of this tradeoff for Tanzania and several post-socialist states is its historical timing: democratization movements following the end of the cold war may have led to "more democratically constituted societies, but global interdependence may mean that those collectivities have very little to indeed decide and determine" (Wagner, 2012, x).

Research of and in the post-peripheries carries an incoherent and often mutually exclusive weight of theories and narratives of modern and postmodern, socialism and post-socialism and colonial, imperial and post-colonial. However, rarely do the perspectives applied originate from the regions' positions in the world-system, whereas the applied core and semiperipheral narratives and models are derived from attempts at explaining their privileged or dependent position. It would be a fair assessment that we are groping in the dark in terms of what is globally local for these post-peripheries. Sarah Amsler (2007) points this out in her book about knowledge production in the post-Soviet periphery, one of the few, on the topic. She writes that sociologists of knowledge and science who in the past have mobilized en masse to analyze lesser upheavals in scientific and intellectual life have remained curiously silent about the fate of ideas in post-Soviet societies. Perhaps this is because they have fallen beyond the grasp of knowledge that is relevant in the world-system today.

Post-socialist debates themselves over the role of knowledge promote a paradoxical dichotomy. On the one hand social scientific knowledge is seen as not sufficiently national and yet on the other hand national traditions are seen as backward whereas Western credentials and concepts are considered the hallmark. As mentioned, expanded space for intellectual experimentation following the fall of the Soviet Union in fact incapacitated social scientists because imagining what that might entail was difficult and continues to be so. Therefore the reconstruction of boundaries of legitimate knowledge was and is experienced as a crisis instead of an opportunity (Amsler, 2007). This, when situated into the world-system, prompts me to expand our analytic frame one way or another.

Statehood, World-System and Agonistics of Potentiality

Albert Bergesen (2000) has argued that hegemonic domination in the world-system has always been accompanied by a specific cultural framework and as cultural frameworks actively change so do social theories. Bergesen's analysis, however, needs to be extended to a world-system in crisis.

For Bergesen postmodernism is the cultural framework of the contemporary world-system, one that represents heightened intercapitalist rivalry. However, Bergesen sees this as the appearance of multiple competing voices, while I turn my attention to the limits and possibilities to participate in that competition in the first place. Therefore I combine the term agonistics with the term potentiality. Together they refer to a mode of organization caused by the tension of perpetual competition with a plurality of diminishing returns. Especially when connected to the structural crisis of the world-system, it appears that while creating more space for alternative positions, the crisis and competition also demands more capabilities and faster adaptation from any actor(s) desiring to advance their mode of politics. Especially access to structures of knowledge of the core, which facilitate cultural frameworks, is becoming increasingly limited, a scarce resource.

58   *Juho T. Korhonen*

The most worrying side of this investigation is that it implies that inclusion even into the dependent relations of the global society has become a privilege. As Boswell et al. (2000, 297) point out, while states have always balanced between upholding domestic standards and global competition, recently world-economic integration has risen to such a level, and continues to escalate so rapidly that global competition has won in importance. At the same time, as Wallerstein argues, complexity and competition have intensified in the modern world-economy whilst fluctuations between markets, currencies and power alliances have become manifold and faster, resulting in unpredictability (Wallerstein et al., 2013). Therefore, I believe that also the requirements to participate in the competition have become increasingly high, so high that not all can participate even in a dependent role. This situation has then excluded actors all together, such as some post-socialist states, as they possess little cultural or political means to influence the fluctuations or adapt to unpredictable swings. The struggle to provide affordable AIDS medication is one well-known example of the capacities and connections required to navigate successfully the tension of knowledge production and political struggles within global competition (see Chorev, 2012).

Then, just as the creation of the states' structure was part and parcel of the creation of a capitalist world-economy (Wallerstein, 1998, 10), now, not the disintegration as such, but devaluation, especially where politics and knowledge are concerned, of the states' structure is part and parcel of the world-systemic crisis. I believe that some post-socialists states are an example of this trend in their incapacity to participate in what William Connolly has, in other words, described as "dependent uncertainty" (Connolly, 2002, 22). This stands in contrast especially to dependent development (see Cardoso, 1972). Connolly specifically refers to the position of the most powerful states in driving this as they are forced to muster more power to remain self-governing. He recognizes this condition as rendering "anachronistic and dangerous" the "classic-modern conceptions of the state as a sovereign of a self-subsistent entity . . . with the efficacy to control the collective destiny" and thereby leading to a "gap between world systemacity and state efficacy" (Connolly, 2002, 24).

This condition is present worldwide. For example, Pierre Nora's popular work on French collective memory "Les lieux de mémoire" begins with a description of this predicament in the French case as well: "Just as the future—once a visible, predictable, manipulatable, well-marked extension of the present—has come to seem invisible, so we have gone from the idea of a visible past to one of an invisible past . . . given to us as radically other, the past is a world from which we are fundamentally cut off" (Sewell, 2009, 70). But the French had the capacity to alleviate this loss via new compacts within the core, facilitated by access to world centers of knowledge and a politically rekindled European project, while many post-socialist societies developed an excruciating relationship to the different tools and concepts, hegemonic or counter-hegemonic, that had promised them the visible, predictable, manipulatable and well-marked future as an extension of the past. This is roughly the wider condition that I see as the cause for agonistics of potentiality. It means that in a world-system where the state is considered to be the facilitator of power and resistance, that constitutes and reproduces the system, it is also crucial to investigate the limitations and possibilities of the facilitators themselves to engage that system. It calls for analytical preparedness to account for states that are unable to bridge the gap between world systemacity and state efficacy from either the side of sovereignty or dependency.

As the gap widens world-systemic knowledge networks and the world-economy no longer concern themselves with expansion to all political and societal spheres. Some societies and their political systems no longer have anything to offer to lower the basic costs of production as doing so has become an increasingly complex matter in terms of the connections that knowledge(s), capitalism and statehood have with each other. On the contrary, such integration might threaten the prevailing processes of renegotiation that are already burdened with structural uncertainty. It is to me an example of bifurcation and pluralization that has hurled different forms of knowledge and statehood to divergent trajectories, some still participating in a plurality of ways in the world-system while others are expulsed beyond dependency.

Moreover, we should not necessarily expect the crisis to end. Rather, a new compact might be formed between knowledge and politics. One that simply renders the continuing crisis more predictable. Then, just as the nation-state was not originally intended for all and was universalized only through socialist and anti-colonial struggles (Manela, 2007), the question is who will be excluded from any new compacts.

This gives me reason to believe that the form of the question about the successor system posed by Wallerstein—Porto Alegre or Davos as the ideatypical possibilities—might not provide the whole picture. Instead, it could as well be that multiple systems emerge from the structural crisis or that one or two dominant systems are able to maintain their internal logics while swaths of societies descend to a perpetual limbo beyond dependency.

The consideration of multiple logics and systems is crucial for defining critically "possible prospective scenarios of the future evolution of the capitalist world-system" (Wallerstein et al., 2013, x). There must be present a constant realization that we might have to rethink all of our analytical and conceptual tools even if at the moment the intensifying struggle between the contradictory logics of the system and consequentially the renegotiation of social compacts is a most pressing issue. In this sense I question the straightforward assumption made by Carlos Antonio Aquirre Rojas about the usefulness of intellectual tools based on a portrait of the past and present in keeping an eye on the possible future scenarios, especially I question this assumption in terms of a "forward projection of those tendencies operating today" (Wallerstein et al., 2013, xviii).

Conclusion

Preliminary empirics from post-peripheries suggest that some knowledge work has lost its all-encompassing grounding in the so-called redemptive epistemologies of modernity and progress. This dissociation came with an agonistic stress on freedom, as Wenman discusses (2013, 299–300), "without producing an alternative conception of the temporality of the post-modern republic". Instead, Wenman suggests, a trap arises from the tension between the alternativelesness of the present system and a knowledge of politics that is bereft of new ideas. The symbolic pedestal without a statue.

Knowledge and its production is the regulation of agonistics, while potentiality is dependency on alternatives, be they capitalistic or antisystemic. A literary analogue to an agonistics of potentiality in action could then be Voltaire's Candide, had his journey never ended and had he kept repeating the mantra of his teacher Pangloss.

Recently world-systems analysis has pointed out that the current crisis is in fact a multiplicity of crises (see Chase-Dunn, 2013; Brewer, 2012), signaling towards the idea of uncertainty and plurality of modernity that distances the past from the future and alternatives from one another. Such a situation may call for a united alternative to arise, as Chase-Dunn proposes, or for similarly complex and interrelational work connecting a multiplicity of expressions for political change, as Rose Brewer calls for. Be it either way, such activity hinges upon cognitive resources and network building, that is on both the capacity to wage discursive struggles against capitalism as well as the capacity to advance alternative visions, strategies and potential, as Carroll and Sapinski have argued (2013). This takes place within in a global society and against capitalist disembedding. It is not centered upon national states and has an emphasis "on constructing critical knowledges and solidarities, across borders" (Carroll et al., 2013, 214). An agonistics of potentiality then describes a condition within systemic crisis that lacks capacity for this type of action, caused by the crisis that has not yet abandoned its past or presented new alternatives for the future that would be legitimized in the form of a renewed social compact; a new legitimate and known way for constituting power.

As Giorgio Agamben and Antonio Negri have pointed out, "the unresolved dialectic between constituting power and constituted power opens the way for a new articulation of the relationship between potentiality and actuality, which requires nothing less than a rethinking of the ontological categories of modality in their totality" (Agamben, 1998, 31). However, first, there is no knowing if and when a rethinking might consolidate itself and, second,

Statehood at the End of the Rainbow? 61

whether that would take the form of a single or multiple competing political organization(s), and lastly, whether any such modalities would be inclusive and accessible.

Because of these three uncertainties I propose that we must also consider how a world-system in crisis and undergoing transformation does not only present itself as increased and more complex stratification but also as tensions—between the past and future, knowledge and politics—that produce incapacity.

Note

1 Giorgio Agamben, a leading theorist of potentiality, points to the tension I seek to conceptualize in the following manner: "until a new and coherent ontology of potentiality (beyond the steps that have been made in this direction by Spinoza, Schelling, Nietzsche and Heidegger) has replaced the ontology founded on the primacy of actuality and its relation to potentiality, a political theory freed from the aporias of sovereignty remains unthinkable." (Agamben, 1998, 31).

References

Agamben, Giorgio. 1998. *Homo Sacer: Sovereign Power and Bare Life*. Stanford, CA: Stanford University Press.

Amsler, Sarah. 2007. *The Politics of Knowledge in Central Asia: Science Between Marx and the Market*. London and New York: Routledge.

Bergesen, Albert. 2000. "Postmodernism Explained." In Hall, Thomas (ed.), *A World-Systems Reader: New Perspectives on Gender, Urbanism, Cultures, Indigenous Peoples, and Ecology*. Oxford: Rowman & Littlefield Publishers.

Blommaert, Jan. 1997. "Intellectuals and Ideological Leadership in Ujamaa Tanzania." *African Languages and Cultures*, 10(2): 129–144.

Boswell, Terry and Christopher Chase-Dunn. 2000. "From State Socialism to Global Democracy: The Transnational Politics of the Modern World-System." In Hall, Thomas (ed.), *A World-Systems Reader: New Perspectives on Gender, Urbanism, Cultures, Indigenous Peoples, and Ecology*. Oxford: Rowman & Littlefield Publishers.

Brewer, Rose. 2012. "Political Economy of the World-System: The Imperative of African-Centered Utopias." *Journal of World-Systems Research*, 18(2): 146–150.

Cardoso, Fernando Henrique. 1972. "Dependency and Development in Latin America." *New Left Review*, 74: 83–95.

Carroll, William and Jean Philippe Sapinski. 2013. "Embedding Post-Capitalist Alternatives? The Global Network of Alternative Knowledge Production and Mobilization." *Journal of World-Systems Research*, 19(2): 175–180.

Chase-Dunn, Christopher. 2013. "Five Linked Crises in Contemporary World-System." *Journal of World-Systems Research*, 18(2): 146–150.

Chorev, Nitsan. 2012. "Changing Global Norms through Reactive Diffusion: The Case of Intellectual Property Protection of AIDS Drugs." *American Sociological Review*, 77(5): 831–853.

62   Juho T. Korhonen

Connolly, William. 2002. *Identity/Difference: Democratic Negotiations of Political Paradox*. Minneapolis: University of Minnesota Press.

Kennedy, Michael. 2014. *Globalizing Knowledge: Intellectuals, Universities and Publics in Transformation*. Stanford: Stanford University Press.

Levitas, Ruth. 2013. *Utopia as Method: The Imaginary Reconstitution of Society*. Hampshire: Palgrave Macmillan.

Manela, Erez. 2007. *The Wilsonian Moment: Self-Determination and the International Origins of Anti Colonial Nationalism*. New York: Oxford University Press.

Nyerere, Julius. 1967. *Freedom and Unity*. London: Oxford University Press.

Nyerere, Julius. 1974. *Freedom and Development*. New York: Oxford University Press.

Pitcher, M. Anne and Kelly M. Askew. 2006. "African Socialisms and Postsocialisms." *Africa: Journal of the International African Institute*, 76(1): 1–14.

Sewell, William H. 2009. *Logics of History: Social Theory and Social Transformation*. Chicago: University of Chicago Press.

Singh, Bhrigupati. 2015. *Poverty and the Quest for Life: Spiritual and Material Striving in Rural India*. Chicago: University of Chicago Press.

Skocpol, Theda and Margaret Somers. 1980. "The Uses of Comparative History in Macrosocial Inquiry." *Comparative Studies in Society and History*, 22(2): 174–197.

Wallerstein, Immanuel. 1998. *Utopistics: Or, Historical Choices of the Twenty-First Century*. New York: The New Press.

Wallerstein, Immanuel, Charles Lemert and Carlos Aguirre Rojas. 2013. *Uncertain Worlds: World-Systems Analysis in Changing Times*. Boulder, CO and London: Paradigm Publishers.

Wagner, Peter. 2012. *Modernity: Understanding the Present*. Cambridge: Polity Press.

Wenman, Mark. 2013. *Agonistic Democracy: Constituent Power in the Era of Globalisation*. Cambridge: Cambridge University Press.

5

MIGRATION AS A RESPONSE TO GLOBAL INEQUALITY

Vilna Bashi Treitler

Migration as a Response to Global Inequality

Subscribers to World-Systems Theory have long understood that nations are connected and unequal in power and wealth. They argue that this inequality—between richer and more powerful core nations, and poorer and less powerful peripheral nations—stems from a history of imperialism and colonialism that transferred wealth to the core, along with material resources, and labor (although labor is not as free to travel the global capitalist world system as are capital and resources). The wide and ever-widening global income gap between the world's rich and poor follows the core/peripheral divide. (Semi-peripheral states are semi-dependent, and share characteristics of both core and peripheral countries.) Currently, 1% of the world's population holds nearly 50% of the world's wealth, while the bottom half holds less than 1% of the world's riches—a situation that causes pundits to predict widespread social

64 *Vilna Bashi Treitler*

unrest (Resnikoff, 2014). Of the world's wealth, North America holds 34.7%, Europe 32.4% (Credit Suisse, 2014). While the world's poorest may not have the means to move, those that can move often take advantage of opportunities to enter core countries (that is, Europe and North America) and create for themselves better lives.

At one time the prevailing scientific models presumed migration to be best measured as discrete events undertaken according to a rational-actor decision-making rubric and occurring unidirectionally between an origin and a destination. Now, it is no longer news when social scientists configure migration as a transnational process having ripple-effects in both origin and destination sites. Further, we now understand migration to be rooted in webs of kith and kin linked across households in two or more countries, who together share knowledge and resources that affect the collectivity in positive and sometimes in negative ways. We call the webs *networks*, and the shared resources *social* or *economic capital*, and together network capital is considered to be of great importance in understanding how geographic, social and economic mobility occurs. When resources are sufficient, networks facilitate migrants' abilities to cross borders, create labor market niches, start their own businesses, as well as offer nonmaterial social support and influence politics (Tilly and Brown, 1967; Kuo and Tsai, 1986; Basch, 1987; Massey, 1998; Gilbertson and Gurak, 1992; Ho, 1993; Hagan, 1994; Waldinger, 1996; Koser, 1997; Glick, 1999; Levitt, 1999; Waters, 1999; Bashi 2007; Menjivar, 1997 and 2000 for discussions of the alternative capital-poor case). Networks can be so effective at aiding migrants that they encompass increasingly wider swathes of the sending society such that they may even successfully thwart laws and policies meant to control or prevent flows to individual states (Donato, Durand, and Massey, 1992; Massey, 1998; Bashi, 2007). It is still news, however, to have social scientists study and understand migration as a global phenomenon (rather than a process that is best studied between paired binary origin-destination states) that contextualize that analysis in global inequality (as opposed to acknowledging only the relative poverty in the destination from which migrants originate) and acknowledge that this inequality has a racial bias (born when Europeans traveled and encountered those they deemed "other" and chose to conquer). I argue that taking a network approach to understanding migration can allow scholars to keep global inequality in context—perhaps qualitative network analysis is useful to migration scholars who are open to the influence of World-Systems Theory.

What Do We Mean by Inequality, and When Is It Global?

International migration is a global process not only because movement occurs between one nation and another, but also because individual nations are linked in ways that have global effects. We live in an unequal global economy in which nations are ranked hierarchically according to their power to control capital and labor and set prices for these inputs to production. People in search of a better life move within a world system that left many marred by legacies of colonization: ruining indigenous peoples with practices ranging from marginalization to genocide, grabbing control of people, land and resources for exploitation, creating an international division of labor, and organizing the world's wealth so that it enriched Western Europe and those later described as racially white, and causing "underdevelopment" of homelands of those made nonwhite while leaving them with the option to develop mainly in a hobbled or dependent fashion (Rodney, 2011; Galeano, 1997; McMichael, 2000; Wallerstein, 1974). Further, colonizers and their beneficiaries created and employed racial thinking that supported and justified their resource draining exports (Smedley, 1993).

At the same time, migration is also a local-level phenomenon where immigrant incorporation into local hierarchical systems takes place. The same processes that encouraged the global reach of the ideas that humans should be hierarchically valued according to the fallacy of racial superiority and inferiority also caused those ideas to develop local variations that shaped the development of individual nation states (Marx, 1998). These ideas, though developed centuries ago and proven false many times over, still shape the destinies of the racialized and the racist worldwide and the way science is conducted (Roberts, 2011; Morning, 2011; Muhammad, 2010; Smedley, 1993); they even continue to shape the way social scientists study immigration (Bashi Treitler, 2015).

Inequality is a vague term that can be applied to mean unequal measures on any variable that can have graduated values (Allison, 1978); but normally it is a shorthand term that sociologists use to mark societies that have extremes in the quality of life connected to resources and opportunities available in variable amounts to people in different stations of life both within a single nation, and among the world's nations; it shapes us as pyramids of people—the few who have much are at the top, and the many who have little are at the bottom. The Political Economy of the World System is the branch of the discipline that argues that the stratified system that comprises the nations of the world in unequal fashion focuses on the links among these different kinds of inequality, arguing that two sets of nations (one a poorer periphery dependent upon a wealthy core) are entangled in a capitalist world-economy driven to accumulate capital and condition prices of commodities, labor and capital, and involved in the creation of all modern world institutions,[1] including classes, ethno-national groups, households, states (Wallerstein, 1984, 29) and, I would add, races.

Migrants fight the political and economic stagnation relegated to them in the systemic periphery as they move to resource-rich places in the core; in the process, they battle inequalities that infringe on opportunity and outcomes at global and local levels. Inequalities are not just data (that is, measurable differences in quality of life), but are obstacles blocking access to the very resources hoarded in the core. Migrants who arrange themselves into networks rich in economic and social capital efficiently transmit information, services and goods from the more fortunate to the less fortunate, helping to ensure that global/local inequalities are challenged, and migrant network members are therefore best poised to succeed (Bashi, 2007).

Network Structures

Networks function to allow some of the world's less fortunate people to partake in the resources held in the nations of the world's most fortunate people. By allowing newcomers from countries in the peripheral regions of the global economy to enter nations in the political-economic core and economically succeed, immigrant social networks provide some counterweight to global inequality inherent in the world system. Partly, it is the networks' specific structure that allows this inequality-fighting function to occur. However, in this paper I focus less on that structure, and more on the socioeconomic outcomes relevant to global inequality (Bashi, 2007).[2] The migrant networks I studied were linked transnationally among metropolitan areas surrounding New York, London and Toronto and five islands in the English-speaking Eastern Caribbean.

Because I sought to study the connections between persons in transnational networks, I needed a method of data collection that could study how network links are made and what processes travel across those links. I found that quantitative methods of network analysis could not allow me to answer the questions that I posed about network building processes and mechanisms. I needed a method akin to the grounded theory approach to ethnography since I wished to understand their social relations from members' own standpoint (surmising that capturing this perspective is the only way I could understand both how they created and maintained their networks, but also why they did so). On the other hand, because network connections and operations are not visible to the naked eye—not in the way street life or social systems revolving around singular spaces like restaurants might be (see Anderson, 1992; Duneier, 1994, for examples)—immersing myself in an immigrant community would be insufficient, and certainly it was prohibitive to immerse myself in several different such communities in several different countries. For this reason, I employed a new method of research that interrogated individuals' oral histories to understand the connections they themselves knew intimately and could explain to me. For data collection, I employed what I have named "ethnographic interviewing," a method where researchers enter the field guided by the premise that those who live in field have the best available accounts of and explanations for the social phenomena in which they are immersed daily; a conversational style is employed to collect oral histories to be used to generate robust propositions about the field's social, economic and political life. Using this method, I mapped the transnational networks and collated the various types of aid network members gave to one another; rather than defining aid in advance, I asked them explicitly how they were "helped" by others, and I asked them to tell me who they had "helped" and how. The data produced by these methods certainly did not lend themselves to applications of rational-actor models of individual decision makers that have traditionally been applied to the study of migration streams; indeed, they enabled a vision of how migrants built networks, and allowed me to see under which conditions migrants and potential migrants failed to build networks. By inquiring of migrants how they defined help (that is, how they were helped to leave one place, enter another and integrate into destination communities while keeping relations with home communities) I learned about the central figures (the aforementioned "hubs") who, with the help they offered, veritably ensured the success of newcomers through their active selection of potential migrants. (This finding is in direct contrast to those migration models that give primacy to self-selection as a driver of future migration.) I credit my research method with allowing me to gather the data that brings me to this alternative explanation. In the data analysis portion of the research, I found that I could collate migration network socioeconomic successes specific actions that each directly aid network members in inserting themselves into positions higher in the hierarchy of nations. The remaining sections of this paper detail these socioeconomically successful outcomes, concluding with an overview of the ways networked immigrants join together to combat global inequality.

How Networks Respond to Inequality

I interviewed migrants in transnational networks involving Eastern Caribbean peoples who move to three Western cities: Toronto, in Ontario, Canada; New York City, in New York (State), USA; and London, in England, UK. These networked migrants aided each other in five different areas that could be said to directly counter the ways that inequality operates on global and local levels. First, they moved newcomers across national boundaries. This is far from unimportant, as national borders of Western states are barriers to the resources held within the states. After entry, migrants must find ways to stay (particularly if they entered without documentation sufficient to guarantee residency). Physical presence also means varying degrees of incorporation into hierarchical systems of labor, housing and racial and ethnic relations. I take each of these in turn as I review the data from studying these transnational networks.

68 *Vilna Bashi Treitler*

Getting Out of the Periphery and Into the Political-Economic Core

Migrants in immigrant networks use their knowledge of immigration regulations to construct flexible and creative arrangements to send for family members and friends. When I say, "send for," I mean that veteran migrants use legal and extra-legal means to achieve the ends of having a potential migrant join them in the destination (Garrison and Weiss, 1979; Bashi 2007).

In the transnational migration networks I chronicled, newcomers were recruited to join networks in destinations—the potential migrant did not him/herself have the opportunity to choose the destination. One migrant in my sample explained it this way, in describing his anger that his sister did not send for him when she was in the United States and had the opportunity to bring him into the United States.

> She could have done it. She had legal status in this country, she could have easily become a citizen and the laws were much [more] lenient then to allow your mom, your dad, your brothers, and sisters, whoever wanted to come to this country, but she decided to move to Canada [because] quote, unquote, it's cleaner over there. She tried to get me into school in Canada but, you know, things are much different over there.

He concluded by explaining that the requirements to enter Canada were much greater at the time, so he couldn't get there either; he had to wait for another opportunity and another hub to get him into the USA. His is just one example of the ways potential migrants had to wait to be chosen to get aid to go to one of a few destinations; people also migrated to an intermediate place (a different island, or a different Western city) in order to arrive at a more desirable destination in the West. Since people had to move fast in order to take advantage of the opportunities that arose for them, they often had to be flexible in timing their departures, and in the kinds of work they accepted. This led to child fosterage (where children of migrants are left behind—often without informing the children!—to be cared for by relatives or friends), and in people agreeing to do work for which they were little trained (e.g., babysitting/nannying, construction, etc.)

In order to stay after arrival, networks used a few different kinds of schemes. Of course, overstaying visas is one such method but it was not the sole method by which the network ensured a newcomer could remain. Sometimes, network members would develop and proffer legal expertise, helping newcomers to file the paperwork to become "legal." As one of my respondents explained: "Because of my overall knowledge, right, being an auditor, accountant, I do a lot, because of the job, you know. I'm aware of the system—the legal system and the immigration system—so I help all my relatives and all my—they bring their friends and I file the immigration papers to get their sons and daughters up here. I enjoy doing it, so I just do it . . . for nothing."

Migrant networks also used employers to solidify legal status—sometimes the employment was secured even before the migrant had arrived in the destination; oftentimes, the newcomer was illegally there, but employment was secured and the situation was "fixed," either by the employer themselves, or by the aforementioned network self-made legal specialists. Network members also manipulated formal labor recruitment programs to bring in their loved ones—a significant finding considering that these programs are normally understood to be drivers of a separate kind of migration, one that is either wholly unrelated to networks, or one that begins a new network altogether. However, my research shows that veteran migrants unattached to formal recruitment channels in some cases manipulated those channels to bring in newcomers chosen by network hubs. Since I found this to be the case both in the UK and in the US, and therefore unspecific to a single location or to migrants from a single point of origin, I surmise that use of a mix of opportunities—in this case, formal recruitment programs along with job creation, departures from intermediate destinations, arrivals at less-than-optimal destinations, and the employment of a succession of documented and undocumented statuses in succession—is a feature of network migration per se, and not at all a characteristic of the ethnic culture of the migrant group.

Forging Socioeconomic Footholds in Destinations

Spokes—the term I used to describe newcomers aided by hubs who usher them into veteran migrant networks—are aided in the first instance by co-residence, a key component of contemporary network migration for black Caribbean migrants to Western cities. In fact, spokes are normally brought to stay in the home of the hubs who sent for them, during which time they are given gifts of bed and board and often clothing and other amenities; newcomers then oftentimes return the favors with pay after they begin working. Co-residence is a crucial first step because it creates savings for the spoke, and indebts him/her to the hub (where this last is the basis of good performance in the job the hubs finds for the spoke).

Network connections of course aid newcomers in finding employment in the destination, but perhaps the extent to which the network aided its members is not as widely known. Employment aid in the networks I studied continued well beyond the first job—network information also was used to aid employment moves horizontally (for better pay, more status), and laterally (if a network member needed to escape poor or dangerous working conditions). To accomplish this, a great deal of control over sectors of the labor market would be required—and immigrant groups tend not to have so much power and control. Thus, network "hubs" instead used great flexibility in order to secure employment for those they aided. Sometimes aid was available where migrants are concentrated in the labor market (that is, employment niches), but niches were not always available to black migrants; and in some cases, women and men did not have equally strong niches, nor equally easy access to jobs. (For example, in New York City, women had more powerful control over their labor market niches, while men had fewer labor market niches and had less control over them.) However, to be as successful as they were, network members could not limit themselves to niche sectors; whether in a niche or outside of it, network members could find employment wherever they would avail themselves of it.

Once a spoke had gotten on his/her feet, they are able to move out of a co-resident situation to a rental-housing unit. Oftentimes this meant renting a hub's property, which in fact aided the hub, sometimes to the degree that they could move forward and bring the next person. For example, one of my respondents explained that he rented out his home to people because he knew his co-ethnics would have difficulty finding good housing, saying: "It was very difficult for people to rent; most people don't want to rent [to apartment-seekers] with children; children could be destructive—not could be, they *are* destructive." Another reports:

> When my brother came he stayed [lived] here with me and then we went back home and he come back again. While he was here that house [he points out the window and down the road to a nearby house] went up for sale right here . . . and they called him and we convinced him to get the house rather than paying rent. It costs about the same thing to pay for— pay rent—you have to pay for a mortgage and you're renting and you don't own it. There's no equity—but if you put yourself out, even if you have to lie on the floor [and have no furniture because the money goes to pay the mortgage], there's a roof over your head.

Some spokes eventually purchased homes, and with hubs' aid, they often contributed to the formation of ethnic enclaves. Network members some-times organized themselves into rotating savings associations, whereby asso-ciation members donate into a savings pool and are awarded the pool when it becomes their turn (often before they would have been able to save that amount themselves). These associations were often the source of down pay-ments on homes, but the windfall could be applied to other big ticket items. Many reported emigrating in order to secure educations for themselves, and savings associations aided in tuition payments. Mutual aid was also afforded to those back in the home country, in the form of remittances and barrels of goods that are expensive there but less expensive in the West. And finally, perhaps in the same spirit of the other kinds of social support that the network gives, newcomers also found themselves encouraged to accept help in finding romantic partners.

Managing Social Integration: Racism and Reputations

Racism. Immigration as a subject of public discourse is one where emotions run high. Partly, this is because immigration has always been vulnerable to critiques charging racism since it focuses citizens on how to imagine their nation and question which persons appropriately render that image. At best this race-tinge discourse may hearken to race without making explicit reference to it; at its worst, the discourse veers into xenophobia and perhaps even hate. The idea of racial belonging and ill-fitting has defined migration for centuries (Paul, 1997; Bashi, 2004, 2007), even if some researchers argue that we are in a new phase of global migration (see Castles and Miller, 1993; Massey et al., 1998; United Nations, 2012)).[3] Indeed, two very important historical continuities between the pre- and post-1965 migration eras center on evolving ideas of race.

First, we can mark continuities in migration legislation and policy that have explicitly racially unequal outcomes. For example, the US Immigration Act of 1924 (also known as the National Quota Act) that allotted to racially "white" core nations generous quotas that were so excessively large that migrants from these nations did not fill the quota; by contrast, "non-white" nations in the periphery were given comparatively microscopic quota numbers that were never sufficient to fill the demands to migrate. Scholars for this reason still cite as a historical landmark the 1965 passage of the US Family Reunification Act, which replaced the National Quota Act. The former immigration act was an improvement over the latter: it did not have explicitly racist formulations in its content, and was perceived as race-blind. However, since the migrant pool in the USA was formed by decades of racist immigration law that ensured those pools were filled with whites, and new law allows mainly these migrants to reunite with extended family members, the Family Reunification must then be read as intending to ensure continued preferential entry to whites over nonwhites (Bashi, 2004). Migration policies like these were not privy only to the US. Assuredly racist immigration laws and policies like these were maintained by the USA, Canada and the UK, who together created a virtual global blockade against black migration that both preceded and followed the mid-twentieth century mark. (Bashi, 2004). This kind of intra-state collusion, that racially filters a mobile global populace at Western state borders—rooted as it is in imperial and colonial enterprises that created the West's wealth, and justified with Western racial pseudo-science—leads me to argue that migrants navigate a global racial hierarchy of nations.

Second, we can look to internal processes of post-migration national incorporation that comprise the local hierarchy of races. For example, we may (re)read Western immigration history as waves of racialization of newcomers in ways that suited the needs of a particular era and location, as some migration scholars have done for some time (Castels and Miller, 1993; Sassen, 1999; Bashi Treitler, 2013). Specifically, we now read migrants emigrating from Europe as white, but prior to the mid-century mark, migrants to the United States from the South and East parts of Europe were not deemed white at the time of their migration to the United States (Bashi Treitler, 2013). Similarly, Irish migration to the UK was not free from racialization. Indeed, Irish inclusion in Britain has even been described as "forced" since their post-1962 inclusion certainly did not prevent their racial denigration (Hickman, 1998); instead, Britain was then, like contemporary Ireland is now, conceived of as a "white" nation coercively having to "diversify" (Hickman, 2007). In sum, a race-based ideology of assimilationism is generally applicable to immigrant newcomers in the contemporary period, where we may read assimilationism as a kind of racialized processing of newcomers (Hickman, 2007; see also Bashi Treitler, 2015).

From the point of view of networks, historical phases of migration law are not terribly relevant—what counts is whether one can enter a country, survive and succeed. Networks are made of the social matter that only ebbs and flows as best it can, given migration policies that allow or deny entry to persons who desire to better their lives through geographic relocation. I am not suggesting that the degree of racism in migration policies is entirely irrelevant. But racist immigration policies are a subset of all migration policies, and networks must study policies. But, if survival and indeed economic flourishing is to ensue, networks study policies enough to have them work in network members' favor, or be worked around. Network members adjust their operations to counter and resist those immigration laws and policies that prevent their entry, including the category of policies that have explicit or hidden racist intent. In particular, for the case at hand, English-speaking black Caribbean migrants to global core cities were well aware of the racist ideology of immigration and quite intentionally used their migrant networks to conquer racist policy and legislative obstacles to entry (Bashi, 2007).[4] Migrants in the New York City area nearly always brought up the idea of race spontaneously, without my ever asking about it. (As noted, my research method centered only on learning their oral history of mutual aid in an ethnographic fashion—I let the migrants themselves decide what parts of that history were important to discuss.) Migrants to London did not always bring up the issue without prompting—but these migrants were nonetheless quite literally activist in response to their encounters with racism in England, so their not bringing it up initially in interviews did not mean that racism had no place in their lives. Indeed, immigrants in London echoed the New Yorkers' understandings and experiences of racism as an obstructing force in a black migrant's life, including in the unequal application of border access. Migrants also noted racism in the public school systems, in their workplaces and in their attempts to secure better housing for themselves (Bashi, 2007). As just one example, a migrant in the New York metropolitan area explained,

> We were the first blacks to move into this area many years ago, and the day of the closing, close to the night, they attempted to destroy this house. . . . They attempted to destroy it with water. They flooded the whole house, and throw [*sic*] a can of black paint through the picture window. Therefore, it destroyed the walls of the dining room and the rugs in the dining room and sitting room.

Migrants' networks enable network members a degree of detachment from racism and even explicit racial acts because they are able to insulate themselves: they can get together with co-ethnics for social support that makes them feel more at home than they might otherwise be in a place that is unwelcoming to them. Network membership also helps migrants to achieve what looks like economic success—at least in the US, especially when compared with persons left back home, and perhaps African Americans as a group, where ethnic social distancing allows for increased ethnic status; in the UK, since Afro-Caribbean people have no such black ethnic group to which they may be favorably compared, the network does not give the same benefits in buffering against racism (Bashi, 2007; Bashi Treitler, 2013).

Reputations. Networking veteran migrants make great sacrifices to aid those they left behind, and some (that is, "hubs") sacrifice further, bringing along newcomers and helping them resettle in destination societies. Aid begins with "sending for" someone (choosing a prospective migrant and gaining them entry), and can include co-residence, securing winter clothing, employment (initial and subsequent, that together can make an upward career trajectory), savings associations, housing arrangements (both initial and subsequent, that mark bigger and more secure living arrangements and even further wealth building), etc. Collectively these networks—when the resources are ample and the racial dynamics favorable—can enable socio-economic success that indicates upward social mobility on a global scale. Indeed, these arrangements secure the reputations of the hubs themselves, who gain reputations as the "go to" person for all manner of migration assistance, which can be especially rewarding for migrants who begin as pioneers (some of the first in one's village or one's family to migrate). In the course of ushering responsible newcomers into neighborhoods and job sites, hubs—who selectively bring one person at a time in a manner that coerces migrants into appropriately auspicious behaviors—create networks that build favorable reputations for the ethnic group. Specifically, employers and neighbors see them as positively ethnically distinct from others; but this networks success obtains only when resources are not too scarce and racial hierarchies are such that affirmative ethnic group distinction is possible (Bashi, 2007, 2013). While upward mobility on a global scale is possible for successfully networked groups like the Afro-Caribbean diaspora I studied, their relative successes are tempered by the local dynamics of inequality (including, but not limited to, race, gender and labor- and housing-market stratification systems) that can constrain network processes.

Summary and Conclusion

Migrants use geographic relocation to fight against the global inequality that leaves their home economies struggling with scarcity and obstacles that global dominants place in the way of opportunities for sharing resources hoarded by the more developed Western economies. Networks are one of the most effective mechanisms enabling migrants to surmount or remove these obstacles. In this paper, I have specifically focused on network achievements that enhance that quest for increased equality: geographic mobility, mobility in labor markets, mobility in housing, social support and ethnoracial solidarity against racism.

Lest the reader think that network mechanisms like these are specific to Caribbean nationals, evidence abounds that migrants from resource-poor regions of the world have been organizing themselves in this way for decades. I raked the historical literature on migrant networks, and showed that the hub-and-spoke model I had developed has application to several groups in the historical and contemporary literature on migration (Bashi, 2007).

While networked migrants of all ethnicities and time periods seem to struggle against their place in a global hierarchy of nations, networking for success is not exactly the same as overturning global and local inequalities. Because networks are selective in membership, choosing to aid only very specific potential migrants, the social capital inherent in network relations is not available to all potential migrants (Bashi, 2007). Indeed, even those potential migrants that have access to veteran migrants in networks are to some degree at the mercy of those veterans; and even the most social capital-rich migrant surely does not control the levers of power that provide access to nations with economic strength in the global system. Migrant networks have notable effects on members' own positions in the global political economy, and even help to redistribute monetary resources with remittances they send to their countries of origin in ways sufficiently strong enough to restructure peripheral economies. However, network activities pose no long-term permanent, widespread and sufficiently redistributive solution to the problem of global inequity.

Notes

1 Wallerstein (1984, 28–9) writes, "I believe one can argue the case for integrated production processes as constituting this heuristic criterions, and I shall use it to draw the boundaries which circumscribe a concrete 'historical system,' by which I mean an empirical set of such production processes integrated according to some particular set of rules, the human agents of which interact in some 'organic' way, such that changes in the functions of any group or changes in the boundaries of the historical system must follow certain rules if the entity's survival is not to be threatened. This is what we mean by such other terms as a social economy or a specific social division of labor . . . This is a long preface to a coherent analysis of the role of states in the modern world . . . The capitalist world-economic constitutes one such historical system . . . [and] has involved the creation of all the major institutions of the modern world: classes, ethnic/national groups, households—and the 'states.'"

2 I have argued elsewhere (Bashi, 2007) that immigrant social networks have a specific structure—i.e., a veteran immigrant with a great deal of knowledge about entering the destination country and succeeding there (someone I labeled a "hub") makes a conscious decision to offer that aid to newcomers (who I named "spokes") in culturally specific ways (that I labeled a "culture of reciprocity"). The hub and spokes engage in migration-related transactions that bring reputations to the former and socioeconomic successes to the latter through linkages that traverse the globe. These hub-and-spoke networks of kin, fictive kin, and friends joined together to increase their potential for survival and a better quality of life.

3 These authors see this recent phase of migration as marked by an increasing rate of postindustrial international movement that began in the mid-1960s and has been dominated by outflows from developing nations from the southern hemisphere and Asia.

4 Walter et al. (2002), too, found that Irish persons in Britain constructed their identities knowing that they were racialized, even when public and private education failed to provide the populace with the history of racialized colonization, leading to a silence about that history in the public sphere.

References

Allison, Paul D. 1978. "Measures of Inequality." *American Sociological Review*. 43(6, December): 865–80.

Anderson, Elijah. 1992. *Streetwise: Race, Class, and Change in an Urban Community*. Chicago, IL: University of Chicago Press.

Basch, Linda. 1987. "The Vincentians and Grenadians: The Role of Voluntary Associations in Immigrant Adaptation to New York City." *New Immigrants in New York*, Nancy Foner, editor. New York: Columbia University Press. Pp. 159–93.

Bashi Treitler, Vilna Francine. 2004. "Globalized Anti-Blackness: Transnationalizing Western Immigration Law, Policy, and Practice." *Ethnic and Racial Studies*. 24(4, July): 584–606.

Bashi Treitler, Vilna Francine. 2007. *Survival of the Knitted: Immigrant Social Networks in a Stratified World*. Stanford, CA: Stanford University Press.

Bashi Treitler, Vilna Francine. 2013. *The Ethnic Project: Transforming Racial Fiction into Ethnic Factions*. Stanford, CA: Stanford University Press.

Bashi Treitler. 2015. "Social Agency and White Supremacy in Immigration Studies." *Sociology of Race and Ethnicity*, vol. 1 (no. 1) pp. 153–165.

76   *Vilna Bashi Treitler*

Castels, Stephen, and Mark J. Miller. 1993. *The Age of Migration: International Population Movements in the Modern World*. Second edition. New York: Guilford Press.

Credit Suisse. 2014. *Global Wealth Report 2014*. (October). https://publications. credit-suisse.com/tasks/render/file/?fileID=60931FDE-A2D2-F568-B041B58 C5EA591A4.

Donato, Katharine M., Jorge Durand, and Douglas S. Massey. 1992. "Stemming The Tide? Assessing the Deterrent Effects of the Immigration Reform and Control Act." *Demography.* 29(2, May): 139–57.

Duneier, Mitchell. 1994. *Slim's Table: Race, Respectability, and Masculinity*. The American Studies Collection Series. Chicago, IL: University of Chicago Press.

Galeano, Eduardo. 1997 [1972]. *Open Veins of Latin America: Five Centuries of the Pillage of a Continent*. New York: Monthly Review Press.

Garrison, Vivian, and Carol I. Weiss. 1979. "Dominican Family Networks and United States Immigration Policy: A Case Study." *International Migration Review.* 13(2, Summer): 264–83.

Gilbertson, Greta, and Douglas T. Gurak. 1992. "Household Transitions in the Migrations of Dominicans and Colombians to New York." *International Migration Review.* 26(1, Spring): 22–45.

Glick, Jennifer E. 1999. "Economic Support from and to Extended Kin: A Comparison of Mexican Americans and Mexican Immigrants." *International Migration Review.* 33(3): 745–65.

Hagan, Jacqueline M. 1994. *Deciding to Be Legal: A Maya Community in Houston*. Philadelphia, PA: Temple University Press.

Hickman, Mary J. 1998. "Reconstructing Deconstructing 'Race': British Political Discourses about the Irish in Britain." *Ethnic and Racial Studies* 21(2, March): 288–307.

Hickman, Mary J. 2007. "Immigration and Monocultural (Re)Imaginings in Ireland and Britain." *Translocations: The Irish Migration, Race and Social Transformation Review.* 2(1): 12–25.

Ho, Christine. 1993. "The Internationalization of Kinship and the Feminization of Caribbean Migration: The Case of Afro-Trinidadian Immigrants in Los Angeles." *Human Organization.* 52(1): 32–40.

Koser, Khalid. 1997. "Social Networks and the Asylum Cycle: The Case of Iranians in the Netherlands." *International Migration Review.* 31(3): 591–612.

Kuo, Wen H., and Yung-Mei Tsai. 1986. "Social Networking, Hardiness and Immigrant's Mental Health." *Journal of Social Health and Social Behavior.* 27(2, June): 133–49.

Levitt, Peggy. 1999. "Social Remittances: A Local-Level, Migration-Driven Form of Cultural Diffusion." *International Migration Review.* 32(124): 926–49.

Marx, Anthony W. 1998. *Making Race and Nation: A Comparison of South Africa, the United States, and Brazil*. Cambridge, UK: Cambridge University Press.

Massey, Douglas S. 1998. "March of Folly: U.S. Immigration Policy after NAFTA." *The American Prospect.* 37(March/April): 22–33.

Massey, E.J., Douglas S., Joaquin Arango, Graeme Hugo, Ali Kouaouci, Adela Pellegrino, and J.D. Taylor. 1998. *Worlds in Motion: Understanding International Migration at the End of the Millennium*. Oxford, UK: Clarendon Press.

McMichael, Philip. 2000. *Development and Social Change: A Global Perspective*. Second edition. Thousand Oaks, CA: Pine Forge Press.

Menjivar, Cecilia. 1997. "Immigrant Kinship Networks and the Impact of the Receiving Context: Salvadorans in San Francisco in the Early 1990s." *Social Problems*. 44(1): 104–23.

Menjivar, Cecilia. 2000. *Fragmented Ties: Salvadoran Immigrant Networks in America*. Berkeley and Los Angeles: University of California Press.

Morning, Ann. 2011. *The Nature of Race: How Scientists Think and Teach about Human Difference*. Berkeley, CA: University of California Press.

Muhammad, Khalil Gibran. 2010. *The Condemnation of Blackness: Race, Crime, and the Making of Modern Urban America*. Cambridge, MA: Harvard University Press.

Muhammad, Khalil Gibran. 2011. *The Condemnation of Blackness: Race, Crime, and the Making of Modern Urban America*. Cambridge, MA: Harvard University Press.

Paul, Kathleen. 1997. *Whitewashing Britain: Race and Citizenship in the Postwar Era*. Ithaca, NY: Cornell University Press.

Resnikoff, Ned. 2014. "Global Inequality Is a Rising Concern for Elites." *Al Jazeera America* (14, November). http://america.aljazeera.com/articles/2014/11/11/global-inequalityisarisingconcernforelites.html.

Roberts, Dorothy. 2011. *Fatal Invention: How Science Politics, and Big Business e-create Race in the Twenty-First Century*. New York: The New Press.

Rodney, Walter. 2011 [1972]. *How Europe Underdeveloped Africa*. Baltimore, MD: Black Classic Press.

Sassen, Saskia. 1990. *The Mobility of Labor and Capital: A Study in International Investment and Labor Flow*. Cambridge, UK: Cambridge University Press.

Sassen, Saskia. 1999. *Globalization and its Discontents: Essays on the New Mobility of People and Money*. New York: The New Press.

Smedley, Audrey. 1993. *Race in North America: Origin and Evolution of a Worldview*. Boulder, CO: Westview Press.

Tilly, Charles, and C. Harold Brown. 1967. "On Uprooting, Kinship, and the Auspices of Migration." *International Journal of Comparative Sociology*. 8(2, September): 139–164.

United Nations. 2012. "Migration by Origin and Destination: The Role of South-South Migration." *Population Facts*. No. 2012/3 (June). Department of Economic and Social Affairs, Population Division. www.un.org/esa/population/publications/popfacts/popfacts_2012-3_South-South_migration.pdf.

Waldinger, Roger. 1996. *Still the Promised City? African Americans and New Immigrants in Postindustrial New York*. Cambridge, MA and London, England: Harvard University Press.

Wallerstein, Immanuel. 1974. *The Modern World System*. New York: Academic Press.

Wallerstein, Immanuel. 1984. *The Politics of the World-Economy: The States, the Movements and the Civilizations: Essays by Immanuel Wallerstein*. In the Series Studies in Modern Capitalism. Cambridge, UK: Cambridge University Press.

Walter, Bronwen, Sarah Morgan, Mary J. Hickman, and Joseph M. Bradley. 2002. "Family Stories, Public Silence: Irish Identity Construction amongst the Second-Generation Irish in England." *Scottish Geographical Journal*. 118(3): 201–217.

Waters, Mary C. 1999. *Black Identities: West Indian Immigrant Dreams and American Realities*. New York: Russell Sage Foundation.

6

LONG WAVES AND CHANGES IN THE STRUCTURE OF THE CAPITALIST WORLD SYSTEM

Zenonas Norkus

Does the structure of the capitalist world system (CWS) change in the course of time, as this most encompassing social system is growing "older", "maturing" and "ageing" (or maybe repeatedly "rejuvenating")? This is the research question of this paper. By "changes in the structure of the CWS", I mean changes in the number of the categories of structural position in the CWS, which I will alternatively designate as classes (or "mega-classes") of the CWS member societies. By emergence and disappearance of classes I mean the change of structure in the strong sense, which I distinguish from change in the CWS structure in the weak sense: change in relative numbers of countries taking different positions, while the number of position types remains constant. Technically, the change of structure in the weak sense means a difference between the row and column marginals in a mobility table (see e.g. Hout 1983), while structural change in the second or strong sense is reflected by the difference in the number of rows and columns in a mobility table.

I will start with the discussion of the parallels and affinities between the theoretical problems and alternatives in the analysis of the stratification of country level societies and that of the CWS. In the second section, I recall selected findings of empirical (bottom up) research on the stratification of the CWS as we know it during the last 50 years, focusing on the work which uses relational (network) data. In the third section, I will recall the Kondratieff 1999 (1928) wave theory, which is a main theoretical resource to explain or provide theoretical (top down) rationale on why findings of empirical research on the zoning of the CWS deviate from the orthodox trichotomous Wallersteinian schema (core-semiperiphery-periphery). This explanation is elaborated in more detail in the fourth section, where I also draw on the ideas of Neo-Weberian class analysis. I will also provide here the interpretation of the recent inductive (bottom up) research findings (Mahutga and Smith, 2011) on the mobility in the CWS to illustrate my points about the structural change of CWS which should be distinguished from the pure or net mobility.

How Many Classes Are There? Does Class Matter?

The existence of ("real") classes is a main topic in the debates on the social structure of national societies. The main alternatives in the macroanalysis of social structure are categorical (relational or class analytical) approach and continuity approach, represented by various versions of the social stratification analysis. The continuity approach is grounded in the concept of socio-economic status, measured by index values at the interval or ratio level. The celebrated book by Peter M. Blau and Otis Dudley Duncan (1967) on mobility in the American occupational structure is maybe the most famous example of the continuity or stratificational approach in the analysis of social structure. According to this approach, there are no real categorical divisions in a society, only a continuously graded hierarchy of income or socioeconomic status, with "low", "lower middle", "upper middle" and "high income" "classes" as purely nominal classification units or statistical aggregates.

According to both versions—neo-Marxian (e.g. Wright 1989 [1984], 1997) and neo-Weberian (e.g. Erikson et al. 1979; Erikson and Goldthorpe 1992)—of categorical approach, the question of how many (and which) classes there are in a society is real and is even the central issue for sociological analysis as a distinct research perspective. It is rather similar to the question of how many chemical elements or elementary particles exist? Or how many bird species are living in March 2014 (for example) on Bornholm

80   *Zenonas Norkus*

island? Even if kindred elements or species belong together as elements of the taxons of higher order, they cannot be "merged" or "defined out of reality" by the researcher's fiat. The discovery of new life species or the synthesis of a new chemical element is a rare and important event in the natural sciences, worthy of a report in "Nature".

The advocates of the continuity approach refer to the weakness or lack of "class consciousness" in most contemporary societies. However, the classics of class analysis never considered "class consciousness", "class identity" or "class action" as part of the definition of the class concept. Karl Marx famously distinguished between "classes in itself" from "classes for itself". Max Weber considered a collective identity as a distinctive feature of status groups and political groups, not of classes. For both of them class was not an emic but an etic concept.

I would argue that the assumption about the specific number of mega-classes is one of the "hard core" assumptions of the World System (WS) analysis as a distinctive research programme in the sense of Imre Lakatos.[1] Such assumptions are basic tenets that cannot be rejected without abandoning the programme in question. They should be distinguished from the auxiliary hypotheses, which constitute "protective belts" around the "hard core" assumptions. The three Newtonian laws of motion can serve as examples of such "hard core" assumptions in the most successful research programme in physics (Lakatos 1978). The trichotomous view of the world system (periphery-semiperiphery-core) structure is the trademark of the WS analysis founded by Immanuel Wallerstein. This assumption distinguishes Wallersteinian WS analysis from its ancestor and closest kin—Dependency theory, characterized by a dichotomic vision of the world system, distinguishing the core with autocentric and the periphery with extroverted accumulation of capital.

Findings of Empirical Research: Some Anomalies for the Wallersteinian Research Programme

There are two lines of research aiming to test Wallerstein's trichotomous model of the structure of the WS. One of them works with attribute (income) data. Two of the most important contributions from this line of research are the famous paper by Giovanni Arrighi and Jessica Drangel (1986), and the work by Salvatore Babones (2005, 2009). Their common finding is the trimodal distribution of the world population, emerging from the hologeistic[2] comparison of national income per capita of the countries. The authors consider this finding as evidence confirming the trichotomous WS structure model.

However, another line of research, using relational or network data provides a more ambiguous picture. This line of research goes back to the famous paper by David Snyder and Edward L. Kick (1979). Actually, by applying the CONCOR algorithm to four types of international networks (trade flows, military interventions, diplomatic relations and conjoint treaty membership) data in circa 1965, they derived 10 block models. Then they merged this most specific model into an orthodox 3 block model in an informal way (see also Clark and Beckfield 2009, 9). In his later research (with Byron L. Davis), comparing global networks and economic growth across two time periods 1960–1965 and 1970–1975, Kick found 11 blocks, collapsing them into 5 "mega-blocks" (Kick and Davis 2001): (1) Capitalist core; (2) Socialist semi-core; (3) Capitalist semi-core; (4) Semiperiphery; (5) Periphery.

Importantly, such a deviation from the orthodox Wallersteinian trichotomy is not a single exception, but a rather typical finding in the research using network data. The work of David Smith may serve as a good example. In Nemeth and Smith (1985) the blockmodel analysis of the trade patterns in 5 commodity types of 86 non-centrally planned countries identifies 8 blocks, which are collapsed into 4 mega-classes: (1) Core; (2) Strong semiperiphery; (3) Weak semiperiphery; (4) Periphery. In a next contribution: (1) Core; (2) Semiperiphery1; (3) Semiperiphery2; (4) Periphery1; (5) Periphery2. Matthew Mahutga (2006) detected the same number of mega-classes, giving them different names: (1) Core; (2) Strong semiperiphery; (3) Weak semiperiphery; (4) Strong periphery; (5) Weak periphery. In the very latest contribution published by both authors (Mahutga and Smith 2011), their analysis closes with 6 mega-classes: (1) Core; (2) Core contenders; (3) Upper-tier semiperiphery; (4) Strong periphery; (5) Weak periphery; 6) Weakest periphery.

Formally, all these findings are compatible with Wallersteinian "troika" orthodoxy. It is possible to merge these groupings further to get a "correct answer" (3). However, as the network data-based research finds ever more final or semi-final blocks, it is difficult to avoid the following question: does the number of mega-classes of WS increase because of better data and analytical techniques, allowing us to get an ever more accurate picture of the reality? Or does the number of mega-classes grow because of the changes in the structure of reality itself: the structure of CWS becomes more complex and differentiated? In the following sections I will work to substantiate the second answer.

There is another one possible motion: to drop the question about the "real" number of the CWS classes in favour of the continuity or seamless-web approach. Actually, several studies have produced continuous measures of the network position in the world. They are used in Mahutga (2006) and Mahutga and Smith (2011). Such measures rank countries according to their coreness, like the socioeconomic status index measures rank individuals according to their status. The major problem is that accepting the "seamless web" approach we would have to abandon the most important "hard core" assumption of the WS as distinctive research programme. This is the assumption of social structure. Concepts of structure, structural position and class all

82 *Zenonas Norkus*

are categorical concepts. A continuity approach allows only for two structural positions: ultimate core (coreness = 1) and ultimate periphery (coreness = 0). Everything else (almost all cases) become transitional or residual categories. This may satisfy an advocate of Dependency theory.

The problem is similar to that of classical Marxism. Karl Marx did not deny that existing capitalist societies include more than two classes (capitalists and wage workers). Rather, he just predicted the simplification of the class structure before the final collapse of capitalism, as traditional "middle classes" of small producers will be destroyed and mainly proletarianize. In reality, new middle classes emerged, with class structure of capitalist societies becoming ever more complex. Similarly, classical Dependency theory predicted the polarization between core and periphery. Reality turned out to be more complex. However, the best way to account for this complexity may be not to reject class analysis or to include all intermediate cases into single "semiperiphery". The introduction of semiperiphery was a progressive theoretical shift in comparison with Dependency theory or modernization theory in the 1960s or 1970s. However, as time goes on, semiperiphery becomes increasingly heterogeneous, and the progressive development of WS analysis needs a differentiated class schema to account for "new middle classes" of the CWS.

Theoretical Rationale for Changing N of the Capitalist World System Classes

In the next sections, I will provide the theoretical rationale for research findings which are an anomaly for the orthodox Wallersteinian view of $N = 3$, where N is the number of class positions in the world system. It aims at specifying and substantiating the differences between social actors which should be interpreted as the categorical class divisions. Such rationales are provided in the refinements of classical Marxian (Wright 1989 [1984], 1997) and Weberian (Erikson et al. 1979; Erikson and Goldthorpe 1992) class theories.

To recall, Karl Marx famously argued that the most important difference is between owners and non-owners of the means of production, their specific identities changing with the modes of production. Eric O. Wright's class theory is an attempt to account for the empirical anomaly for Marxian class analysis, which is the increase in the numbers of employed persons whose class membership cannot be accounted for using the distinction between the owners and non-owners of the means of production. Wright designs a more differentiating class scheme, by taking into consideration two more differences between "haves" and "have-nots": that of between possessors and non-possessors of organizational assets and of that between the owners and non-owners of skills valued at the market.

The strongest competitor of neo-Marxian class theory is neo-Weberian class theory. Importantly, Weber's own analysis of labour market classes is incomplete. Drawing a line between employers and employees, he did not set any upper limit to the number of classes. With no such limitation, even the occupations themselves may count as classes, because members of each occupation take a specific position in the labour market. Neo-Weberian Erikson-Goldthorpe-Portocarero's (EGP; Erikson et al. 1979; Erikson and Goldthorpe 1992) theory corrects this defect in Weber's original theory, adding another five distinctions to the basic distinction between employers, employees and the self-employed: (1) Asset specificity; (2) Difficulty of monitoring; (3) Superior/subordinate; (4) Economic sector: Agriculture/non-Agriculture; (5) Manual/non-manual work. Using all six dimensions, it is possible to reduce the variety of occupations in the labour market to a limited number of classification units, each of them embracing the most similar occupations.

Looking for theoretical rationale to account for the findings of the empirical research about the growing number of the WS classes, I will draw upon Weber's theoretical ideas on class. However, this is only one of two theoretical sources that I will use to account for the empirical anomalies of the Wallersteinian research programme. Another (and most important) is drawn from this programme itself. This is an essential point: the theoretical rationale for empirical anomalies of a research programme can claim to represent a progressive move or shift in its development, if it is enacted using its own conceptual resources as the main source of innovation, while other ideas serve only an auxiliary role.

Does WS theory have such resources? I will argue that it is indeed the case: this is another "hard core" assumption of the WS analysis: Kondratieff waves (or Long waves) theory. I. Wallerstein writes: "A- and B-phases of Kondratieff cycles seem, therefore, to be a necessary part of the capitalist process. It follows that they should logically be part of its operation from the very beginning of the existence of a capitalist world economy" (Wallerstein 2011 (1989), XVI). This is a very strong statement, suggesting that Long waves are part of the "hard core" of the WS analysis.

Up to five "long waves" can be identified in the history of technologically advanced capitalism in the CWS core, beginning with the last quarter of the XVIIIth century (see e.g. Freeman and Louçã 2001; Norkus, 2012: 97–107; 2013; Perez 2002). Basing on their emblematic products, new progressive technologies or carrier branches, they can be described as follows:

1. water-powered machines and the textile industry (upswing 1780s–1815, downswing 1815–1848),
2. steam-powered machines, steam ships and railways (upswing 1848–1873; downswing 1873–1895),
3. electricity, electrotechnics and inorganic chemistry (upswing 1895–1918; downswing 1918–1945),

84   *Zenonas Norkus*

4. motorization, organic and synthetic chemistry (upswing 1945–1973; downswing 1973–1993),
5. computerization and telecommunications waves (upswing since 1993).

In the original (Wallersteinian) version of the WS analysis, Kondratieff waves are part of the explanation of the struggles for hegemony in the core of the WS as well as of the vertical mobility from the semiperiphery into the core. During B or descending phases, the contenders for hegemony challenge incumbents, and even if they fail, the hegemon can change (as in the case of the U.S. rise to hegemony as a side effect of British-German struggles). Windows of opportunity open for semiperipheric powers to join the core. However, the basic trichotomous structure remains unchanged.

I will argue that Long waves theory is a still an underused resource in WS analysis and demonstrate how it can be applied to account for anomalous findings of the empirical research. Kondratieff waves do change the class structure of the WS, multiplying the number of structural positions and mega-class divisions in the CWS. However, for such an application of the Long waves theory, mega-classes of the WS should be conceived in the Weberian rather than in the Marxian way.

Ideas for a Neo-Weberian Analysis of the Structure of the Capitalist World System

The main difference between Marxian and Weberian approaches in the analysis of social structures is not about the number of classes, but how they conceive class relations. They share a relational conception of classes as categories of positions in the structure defined by their relations. According to the Marxian view, the relations between classes are those of exploitation: ownership of the means of production (according to Marx himself) as well as possession of organizational assets and skills (according to Wright's extension) enables owners/possessors to exploit non-owners/non-possessors. According to Marx and Marxists, there is no capitalism without exploitation. According to some Marxists (e.g. Wright), even socialism is not safe from exploitation, because also under socialism there are subordinates and superiors, skilled and unskilled workers.

According to the Weberian view, there is no real or really existing capitalism without exploitation, while ideal capitalism without exploitation (grounded in the perfectly competitive markets) is thinkable as a matter of principle. Exploitation is conditional on the monopolistic appropriation of market opportunities (*Marktchancen*), their usurpation and closure. Under perfect capitalism, there are classes (categories of incumbents of different and interrelated market positions), but there is no exploitation. Thus, although

Long Waves and Changes   85

there may be no alternative to capitalism, there may be good and bad varieties of capitalism.

Key concepts in Weber's analysis of class relations are closure and usurpation (Weber 1978 (1922), 43–46). Closure is the process by which holders of positions providing rents seek to maximise rewards by restricting access to resources and opportunities to a limited circle of eligibles. The incumbent monopolist (or oligopolists) works to exclude competitors, competitors struggle to usurp rent-bringing positions. Usurpation is the struggle for entering closed market positions, which may eventually end in their complete opening. If usurpations fail, classes mutate into status groups and society itself transforms into status society, ceasing to be a class society. This Weberian approach is elaborated in the most detail in the work of the British sociologist Frank Parkin (e.g. Parkin 1979). Along with Kondratieff waves theory, which is part of the CWS analysis as a research programme, I will use it for the analysis of the changes of the structure of the CWS.

The most powerful attempt to construct "a theory of semiperiphery" by Giovanni Arrighi and Jessica Drangel (1986) is unmistakably Weberian, because they describe monopolization of opportunities or market chances for insiders and exclusion of outsiders as the mechanism of the "core boundary construction". Although they do not use the terms "closure" and "usurpation", this is to what their justly famous description of the core-periphery relations refers to, in fact:

> In our view, the use of the term "surplus" is neither necessary nor helpful in defining core-periphery relations. All we need is to assume that economic actors (irrespective of whether they seek a remuneration for labor-power, assets, or entrepreneurial energies), far from accepting competition as a datum, continuously endeavor to shift, and some succeed in shifting, the pressure of competition from themselves onto other actors. As a result, the nodes or economic activities of each and every commodity chain tend to become polarized into positions from which the pressure of competition has been transferred elsewhere (core-like activities) and positions to which such pressure has been transferred (peripheral activities).
>
> (Arrighi and Drangel 1986, 17)

According to Arrighi and Drangel, the core of the CWS includes states with a high concentration of "core-like" economic activities. Periphery includes countries concentrating only on "periphery-like" economic activities. Semiperipheric states host mixes of core-like and periphery-like economic activities. The problem with this definition is the flavor of tautology. Happily, Arrighi and Drangel themselves provide the hint, on how the specification problem can be solved. "Any activity can become at a particular point in time core-like or periphery-like, but each has that characteristic for a limited period.

86 *Zenonas Norkus*

Nonetheless, there are always some products and techniques that are core-like and others that are periphery-like at any given time" (Arrighi and Drangel 1986, 18).

I would like to follow this hint by proposing to use Kondratieff wave theory as the guideline to identify core-like products and techniques for each specific period. We must just know the phase of the development of technology at the technological frontier at the point of time or period of interest to find out which activities and products are core-like at a particular time. I will continue with the series of Weber-style definition schemes of the key structural positions in the CWS. I call them "schemes" because they include the variable "N" referring to the order number of the actual Kondratieff waves as well as the indexical expressions "actual", "future" and "recent".

A definition scheme becomes a fully-fledged definition after the substitution of N and indexical expressions by the proper names connecting it to world historical time. My elaboration aims to temporalize the class structure of the CWS by embedding it into the historical time. Incumbent core members can cease to belong to the core by being superseded by "new" or "young" contenders, if they succeed to catch and ride the new Kondratieff wave, usurping the advantages of the "first comer" (cp. Giedraitis et al. 2012). So "moving in time" means becoming "old", "outdated", "superseded", "outmoded" or "traditional", while core is where most globally new or advanced activities concentrate. New in the world historical sense means: they have the power to make already existing things outdated, even if these things are still new in a physical sense (freshly made). Speaking of the Arrighi-Drangel "activities mix" terminology, "core" is the structural position where most new or advanced activities are concentrated. "Core" at N is the world historical "outdater" of the "Rest"—that power which transforms the rest of CWS into "Rest". Periphery hosts oldest and most outdated activities. While core hosts creative aspects of Schumpeterian "creative destruction", the periphery is the place were destruction prevails (Korzeniewicz and Moran 2009, 74; Schumpeter, 1939). In between there are mixes of "new" and "old" activities, which differentiate according to how much "new old" or "old old" things they include.

So *Core* of the CWS are structural positions occupied by the states successfully claiming the monopoly or oligopoly of the *actual (Nth)* long wave core-like economic activities and world market positions, clustered in their territories, and having the best chances to usurp the **next (N+1)** Kondratieff wave of core-like activities.

Periphery are structural positions occupied by the countries excluded from participation in the *actual* core-like activities and world market positions and hosting clusters of purely peripheric or *very old* (first two Kondratieff wave times) core-like economic activities.

Middle positions of the CWS are taken by states, hosting core-like activities characteristic for the former Kondratieff waves, that is, traditional industries (***N-1, N-2, . . . , where N is the order number of the actual Kondratief wave***).

With each new Kondratieff wave, the number of middle structural positions grows. But arguably, the CWS semiperiphery started to differentiate internally into "old" and "new" middle classes only after the second industrial revolution (latter half of XIX century—1920), which made the technological application of science (R&D) the main driving force of economic growth (the source of the "Solow residual" or "Romerian growth") in the CWS core countries. During the third Kondratieff wave, there was a strong industrialization drive in the semiperiphery. The successful industrialization of Russia is the most important case in in this regard. However, at the same time industrialization ceased to be the entrance ticket to the CWS core. After successful industrialization, newly industrializing countries had repeatedly discovered bitterly that they only host carrier industries from former Kondratieff waves, while the core incumbents managed to leap and ride a newly emerging Kondratieff wave. So the correct formula for finding the number of middle structural position is N-2, which implies that the CWS at the time of current 5th Kondratieff wave (or CWS 5.0) includes (besides core and periphery) three middle class positions, while in the CWS 4.0 (1945–1993) there were two "middle classes".

Figure 1 depicts the relation between the structure and history of the CWS as described above.

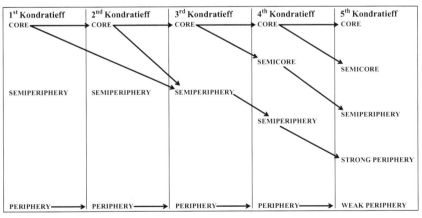

Figure 6.1 The relation between the history and structure of the CWS.

Vertical lines stand for structure of the CWS at specific time points, horizontal lines—for transitions from one Kondratieff wave to another, inclined lines—for sedimentation of the history in the newly emerging ranks or layers of the CWS structure.

88 *Zenonas Norkus*

The model of the (mega-class) structure of the CWS as of 1993–2015 or during the A-phase of the 5th Kondratieff wave is as follows:

Core includes states in monopolist or oligopolist control over 5th Kondratieff wave core-like activities and carrier high tech industries (mainly ITC), and with best chances to become leaders in the next technological revolution, launching a 6th Kondratieff wave.

Semicore contains countries with competitive advantages in the 4th KW Kondratieff wave (1945–1970 "high tech"), carrier industries, struggling to usurp 5th KW activities, as well as displaying potential to participate in the 6th Kondratieff wave core-like activities.

Semiperiphery comprises states that display competitive advantage in the 3rd Kondratieff wave type carrier industries (Second industrial revolution type "high tech").

Strong periphery states host economic activities clustering around 1–2 Kondratieff wave carrier industries ("high tech" from the times of the First industrial revolution).

Weak periphery countries host purely peripheric activities (still unindustrialized).

I am closing by applying this theoretical schema to interpret recent findings of bottom-up (inductive) analyses of the CWS structure in Tables 6.1 and 6.2. I am drawing upon recent measurements of the WS ranks in 1965 and 2000 in Mahutga and Smith (2011), with the single difference: their "weak" and "very weak" periphery positions are merged into a single "weak" periphery position.[3] I do not dispute that two strata or tiers can be distinguished within weak periphery. One of them includes countries with exportable natural resources. Benefiting from the resource rent they may not be poor in terms of income per capita. Another strata includes very poor international aid dependent countries with no exportable resources. I do not designate them as two different classes, because my argument only provides the reasons for the internal structural differentiation of the semiperiphery in world historical time. There may be underway also the structural differentiation of the periphery, but this is a different theoretical and empirical research problem.

In all tables, rows represent the distribution of countries across the positions in the "departure" or "outflow" year 1965, while columns are "arrival" or "inflow" positions in 2000. Diagonal cells host the countries with an unchanged CWS position (i.e., "stayers"). Percentages in the diagonal cells describe the numbers of stayers in relative terms: which part of countries, taking specific positions in 1965, remained in the same position in 2000. The only way out of the top is to move down, and the only way out of the very bottom is to go up. So the cells to the left from the diagonal host the

Table 6.1 Mobility in the CWS 1965–2000: 5 × 5 classes model

	Core	Semicore	Semi-periphery	Strong periphery	Weak periphery	N	%
Core	9 (81%)	2	0	0	0	11	11.7
Semicore	1	10 (83%)	1	0	0	12	12.8
Semiperiphery	0	9	6 (31.5%)	3	1	19	20.2
Strong periphery	0	0	1	12 (50%)	11	24	25.5
Weak periphery	0	0	1	1	26 (93%)	28	29.8
N	10	21	9	16	38	94	100
%	10.6	22.3	9.5	17.0	40.4	100	

Data source: Mahutga and Smith 2011, 263.

countries which moved up, and those to the right contain the downwardly mobile cases. According to Table 6.1, semiperiphery and strong periphery were most unstable positions, the former providing best chances of upward mobility (9 countries moved up), and the latter harbouring the gravest perils of downward mobility (11 countries moved down). In contrast, both extreme (weak periphery and core) positions have relatively stable inhabitant populations (with 81% and 93% stayers respectively). Semi-core position with only one case of downward mobility is a safe harbour too.

The overall picture gives some support for classical Dependency theory, which emphasized (in a way reminiscent of classical Marxism) the instability of the "middle" positions. However, mobility takes place mainly between middle and peripheral positions, while breaking into the core is an extremely difficult challenge. Only one country (Spain) was successful in joining the core of CWS during the period under consideration. This is also what the comparison of row and column marginals attests. Here, cells with underlined column percentage numbers represent the "expanding" classes, while those containing numbers in italics represent "contracting" classes. Somewhat out of tune with classical Dependency theory, the number of vertically mobile countries (13) is relatively significant, although less than that of downwardly mobiles (17). By 2000, weak periphery countries (40.4%) were almost an absolute majority. Actually, vertical mobility from the very "bottom" is nearly as difficult a task as ascending to the very top, because there were only two success stories of that kind—Cyprus (to strong periphery) and Saudi Arabia (to semiperiphery). However, it may not be wise to dramatise these findings, as Mahutga and Smith include only the half of the world's nations in their sample (N = 94), with the very unfortunate underrepresentation of the communist and former communist countries.

The obvious excuse for their omission is the very absence of many former communist countries on the political world map in 1965. They emerged

90   *Zenonas Norkus*

Table 6.2 Mobility in the CWS 1965–2000: 4×5 classes model

	Core	Semicore	Semi-periphery	Strong periphery	Weak periphery	N	%
Core	9	2	0	0	0	11	11.7
Semicore	1	10	1	0	0	12	12.8
Semiperiphery	0	9	6	3	1	19	20.2
Periphery	0	0	2	13	37	52	55.3
N	10	21	9	16	38	94	100
%	10.6	22.3	9.5	17.0	40.4	100	

Data source: Mahutga and Smith 2011, 263.

in 1990–1992 as several composite political bodies split, complicating the life of researchers who need for their conclusions research designs involving analysis of long time series. The message of my paper is that there may be another complication: if polities split, why cannot classes? This possibility is explored in Table 6.2. The difference in the number of rows and columns means that between 1965 and 2000 a structural change in the CWS took place: periphery did split into two world "mega-classes": weak periphery and strong periphery.

Weak periphery is "old" or "traditional periphery", which includes exporter countries of primary products as they are described in the ideal typical way in the Dependency theory tradition, or just "failed states" with strong "push" type emigration. In the CWS 5.0, the strong periphery includes late industrializing countries hosting industries of the First Industrial revolution profile, which means a three Kondratieff waves long underdevelopment gap with respect to the CWS core. For semiperiphery countries, this gap is only two Kondratieff waves gap long, and semi-core countries are just behind the actual Kondratieff wave. The rough indicator to differentiate between periphery and semiperiphery countries is the presence or absence of the unified national electric grid. Vladimir Lenin famously declared that Communism = Soviet power + electrification. Actually, the still incomplete electrification by 2000 indicates peripheric capitalism.

According to the 5 × 5 classes model (Table 6.1), there was a rather significant downward mobility in the CWS, with nearly half (11 from 24) strong periphery countries joining the weak periphery in 1965–2000. According to the 4 × 5 model (Table 6.2), real change involved the differentiation of the "periphery without adjectives" into strong or new (industrialized) periphery and weak or old periphery. The exploration whether this interpretation is compatible with Mahutga and Smith data[4] would need a case-oriented analysis, going through the list of states which they classify as strongly, weakly and very weakly peripheric, and considering in detail their economic histories between 1965–2000. This would explode the space of single paper. Instead, I will end with a few points in favor of the idea of the "strong" change of the structure of the CWS and empirical implications of the proposed grounding of the analysis of the CWS structure in the long waves theory.

Conclusions, Implications for Further Research and the Forecast

1. My analysis of the contemporary structure of the WS invites us to distinguish between the absolute (or structural) and relative (or net) mobility in the CWS. Much of the current research on the mobility in the CWS misperceives or misdescribes changes in the structure of the CWS as vertical mobility in the CWS.
2. There should be a rough correlation between the CWS positions of countries as measured by Mahutga and Smith (2011) using relational data and the data about comparative advantage or competitiveness in the industries from different Kondratieff waves.
3. Instead of unconditional convergence predicted by neoclassical economists as the final outcome of globalization, there will be a multiplication of the structural positions in the CWS, with the CWS "middle class" both growing in relative terms and internally differentiating.
4. By 2040, there will be 6 − 2 = 4 middle mega-classes in the CWS.

Notes

1   This is not how Immanuel Wallerstein himself describes WS analysis, but this does not necessarily mean that he is the ultimate epistemological authority in the discussion about what WS analysis is. See Babones 2015 for most recent contribution to this discussion.

2   Famous (among cultural anthropologists) methodologist of cross-cultural studies Raoul Naroll (1920–1985) called "hologeistic" research design where a researcher works (but not necessarily succeeds at this) to include into his N all available cases on the globe (whole planet Earth or Gaia). See Naroll 1972, 211–212; Naroll et al. 1976.

3   Smith and Mahutga's "core contenders" correspond to my "semi-core" countries, while their "upper-tier semi-periphery" is called "semi-periphery" in my CWS class schema.

4   Actually, their country rankings are "data" only with big reservations, because they are outputs of a very complicated and sophisticated processing of real "raw" data.

References

Arrighi, Giovanni and Jessica Drangel. 1986. "The Stratification of the World-Economy: An Exploration of the Semiperipheral Zone." *Review (Fernand Braudel Center)*, 10 (1): 9–74.

Babones, Salvatore J. 2005. "The Country-Level Income Structure of the World-Economy." *Journal of World-Systems Research*, 11: 29–55.

Babones, Salvatore. 2009. *The International Structure of Income: Its Implications for Economic Growth.* Saarbrücken: VDM Verlag Dr. Müller.

Babones, Salvatore. 2015. "What is World-Systems Analysis? Distinguishing Theory from Perspective." *Thesis Eleven,* 126 (2): 11–18.

Blau, Peter M. and Otis Dudley Duncan. 1967. *The American Occupational Structure.* New York: Wiley and Sons.

Clark, Rob and Jason Beckfield. 2009. "New Trichotomous Measure of World-System Position Using the International Trade Network." *International Journal of Comparative Sociology,* 50 (1): 5–38.

Erikson, Robert and John H. Goldthorpe. 1992. *The Constant Flux: A Study of Class Mobility in Industrial Societies.* Oxford: Clarendon Press.

Erikson, Robert, John H. Goldthorpe, and Lucienne Portocarero. 1979. "Intergenerational Class Mobility in Three Western European Societies: England, France, and Sweden." *The British Journal of Sociology,* 30 (4): 415–441.

Freeman, Christopher and Francisko Louçã. 2001. *As Time Goes By: From the Industrial Revolutions to the Information Revolution.* Oxford: Oxford UP.

Giedraitis, Vincentas, Tom Notten, and Vaida Skurdenytė, 2012. "Innovation in the Context of the Global Economic Core-Periphery Hierarchy: The Potential of the Biotechnology Sector in Lithuania." *Теоретичні та прикладні питання економіки* [Theoretical and Applied Questions of Economics], 27 (2): 116–123.

Hout, Michael. 1983. *Mobility Tables.* Beverly Hills: Sage.

Kick, Edward L. and Byron L. Davis. 2001. "World System Structure and Change. An Analysis of Global Networks and Economic Growth Across Two Time Periods." *American Behavioral Scientist,* 44 (10): 1561–1578.

Kondratieff, Nikolai. 1999 (1928). "The Long Cycle Wave." In Francisco Louçã and Jan Reijnders (eds), *The Foundations of Long Wave Methodology.* Vol. 1. Cheltenham: Edward Elgar, 45–126.

Korzeniewicz, Roberto Patricio and Timothy Patrick Moran. 2009. *Unveiling Inequality: A World-Historical Perspective.* New York: Russell Sage Foundation.

Lakatos, Imre. 1978. *The Methodology of Scientific Research Programmes.* Cambridge: Cambridge UP.

Mahutga, Matthew. 2006. "The Persistence of Structural Inequality? A Network Analysis of International Trade, 1965–2000." *Social Forces,* 84 (4): 1863–1889.

Mahutga, Matthew C. and David Smith. 2011. "Globalization, the Structure of the World Economy and Economic Development." *Social Science Research,* 40: 257–272.

Naroll, Raoul. 1972. "A Holonational Bibliography." *Comparative Political Studies,* 5 (2): 211–230.

Naroll, Raoul, Gary L. Michik, and Frada Naroll. 1976. *Worldwide Theory Testing.* New Haven: HRAF Press.

Nemeth, Roger and David Smith. 1985. "International Trade and World-System Structure: A Multiple Network Analysis." *Review (Fernand Braudel Center),* 8: 517–560.

Norkus, Zenonas. 2012. *On Baltic Slovenia and Adriatic Lithuania: A Qualitative Comparative Analysis of Patterns in Post-Communist Transformation.* Budapest: Apostrofa/CEU Press.

Norkus, Zenonas. 2013. When the Kondratieff Winter Comes: An Exploration of the Recent Economic Crisis from a Long Wave Theory Perspective." *Przestrzeń społeczna*, 5 (1): 47–69.

Parkin, Frank. 1979. *Marxism and Class Theory: A Bourgeois Critique*. New York: Columbia UP.

Perez, Carlota. 2002. *Technological Revolutions and Financial Capital: The Dynamics of Bubbles and Golden Ages*. Cheltenham, UK: Edward Elgar.

Schumpeter, Joseph A. 1939. *Business Cycles: A Theoretical, Historical and Statistical Analysis of the Capitalist Process*. Vol. 1–2. New York: McGraw-Hill.

Smith, David A., and Douglas R. White. 1992. "Structure and Dynamics Of The Global Economy: Network Analysis Of International Trade 1965-1980". *Social Forces* 70 (4): 857.

Snyder, David and Edward L. Kick. 1979. "Structural Position in the World System and Economic Growth, 1955–1970: A Multiple-Network Analysis of Transnational Interactions." *American Journal of Sociology*, 84 (5): 1096–1126.

Wallerstein, Immanuel. 2011 (1989). *The Modern World-System, Vol. III: The Second Era of Great Expansion of the Capitalist World-Economy, 1730s-1840s Mercantilism*. San Diego: Academic Press.

Weber, Max.1978 (1922). *Economy and Society*. Ed. by Guenther Roth and Claus Wittich. Berkeley: University of California Press.

Wright, Erik O. 1989 (1984). "General Framework for the Analysis of Class Structure." In Erik O. Wright et al. (eds.), 1989. *Debate on Classes*. London: Verso, 3–43.

Wright, Erik O. 1997. *Class Counts: Comparative Studies in Class Analysis*. Cambridge: Cambridge University Press.

7

"CREATIVE DESTRUCTION" FROM A WORLD-SYSTEMS PERSPECTIVE

BILLIONAIRES AND THE GREAT RECESSION OF 2008

Scott Albrecht and Roberto Patricio Korzeniewicz

This paper explores how to effectively use Joseph Schumpeter's notion of "Creative Destruction" within a world-systems perspective—that is, a perspective that calls for focusing on the world-economy as a whole as the relevant unit of analysis for understanding the relationship between economic growth and social inequality. This article both draws upon and further operationalizes the concept of Creative Destruction to track recent changes in the epicenters of wealth accumulation across the world. More specifically, we draw on an original source of data to argue that the rise and fall of billionaires allows us to identify and map key changes in the accumulation (and redistribution) of income and wealth across the world-economy, changes that have substantive implications for existing patterns of social stratification. Focusing on what Fernand Braudel (1979, 1984) called the "top layers" of production, trade and exchange, data on billionaires provide a unique empirical basis for mapping sites of accumulation and for providing greater historical specificity to Joseph Schumpeter's (1942) concept of Creative Destruction.

Background and Theoretical Framework

In their popular recent contribution, *Why Nations Fail: The Origins of Power, Prosperity, and Poverty*, Acemoglu and Robinson (2012) argue that differences in the long-term sustained growth of nations, and thereby inequality between nations, are a consequence of whether institutions within these nations promote or hamper what Joseph Schumpeter called "Creative Destruction." We argue that while such arguments are productive in bringing concerns about politics and inequality to the forefront of debates about development, they nonetheless reproduce the less useful assumption that all the relevant phenomena, and most importantly "Creative Destruction" itself, are shaped primarily by social and political processes that are largely internal to nations.

For Schumpeter (1942: 82–83), indeed, the constant churn of Creative Destruction is central to capitalism:

> [c]apitalism . . . is by nature a form or method of economic change and not only never is but never can be stationary . . . The opening up of new markets, foreign or domestic, and the organizational development from the craft shop and factory to such concerns as U.S. Steel illustrate the same process of industrial mutation—if I may use that biological term—that incessantly revolutionizes the economic structure from within, incessantly destroying the old one, incessantly creating a new one. This process of Creative Destruction is the essential fact about capitalism.

Moreover, Schumpeter was careful to differentiate his notion of Creative Destruction from "textbook picture" competition, "competition within a rigid pattern of invariant conditions, methods of production and forms of industrial organization in particular" (1942/1950: 84–85). Instead, Creative Destruction entails:

> [c]ompetition from the new commodity, the new technology, the new source of supply, the new type of organization (the largest-scale unit of control for instance)—competition which commands a decisive cost or quality advantage and which strikes not at the margins of the profits and

the outputs of the existing firms but at their foundations and their very lives. This kind of competition is as much more effective than the other as a bombardment is in comparison with forcing a door, and so much more important that it becomes a matter of comparative indifference whether competition in the ordinary sense functions more or less promptly; the powerful lever that in the long run expands output and brings down prices is in any case made of other stuff.

Framing Creative Destruction within a nation-centered analysis, Acemoglu and Robinson argue that inclusive institutions—centralized but pluralist government, secure but broadly distributed property and political rights, the unbiased application of law and competitive markets—allow in some nations (but not in others) for economic incentives that give free reign to Creative Destruction and, hence, to constant, wealth-augmenting innovation. Robust inclusive institutions prevent any specific social force (like entrenched elites) from trying to limit competitive pressures or controlling the impact of innovations, and in doing so preserve and foster the creative force of the market. In nations that move towards the adoption of inclusive institutions, Creative Destruction—the constant destruction of existing ideas, institutions, organizational strategies, and firms, and the simultaneous creation of new ones—becomes the norm, and constant, long-term growth becomes pervasive.

This institutional approach has marked similarities with the modernization arguments that decades ago tended to focus on development as a universal path of growth followed autonomously and independently by all "societies" (e.g., Hoselitz 1960; Rostow 1963; Eisenstadt 1974; Inkeles and Smith 1974; but see Firebaugh (2003) for a more recent version). In the modernization approach, economic development is linear, from agriculture to industry to service, and innovation is sequential. Those regions of the world that are most innovative are the wealthiest; those innovations then diffuse to the rest of the world, encouraging technological and economic convergence. In the modernization perspective, some cultural and social characteristics (modernity and/or universalism) were more likely to promote rationality and merit-based hierarchies, while other cultural and social characteristics (such as traditional attitudes and/or fatalism) were more likely to impede growth and entrench inequalities based on ascribed characteristics. While Acemoglu and Robinson's perspective shifts attention to political processes and power relations as key to the prevalence of growth or stagnation among nations, their analysis shares with modernization perspectives a nation-centered analysis of the processes at hand.

A world-systems perspective leads us in a different direction. As framed by the Schumpeterian notion of Creative Destruction, innovation is not a sequential and progressive linear development from raw material production to industry. Schumpeter was explicit in not restricting his notion of innovation to technological change or manufacturing. New forms of raw material production, the capacity to engage in innovative forms of deploying territorial or political power, or even rent-seeking behaviors, are just as likely to be a source of creation and destruction as any other innovation labeled by some as more "productive." As noted by Arrighi (1994), periodical reconfigurations of the world-economy are just as likely to be driven by processes of Creative Destruction centered around finance—or even corrupted, rent-seeking behaviors—as they are by purportedly more "virtuous" forms of innovation (such as technological changes centered around manufacturing).

Moreover, innovation and Creative Destruction are embedded not only temporally, but spatially. Successful innovation requires a co-location of technologies, organizations, skills, resources, institutions, etc. There are major hurdles to diffusion, innovations must be adapted to local conditions, and diffusion will not drive new wealth accumulation (Arrighi and Drangel 1986). For a long time, more critical perspectives have sought to emphasize how the existence of wealth in some countries is associated with the prevalence of poverty in others (Prebisch 1950; Myrdal 1964; Frank 1966; Emmanuel 1972; Wallerstein 1974, 1979, 1983). In this strand of analysis, some authors have explicitly drawn on Schumpeter's notion of Creative Destruction to explain global patterns of wealth accumulation (e.g., see Arrighi 1991; Arrighi and Drangel 1986; Korzeniewicz and Moran 2005, 2009).

But although Schumpeter's notion of "Creative Destruction" can be of critical assistance to constructing an effective world-systems perspective on the relationship between growth and inequality, the social sciences have lacked the longitudinal and global data to trace how processes of innovation have shifted the frontiers of wealth accumulation over time so as to arrive to a more precise, historically grounded theoretical understanding of Creative Destruction and its implications for economic inequality, social stratification and social mobility. Instead, researchers tend to rely on *a priori* assumptions to trace what they already presuppose to be true epicenters or trajectories of wealth accumulation (e.g., from raw material production to manufacturing, or from the local to the global).

We propose that available data on very wealthy individuals (that is, billionaires) can help us advance a better understanding of where, when and how the epicenters of wealth accumulation have shifted in recent decades. To map these processes, we repurpose data on the world billionaires to identify the spatial and temporal patterns of creative destruction over the 1987–2012 period. Such a dataset can offer important correctives to current understandings of global social stratification. For example, whereas Schumpeter emphasized that epicenters of wealth shifted constantly and are not associated with any single particular array of products, market networks or institutional arrangements, even the most critical perspectives on development have tended to assume (rather than empirically assess) the character of such epicenters. Thus, critical

98 Scott Albrecht et al.

studies often end up sharing with modernization perspectives the assumption that high levels of wealth accumulation are secured to a much greater extent by manufacturing production rather than raw material production, or by production for domestic consumption rather than by production for export. On the other hand, finance is viewed as the antithesis of real wealth accumulation, an appropriation by elites that tends to work against truly productive investments.

To anticipate some of our findings, our study of billionaires indeed provides considerable evidence that we are in the midst of a new temporal-spatial configuration of wealth accumulation. In the last decade, the number of billionaires globally has increased 250% and their net worth has tripled. We also find that billionaires as a class were hit hard by the Great Recession, but most recovered fairly quickly. Consequently, the period was not associated with an exceptional rate of change in the overall wealth commanded by the world's billionaires. On the other hand, we find that the Great Recession marked a turning point after which new billionaires increasingly originate in non-core countries. This suggests that there continues to be considerable elite circulation, not necessarily within countries, but linked to broader transitions in the distribution of income and wealth between nations.

Data and Methods

To track the impact of the Great Recession on the world's wealthiest we draw on *Forbes* annual list of billionaires.[1] Since 1987, the magazine has tracked the financial activities of the world's richest individuals: "the deals they negotiate, the land they're selling, the paintings they're buying, the causes they give to" (Dolan 2012: 1). Dozens of reporters in countries around the world interview "employees, rivals, attorneys and securities analysts" (p. 1) and the billionaires themselves—some are cooperative, others are not—to estimate the value of an individual's assets minus debt. Net worth is reported in US dollars and, to control for market fluctuations, reflects a snapshot from a single day.

The very wealthy often have strong incentives to obscure their private holdings, and some assets are difficult to appraise. Because their holdings are often diversified and extensive, billionaires and the not-quite billionaires might not always have a solid estimate of their own net worth. In other words, the *Forbes* reporters face the challenges that come with any economic survey and a few additional hurdles when generating their annual list of the world's billionaires. But 25 years of experience and a reputation built on generating lists of the world's richest makes the *Forbes* list the best available source for this information. In looking at the impact of the Great Recession, we use the lists published by *Forbes*' lists between 2006 and 2012, but we also draw on a larger selection at times to offer some historical context.

"Creative Destruction" 99

Table 7.1 Number and Characteristics of Billionaires, 2006–2012

	1987	2002	2006	2007	2008	2009	2010	2011	2012
N	151	497	793	946	1125	793	1011	1210	1226
Net worth ($b)	311	1,539	2,646	3,452	4,381	2,415	3,568	4,496	4,575
Average ($b)	2.1	3.1	3.3	3.6	3.9	3.0	3.5	3.7	3.7
Top 100 ($b)	262	847	1,150	1,430	1,720	1,050	1,440	1,700	1,720
Countries	24	43	51	55	56	54	56	56	59
N ('87 $b)	151	313	479	601	701	419	568	687	701
Net worth ('87 $b)	311	888	1,347	1,755	2,147	1,095	1,645	2,036	2,035
N ('06 $b)			793	907	1,056	692	914	1,084	1,086
Net worth ('06 $b)			2,646	3,321	4,035	2,173	3,185	3,903	3,888

Source: **Forbes 2012**

Note: Adjustments using CPI-U-RS from the month Forbes reported their list of billionaires. Reported net worth is rounded and does not represent the true distribution of wealth among billionaires, and the cut-off point after adjusting for inflation is artificial. To accommodate, we use locally weighted scatterplot smoothing on the curvilinear relationship between worth and billionaire rank (with randomly allotted unique ranks in the case of a tie), to simulate a more realistic distribution.

As indicated in Table 7.1 below, the total number of billionaires listed increased from 793 in 2006 to 1,125 in 2008, dropped back to 793 in 2009 and rose again to 1,226 in 2012.[2] In the seven lists from 2006 to 2012, 1,724 different individuals[3] make an appearance, and 518 names appear on all seven. Likewise, the net worth of billionaires grew from $2.65 trillion in 2006 to $4.38 in 2008 before falling to $2.41 trillion in 2009. As of 2012, the net worth of the world's billionaires was approximately $4.57 trillion.[4]

Some of the increase in billionaires and billionaire net worth over time is a product of a declining standard of billionaire standing. Inflation means that a billion dollars today is not worth as much as it used to be. When we adjust for inflation, we raise the standard for billionaire status for later periods; the earlier the benchmark year, the higher the standard and the more current billionaires that are demoted. As a result, the trend in the number of billionaires will depend not only on whether or not we adjust for inflation, but what year we use for the benchmark. Also, the net worth of the remaining billionaires is reduced to reflect the lower purchasing power of their dollars.

In the bottom half of Table 7.1, we report billionaire counts and net worth using 1987 and 2006 US$. From this we can conclude that the growing number of billionaires is not an artifact of inflation; the number of billionaires and the net worth of those billionaires in 1987 US$ more than doubled between 2002 and 2012. But the adjusted results demonstrate that the raw results overstate the strength of the recovery.

In addition to net worth, _Forbes_ lists billionaires by age, residence, citizenship, and industry. We use citizenship to represent an individual's country of origin. Just fewer than 8% of the world's billionaires reside in a country other than the one in which they claim citizenship, and European countries (Germany, United Kingdom, France, Sweden, and Italy in particular) have a relatively high number of billionaire expatriates.

To assess empirical patterns by sector we divided billionaires into 21 "industries" or sectors (see Appendix A for definitions). These categories are meant to be representative, not definitive. Some individuals change industries over time, some are diversified, and some activities reflect more than one industry. In general, we sought to categorize individuals in that industry in which they (or their benefactor) gained most of their wealth to date. In those cases where no particular industry reflected a plurality we categorized those individuals as "diversified," and an individual receives a designation of "inherited" if the wealth was inherited and the individual has been and is largely economically inactive.

We use Gross National Income and Gross Domestic Product as reported by the World Bank (2013) as measures of national and global income and production for the broader population. The values are reported in current dollars to be consistent with the reporting of billionaire net worth.

Our analysis details the impact of the Great Recession on production and wealth broadly, and then compares these trends to the experience of the world's billionaires. We break the story down geographically and compare the experience of billionaires across high, middle and low-income countries and across regions. We compare the between-country convergence of billionaires per capita and of gross domestic product per capita. Finally, we look at the breakdown of billionaires by industry and evaluate the performance of industries globally and within specific countries. Ultimately, these steps combine to paint a broad picture of processes of "Creative Destruction" in the accumulation of wealth globally against the backdrop of broader global economic trends.

Findings

The Global Financial Crisis

The global economic crisis that took hold in 2007 was no minor hiccup. After four years of global growth between 3.5% and 4% per annum, the world's Gross Domestic Product (GDP) grew only 1.3% in 2008 and then contracted by 2.2% the following year (see Table 7.1). The impact of the financial crisis and subsequent economic crisis of 2007–2009 was concentrated in, but not isolated to, the rich world. GDP in high-income nations, as defined by the World Bank,[5] fell by 3.7% in 2009, while production increased but at a slower rate in the rest of the world (World Bank 2013).

Global GDP growth resumed in 2010, but the world economy fell behind its previous schedule. Using global GDP growth from 2003–2007 to project future growth, we estimate that the recession reduced total production by $10.1 trillion between 2008–2011 (2000 US$). Using a similar method, Better Markets (2012) estimates that the United States alone lost $7.6 trillion worth of production between 2008–2012.

The Great Recession rocked financial markets. For example, between the price peak of October 2007 and the trough of February 2009, the market value of publicly traded companies fell $34.9 trillion dollars, from $64.7 to $29.8 trillion. Stock markets rebounded (or reflated) relatively quickly between early 2009 and early 2011, but stock prices were still 13.5% lower at the end of 2012 than before the crash. The cost of falling prices was not limited to financial assets held disproportionately by the rich. In the United States, the Federal Reserve estimates that median family net worth fell 38.8% and mean net worth 14.4% between 2007 and 2010, and that falling wealth was driven by collapsing house prices (Bricker, et al. 2012).

Billionaires During the Great Recession

The world's wealthiest did not escape the economic carnage. The net worth of the *Forbes* billionaires fell from $4.4 trillion in 2008 to $2.4 trillion in 2009. The ranks of billionaires also fell by 342. If we assume an average net worth of $750 million for those former billionaires, the net worth of 2008's billionaires in 2009 comes out to $2.7 trillion. In other words, the world's wealthiest 1,125 individuals lost $1.7 trillion dollars, 40% of their wealth, or $1.5 billion per person, in that year. Looking further up the distribution, the world's wealthiest 100 lost $670 billion, again around 40% of their net worth, between 2008 and 2009.

Billionaires rebounded well from the recession, but like the rest of the world their net worth still fell well short of where it *could* have been without the Great Recession. The total net worth of the world's billionaires surpassed their 2008 value in 2011, and the average wealth of billionaires was greater in 2012 than it had been in 2008 ($3.7 billion versus $3.6 billion)[6] Adjusted for inflation since 2006, the number of billionaires in 2011 exceeds the number in 2008, but their net worth is still lower in 2012 than in 2008. In current dollars, the net worth of the world's wealthiest 100 climbed back over $1.7 trillion in 2011, from a low just over $1.0 trillion two years earlier; only in 2012 did the net worth of the wealthiest 100 again reach the $1.72 trillion amassed in 2008.

The recession was a serious setback for almost all billionaires, and most have not yet recovered. More than 90% saw their net worth fall between 2008–2009. Of the 342 individuals whose wealth fell below $1 billion in

2009, 40% of them rejoined the billionaire club in 2010, and more than half were billionaires again at some point between 2010–2012. On the other hand, 730 of the 1,125 billionaires in 2008 (64.9%) had a lower net worth in 2012 (see Table 7.3), and the average net worth of 2008's billionaires was down 8.7% in 2012, and that number grows to 14.4% if we adjust for inflation. In short, the number and average wealth of billionaires bounced back to where they were before the recession, but those who were billionaires before the recession are still worse off on average.

Freeland (2012: 145) notes, "moments of revolutionary change are also usually moments when it is possible to make an instant fortune." *Forbes* added 262 billionaires to the list in 2010 but 161 of the new billionaires had been on the list at some point between 2006 and 2008. The ratio of new to old faces jumped after 2010; of the 252 new billionaires between 2010 and 2011, 218 were making their first appearance since at least 2006.

The period just before the Great Recession was also fertile soil for those looking to make a quick fortune. Looking at the world's wealthiest in 2012, 15% of the top 100, with a net worth of $9 billion or more, had not been billionaires in 2006, 34% of the top 500 ($2.5+ billion) and just over half of all billionaires in 2012 were not billionaires in 2006. Going back further, 60% on the list in 2007 were not listed in 2001, and 54% in 2002 were new from 1996.

On the other hand, "billionaire" is not a tenured position. Of the billionaires in 2006, 27% did not make the list in 2012, and 19% of those with a net worth of $2.5 billion or more fell below the $1 billion threshold six years later. By way of comparison, 30% of the list in 2001 was absent in 2007 and 47% dropped out between 1996 and 2002.

Non-billionaires had more success breaking into the upper echelons of global wealth between 2006–2008 than after the recession. For example, 100 or 20% of the wealthiest 500 individuals in 2008 were not billionaires in 2006. Just over half as many of the top 500 by wealth in 2012 were not billionaires in 2010, and around 5% of the top 500 in 2010 were new to the billionaire club since 2008. In short, the world's wealthy elite at each stratum—top 50, top 100, top 500, etc.—were more likely to be relative newcomers in 2008 than in 2010 or 2012.

In essence, there is substantial turnover in identity of the world's billionaires, and this was no truer through the Great Recession than at other recent points in the past. Crises favor the more established elites with the deepest pockets; the rank of the world's wealthiest is more stable as you move up the distribution.

The Geography of the Great Recession

The impact of the Great Recession was not uniform across countries. Specifically, lost production was centered in higher-income countries; low- and middle-income countries increased production by 40% between 2006 and 2011 while high-income countries managed only 6.7% GDP growth (World Bank 2013).

The same is true of the world's billionaires. In 2006, 793 billionaires represented 51 countries by citizenship. Almost half came from the United States; Germany had the second most with 55 representatives, followed by Russia (33), Japan (27), the United Kingdom (24), India (23), Canada (22), and Turkey (21). The percentage of billionaires from the United States fell from 46.8% to 34.6% in 2012 even as the number of billionaires from that country increased from 371 to 424. The number of billionaires from Brazil (37), Hong Kong (38) and India (48) doubled from 2006 to 2012. The number from Russia almost tripled, from 33 to 96, and the number of Chinese billionaires increased twelve-fold from 8 to 95. In 2006, five of the top seven countries by the number of billionaires were members of the OECD (US, Germany, Japan, United Kingdom, and Canada), but in 2012 only two OECD countries remained in the top seven (US and Germany).

This is a dramatic shift from the historical trend. Between 1987 and 2002, the number of billionaires from China, Russia, India, Hong Kong, Brazil, South Korea, Indonesia and Turkey combined increased from 13 to 41; their share of the world total fell from 8.4% to 8.2%. These figures rose to 124 and 15.6% in 2006 and then 385 and 31.4% in 2012. China, India, Indonesia and Brazil, the world's four most populous countries excluding the United States, represented 43.6% of the world's population in 2006 but contained only 6.2% of its billionaires. By 2012 the number of billionaires in those countries quadrupled (from 49 to 197) and their share of billionaires jumped to 16.1%. In all, middle-income countries (with GNI per capita between $1,000 and $10,000) added 237 new billionaires between 2006 and 2012, and the percentage of the world's billionaires from these countries increased from 16.1% to 30.2%.

Another way to look at the uneven and evolving distribution of billionaires across countries is to look at the billionaires per capita. In 2006, low-income countries had 10 billionaires for every billion people, middle-income countries 42 and high-income countries 570 billionaires per billion. By 2012, there were 21 (+11 versus 2006) billionaires per billion population in low-income countries, 119 in middle-income countries (+77.6), and 704 in high-income countries (+134.0 versus 2006). Citizens of the rich world are still more likely to become billionaires, but the number of billionaires in middle-income countries tripled in just six years despite the Great Recession.

The increase in billionaires and billionaire net worth correlates with national economic growth. Low and middle-income countries saw Gross National Income increase more than 80% between 2006 and 2011 and billionaire net worth increase 166% and 222%, respectively (see Table 7.2).

104   *Scott Albrecht et al.*

Table 7.2 A Comparison of Billionaire Net Worth and GNI by Region

Income group	% Change, '07-'11		Net worth/GNI[a]	
	GNI	Net worth	2006	2011
Low income	81.5%	165.5%	6.12	8.96
Middle income	89.7%	222.1%	4.18	7.10
High Income	14.3%	37.6%	5.62	6.77
Region				
East Asia & Pacific	57.8%	182.6%	2.47	4.43
Europe & Central Asia	20.8%	64.8%	4.77	6.50
Latin America & Caribbean	70.6%	196.4%	3.89	6.76
Middle East & North Africa	23.9%	19.4%	8.49	8.18
North America	11.4%	34.5%	8.00	9.66
South Asia	82.0%	149.5%	8.35	11.45
Sub-Saharan Africa	61.5%	242.1%	1.39	2.94
Total	30.9%	69.9%	5.36	6.96

[a]Values multiplied by 100

Source: World Bank 2013; Forbes 2012

Breaking it down by geographic region, East Asia, Latin America, South Asia and Sub-Saharan Africa led the way in GNI growth and added net worth. South Asia and Latin America outgained Sub-Saharan Africa in income growth in percentage terms, but Sub-Saharan African billionaires experienced the most growth in percentage terms of any regional group of billionaires.

Different Rates of Convergence

In the last two columns of Table 7.2 we list the ratio of billionaire net worth to Gross National Income by income level and region for 2006 and 2011. The ratio of billionaire net worth to GNI increased in every income group and region, but not uniformly. Billionaires were especially successful in middle-income countries, increasing their holdings to $7.10 for every $100 of income in 2011 from $4.18 in 2006.

Focusing on the breakdown of GNI and billionaire net worth by income group, the implication is that faster economic growth in middle and low-income countries was potentially outpaced by the even faster accumulation of billionaire net worth. Convergence between high and low-income countries was faster for the very wealthy than for the general population during this period.

In the years before 2006 the opposite was true; convergence in billionaires per capita lagged broader convergence in production between countries.

Roles reversed after 2006 and especially after 2009. While convergence in GDPPC between countries outpaced the same in billionaires per capita from 2000–2006, inequality in billionaires per capita made up that ground by 2011. This is consistent with the findings in Table 7.2, that while income growth has been faster in middle-income countries since 2006, the rise of new billionaires in these countries has been even greater.

Despite evidence of convergence between countries and regions, we should not lose sight of the powerful role nationality continues to play. Citizens of high-income countries were twice as likely as citizens of middle-income countries to become billionaires between 2006 and 2012, and they were many times more likely than those in poor countries. Also, as we detail in the next section, the activities that are generating new billionaires vary meaningfully across countries. In short, supranationality is not new, and nationality continues to play an important role.

The Impact of the Great Recession by Economic Activity

Processes of Creative Destruction are manifested as well in the changing importance of different types of economic activity as epicenters of wealth accumulation. In 2006 and 2012, the industry generating the most billionaires and the billionaires with the most net worth was finance (venture capital, wealth management, "investments", etc.). In 2006, there were 142 billionaires that derived wealth through financial deals; six years later that number had increased by 50%. Finance billionaires also added $277 billion to their net worth. Only media saw declining numbers over the period. The average billionaire media mogul was actually slightly richer in 2012 than in 2006, but there were eight fewer of them.

The biggest winners of the period were those involved in extracting natural resources (oil, gas, coal, metals, lumber, etc.). These individuals added $364.4 billion to their net worth. Extraction was relatively successful from 2006 to 2012 despite the Great Recession, not because of it. These billionaires lost more than half their net worth and more than $250 billion in one year from 2008–2009, but then $373 billion over the next three years.

Billionaires by Economic Activity and Country

Hence, we now turn our attention to the intersection of economic activity and country of resdience. Just as the rise in billionaires was not uniform by country or by industry, the distribution of billionaires is not uniform by industry within countries or by country within industries. Some distributional unevenness is random, but in other cases, the intersection of industry and country

Table 7.3 Billionaires by Industry, 1987–2012

Industry	Wealth							Count						
	1987	2001	2006	2009	2012	2006–2012		1987	2001	2006	2009	2012	2006–2012	
						Δ	Δ%						Δ	Δ%
Agriculture	8.0	13.3	36.4	50.6	93.4	57	157%	4	6	21	22	27	6	29%
Art	0	0	1	1	8.5	7.5	750%	0	0	1	1	4	3	300%
Chemicals	7.3	4.2	21.8	31.2	84.5	62.7	288%	3	2	6	8	25	19	317%
Communications	3.6	101.1	112.6	108.5	212.2	99.6	88%	2	36	30	32	42	12	40%
Construction	5.7	33.9	72.3	59	93.6	21.3	29%	4	17	22	27	37	15	68%
Consumer	22	180.9	250.4	220.7	425.9	175.5	70%	15	55	72	72	99	27	38%
Diversified	23.8	66.8	122.5	108.8	205.7	83.2	68%	14	25	40	31	63	23	58%
Energy	0	5.7	6.4	6.8	14.2	7.8	122%	0	4	4	4	10	6	150%
Entertainment	4.8	32.4	86.3	57.2	102.6	16.3	19%	2	15	29	26	34	5	17%
Extraction	13.2	71.1	219.5	211.1	583.9	364.4	166%	10	33	62	73	121	59	95%
Finance	34.0	270.8	417.8	398.6	694.4	276.6	66%	18	87	142	142	212	70	49%
Health care	15.0	51.0	88.7	85.6	149.4	60.7	68%	9	22	31	30	55	24	77%
High tech	4.5	82.6	88.4	78.3	147.5	59.1	67%	3	25	25	25	42	17	68%
Inherited	1.0	3.7	5.3	2.1	17.7	12.4	234%	1	3	4	2	6	2	50%
Manufacturing	19.3	83.2	144.4	121.7	257.7	113.3	78%	12	26	33	36	65	32	97%
Media	23.2	150.1	153.4	113.1	152.2	−1.2	−1%	11	39	49	40	41	−8	−16%
Real estate	89.2	98.5	186.9	206.8	353.9	167	89%	24	36	75	83	119	44	59%
Retail	30.2	248.7	332.9	327.8	535	202.1	61%	14	49	74	74	115	41	55%
Service	0	45.5	59.1	43.9	68.6	9.5	16%	0	24	25	19	29	4	16%
Software	1.25	182	200.2	149.4	300.9	100.7	50%	1	26	32	30	54	22	69%
Transportation	5.4	12.8	39.2	32.5	72.8	33.6	86%	4	8	16	16	26	10	63%

Source: Forbes 2012; Industries based on authors' designation, see Appendix A.

creates unique and exceptional opportunities to create and control massive amounts of wealth. Mapping changes in the composition of billionaires provides a partial window into the types of activities that made up "Creative Destruction" in recent years.

For analytical purposes, we assume that the distribution of billionaires reflects a latent propensity for concentrated wealth creation that varies by industry and country. Certain countries, due to high levels of economic development, rapid growth, and conducive institutional environments, are able to produce more billionaires. Some industries, due to the scale of demand, innovation creating new growth opportunities, and an inherent tendency for accumulation, allow for more billionaires. Finally, the combination of particular industries in particular countries offers unique opportunities for the creation and accumulation of wealth; the population is better prepared to adopt a new technology, the region is endowed with a particular resource (e.g., oil), etc. The observed distribution of billionaires reflects a latent potential that is the sum of national characteristics, industry characteristics, and unique properties that result from the intersection of the two.

We decompose the count of billionaires by national industry into an expected count by country and industry and an error (the unique contribution of national industry):

$$N_{ic} = E_{ic} + e, \quad E_{ic} = P_i P_c N \tag{1}$$

where N_{ic} is the observed billionaires by country and industry, N the total number of billionaires, and P_i and P_c the share of billionaires in that industry (N_i/N) or country (N_c/N), respectively. In words, if there were no unique national industry effects, we would expect the count of billionaires in a national industry to be equal to the global share of billionaires in that industry multiplied by the share of billionaires in that country multiplied by the number of billionaires. The residual (e) is a combination of a unique national industry effect and luck.

Moving this to change over time, the change in billionaires by national industry over time can be represented as:

$$N_{ic,t} - N_{ic,t-1} = P_{i,t} P_{c,t} N_t - P_{i,t-1} P_{c,t-1} N_{t-1} + e_t - e_{t-1} \tag{2}$$

or

$$\Delta N_{ic} = \Delta N P_{i,t} P_{c,t} (\mathbf{A}) + \Delta P_i N_{t-1} \left(P_{c,t} + \frac{\Delta P_c}{2} \right)(\mathbf{B})$$

$$+ \Delta P_c N_{t-1} \left(P_{i,t} + \frac{\Delta P_i}{2} \right)(\mathbf{C}) + \Delta e(\mathbf{D}) \tag{3}$$

108 *Scott Albrecht et al.*

such that expression *A* is the contribution of a changing global propensity for billionaires, *B* is the unique contribution by industry, *C* is the unique contribution by country, and *D* is the contribution of national industry to the rising or falling number of billionaires. We estimate standard errors for *A*, *B*, *C* and *D* using random sampling with replacement from the original set of data.

Plugging in values for 2006 and 2012, we decompose the changing distribution of billionaires between these years. The effect of *A* across countries and industries is proportional and only shows that it was easier to be a billionaire in 2012 than in 2006 (a third of which was due to inflation lowering the billion-dollar bar). The results from expressions *B* and *C* are consistent with our earlier discussions. China and Russia increased their national propensity by 54.5 and 30.1 billionaires, respectively. Taiwan (+10.5), Indonesia (+9.0), and South Korea (+8.9) also made statistically significant gains. The biggest losers were Germany (−20.4), Japan (−11.5), and the United States (−97.8)—despite adding 52 billionaires between 2006 and 2012 the United States failed to keep pace with the growing number of billionaires globally. In other words, it became easier to be a billionaire globally, but much less so in the United States.

Changes by industry tended to be proportional. Only in two industries was there a statistically significant change: Chemicals (+10.2) and Media (−22.4). In other industries the number of billionaires increased substantially but this change was not significantly different from what we would have expected based on the 54% increase in billionaires globally. Extraction and Manufacturing, for example, added 59 and 32 billionaires, respectively, but only about a quarter of that increase can be attributed to new opportunities in those industries above new opportunities available globally.

Turning to national industries, Table 7.4 lists the 33 national industries that varied substantially (+/−5) from their expected totals in either 2006 or 2012. By focusing on the change in billionaires versus expected (Δe), we can easily identify those areas that are accumulating wealth faster (exceptional creation) and slower (stagnation) than trends among related groups would suggest.

Between 2006 and 2012 the number of Chinese manufacturing billionaires increased from 0 to 14. While some of this increase is a product of new opportunities for billionaires globally, in China and in manufacturing, the decomposition suggests almost two-thirds of the increase was a result of unique opportunities in Chinese manufacturing. Simultaneously, the number of US manufacturing billionaires held steady at 9, a clear case of stagnation, which suggests that the national industry contribution fell from −6.5 (US manufacturing was already underperforming in terms of expected billionaires) to −13.5.

A similar transition took place in real estate. In 2006, the 42 real estate billionaires in the United States was 16.2% more than expected—US real

Table 7.4 Change in Billionaires by National Industry vs. Expected

Destruction		2006		2012		Δe
		N	e	N	e	
China	Finance	0	−1.3***	3	−13.4***	−12.2***
United States	Manufacturing	9	−6.5**	9	−13.4***	−7.0*
United States	Real estate	42	6.8*	43	1.8	−5.0
Germany	Retail	18	12.8***	14	8.9***	−3.9
United States	Chemicals	0	−2.8**	2	−6.7***	−3.8*
Russia	Consumer	0	−2.9***	1	−6.7***	−3.8***
India	Finance	1	−2.9**	2	−6.3***	−3.4*
Hong Kong	Finance	0	−3.2***	0	−6.6***	−3.3**
Russia	Real estate	0	−3.0***	3	−6.3***	−3.3*
United States	Diversified	2	−16.7***	2	−19.8***	−3.0
United States	High tech	18	6.3**	18	3.5	−2.8
Russia	Retail	0	−3.0***	4	−5.0**	−2.0
Saudi Arabia	Finance	7	5.4**	5	3.6*	−1.8
United States	Transportation	4	−3.5*	4	−5.0**	−1.5
United States	Construction	5	−5.3**	6	−6.8***	−1.5
Germany	Finance	3	−7.0***	2	−7.5***	−0.5
United States	Service	19	7.3***	17	7.0**	−0.4
Creation						
United States	Finance	82	15.3***	105	31.6***	16.3*
United States	Software	17	1.9	31	12.3***	10.4**
China	Manufacturing	0	−0.3**	14	8.9***	9.2***
Brazil	Finance	4	1.1	16	9.6***	8.5**
China	Real estate	1	0.3	15	5.8*	5.5
China	Diversified	2	1.6	12	7.1**	5.5
South Korea	High tech	1	0.9	7	6.3**	5.4**
Russia	Extraction	19	16.4***	31	21.5***	5.0
Russia	Construction	1	0.1	8	5.1**	5.0*
Hong Kong	Real estate	9	7.3***	16	12.3***	5.0
India	Health care	2	1.1	8	5.9**	4.7*
Russia	Chemicals	2	1.8	8	6.1**	4.3
Taiwan	High tech	3	2.8*	6	5.1**	2.3
Italy	Consumer	9	7.7***	11	9.7***	2.0
United States	Retail	28	−6.7*	35	−4.8	1.9
Turkey	Diversified	10	8.9***	12	10.2***	1.3

***$p < .01$
**$p < .05$
*$p < .1$, two tailed

Source: Forbes 2012; Industry based on authors' designations (see Appendix A)

110 *Scott Albrecht et al.*

estate was a hot spot of wealth accumulation. By 2012, that was no longer the case. The number of billionaires versus expected fell by 5, a matter of little surprise considering the ties between the recession and US housing market. On the other hand, the number of real estate billionaires increased from 1 to 15, almost 6 more than expected. Hong Kong added another 5 more than expected.

But Chinese finance fell well behind its expected total (adding only 3 when an additional 15.2 were expected based on the growing number of billionaires globally and particularly in China and the high proportion of billionaires in finance), but US finance added 16.3 more billionaires than expected. In short, the accumulation of wealth and creation of billionaires in the United States and China were mirror images of each other through this period; stagnation in one was matched by creation in the other, and often with a similar magnitude.

We find many of the most dynamic areas of economic activity are located exactly where we would expect: finance and software in the US, manufacturing and real estate in China, consumer goods from Italy, technology in Taiwan and South Korea, extraction and construction in Russia. Others are more surprising considering the common sense of the division of labor in the global economy. For example, only Brazil joins the United States in adding significantly more finance billionaires than expected. The number of health care billionaires in India quadrupled and their net worth increased more than six-fold. At the other end, the number of high tech billionaires in the United States held at 18 versus an expected growth of 2.8, and the number of service billionaires in the United States fell from 19 to 17.

Dramatic examples of creation and destruction of billionaire wealth are not unique to the last half decade. For example, Japan real estate moguls were the most numerous billionaire group in 1987 and they controlled an absurd 21% of billionaire wealth in that year. That figure tumbled to 3% over the next five years and under 1% by 2002. Meanwhile, finance billionaires in the United States increased in number from 8 to 50, and their net worth grew from $12 billion to $144 billion, or 3.9% to 9.4% of total billionaire net worth, between 1987 and 2002.

While the wealth from manufacturing is rapidly accumulating in the hands of a few in poorer countries, particularly China, this was not always the case; as late as 2002, most billionaire net worth from manufacturing was located in countries that were richer than average. The same is true for the extraction of raw materials. Those billionaires that made their wealth by mining, logging, drilling, were concentrated in the US, but that changed dramatically with the non-competitive privatization of Russian state-owned firms. These transitions highlight that the geography of wealth accumulation cannot be reduced to simple formula based on rich and poor, core and periphery.

Instead, it is also dependent on the historical and political idiosyncrasies of Creative Destruction.

The Great Recession adversely affected billionaires, and some billionaires have not yet and will not fully recover. New billionaires, particularly from China and Russia, emerged to take their place, and billionaires as a group are slightly wealthier in 2012 than in 2008. Billionaires increased the share of net worth as a percentage of global income, particularly in low- and middle-income countries. As a result, international convergence in billionaires per capita has outpaced convergence in GDP per capita, especially since 2009.

Likewise, the distribution of billionaires has shifted by industry, but particularly in the distribution of billionaires by national industry—the intersection of space and economic activity underpinning processes of "Creative Destruction." From this point of view, changes in the United States and China have mirrored one another: Chinese manufacturing and real estate have added more billionaires than expected, while US manufacturing and real estate have underperformed, but US finance added more billionaires than expected (while finance in China has underperformed). This lends support to Arrighi's argument (1994) regarding the privileged role of finance at the end of a cycle of accumulation.

Discussion

We hope that the brief exercise presented in this chapter serves to illustrate what observers might gain from focusing on billionaires as an indicator of patterns, trends and changes in world-economic accumulation. In the future, our research will turn towards collecting historical data that will allow us to extend back in time the exercise we have presented.

But a few conclusions are warranted. Billionaires proliferated despite the "Great Recession" of 2008. Their number increased 54% over six years from 2006 to 2012, and their net worth increased absolutely and relative to global income. In some cases, the growth of billionaires reflects and/or highlights underlying economic trends; in others, they deviate from these trends. Media moguls performed relatively poorly and producers of industrial chemicals have been very successful. Extraction and Finance continue to generate massive amounts of wealth. Especially in these two areas, the relationship between productive innovation and wealth accumulation deserves scrutiny, as how and where wealth it is being created is not always the same as how and where this wealth is accumulating. Clearly the efficient allocation of capital and extraction of raw materials are critical activities in the global economy, and individuals that increase productivity in these industries can generate large amounts of wealth. But the connection between financial deregulation and rising profits

112 *Scott Albrecht et al.*

in finance in the United States (Tomaskovic-Devey and Lin 2011), as well as the complex politics of the super-rich in Russia, are two examples where the innovations from which billionaires draw their wealth arguably revolves more around rent-seeking behaviors than "productive" investments. But Schumpeter tells us that innovation is not limited to technological advance: we can expand his notion of innovative practices to include new ways of connecting to political networks of patronage, organizing access to opportunities through corruption, and other forms of rent-seeking behavior (and as such, the strategies deployed by new billionaires might provide a more complete window into the empirical origins of capitalist accumulation). This is one important reason why, while billionaires may be globetrotters, they remain tied to the country in which they take their initial steps.

Most billionaires continue to come from a handful of rich countries, led by the US, but that might soon change. Many of the world's new billionaires are hailing from a handful of populous countries, led by China and Russia. The explosion in billionaires in China, from 8 in 2006 to 95 in 2012, is historic, and even more so if we add the 21 new billionaires from Hong Kong and 19 from Taiwan. Indonesia, Brazil and India were also billionaire hotspots. As a group, low and middle-income countries added more new billionaires than the rest of the world.

Notably, the rate of change in the composition of the world's billionaires was a significant deviation from the historical trend, but the overall "churn" of billionaires was not. The Billionaire ranks experienced as much or more turnover before 2006 as after. But before 2006, new billionaires were more likely to come from the same country as the departing billionaires or from other rich countries. Then again, a billionaire half-life of 13.2 years between 2006 and 2012 (or 6.6 years between 1996 and 2002) may represent a significant threat to patrimonial capitalism.

The reconfiguration in the geographical distribution of billionaires might manifest a substantive relocation of some of the epicenters of "creative" wealth accumulation from high to low and middle-income nations of the world. For example, where billionaires by industry in the United States underperformed, they were generally matched by overperforming Chinese billionaires, and vice-versa. This does not mean that "creative" wealth accumulation no longer takes place in high-income nations. Finance in the United States was anything but crippled by the financial crisis of 2008, and there are more billionaires in US finance than in any country besides the United States in the world. But finance is not the sole epicenter of "creative" wealth accumulation, as this varies from country to country. In the former other-superpower, Russia, billionaires are amassing wealth, and these few, often politically connected individuals, are doing so by extracting it out of the ground. In China, the number of new billionaires is growing in industries where the United States is not, and vice versa, and, unlike in Russia, these billionaires are amassing their wealth by making things (manufacturing) and exploiting things built on top of the ground (real estate).

Thus, the character of "creation" and "destruction" should be explored as it evolves in time and space, rather than assuming that one particular set of activities (e.g., manufacturing) represents a more "virtuous" or true source of income and wealth. From a historical perspective, this point is fairly obvious. In their time the transportation of spices, sugar and cotton plantations, and pumping oil from the ground have generated massive amounts of wealth. More recently, we demonstrated that the sites of wealth accumulation from different industries have shifted in the last 25 years. The new billionaires in low and middle-income countries are generating wealth in industries that were previously dominated by high-income countries.

Further, the growing number of US finance billionaires is potentially indicative of a more fundamental change in the global economy. Schumpeter argued that the capitalism entails a constant process of Creative Destruction. These changes historically have entailed spatial reconfigurations within the world-economy and new patterns of social stratification and mobility. The introduction and clustering of innovations constantly transform existing economic and social arrangements, and drive cycles of prosperity (characterized by intense investment in new productive opportunities) and depression (characterized by the broader absorption of innovative practices and the elimination of older activities). The accumulation of financial wealth in the United States and the global shift in the geographic distribution of billionaires in the world-economy suggest that we are undergoing one such period of reconfiguration. One may speculate that it was the misallocation of financial resources as we adjust politically and institutionally to this new reality that ultimately caused the global economy to shudder. In fact, with the massive shift in the national origin of billionaires over the 2000s, one may argue that the 2008 global economic crisis has revealed further the likely shape of things to come.

Notes

1   Others have used this source (e.g., Neumayer 2004).

2   Net worth is measured in current US$, so the real value required to make the *Forbes* list has trended downward over the last 25 years. Using the consumer price index, we estimate that it would require $872 million in 2006 dollars to make the 2012 list.

3   If wealth is distributed among members of a family but can be linked to a single individual as the source of that wealth, the net wealth of the family will be list as a single entry: "Lester Crown & Family". Otherwise, the family members are listed independently.

4   The net worth of the world's three wealthiest individuals at the end of 2010 was roughly equal to the Gross National Income of Pakistan and its 174 million inhabitants (World Bank 2013a; Forbes 2011; UN 2011). The wealth of one individual, Carlos Slim Helú ($73 billion dollars), can buy 14.6 billion hours of labor, or 3 1/3 million years of 12 hour days at $5.00/hour.

114 *Scott Albrecht et al.*

5 "Economies are divided according to 2012 GNI per capita, calculated using the World Bank Atlas method. The groups are: low income, $1,035 or less; lower middle income, $1,036—$4,085; upper middle income, $4,086—$12,615; and high income,$12,616 or more" (World Bank 2013b).

6 Piketty and Saez (2012) note a similar pattern for the United States using tax data.

References

Acemoglu, Daron and James Robinson. 2012. *Why Nations Fail: The Origins of Power, Prosperity, and Poverty.* New York: Crown Publishing Group.

Arrighi, Giovanni. 1991. "World Income Inequalities and the Future of Socialism." *New Left Review* 189: 39–65.

Arrighi, Giovanni. 1994. *The Long Twentieth Century: Money, Power, and the Origins of Our Times.* London: Verso.

Arrighi, Giovanni and Jessica Drangel. 1986. "The Stratification of the World-Economy: An Exploration of the Semiperipheral Zone." *Review* 10: 9–74.

Better Markets. 2012. "The Cost of The Wall Street-Caused Financial Collapse and Ongoing Economic Crisis Is More Than $12.8 Trillion" (September 15). Washington, DC: Better Markets. Retrieved January 15, 2013 (http://bettermarkets. com/sites/default/files/Cost%20Of%20The%20Crisis.pdf).

Braudel, Fernand. 1979. *The Wheels of Commerce.* New York: Harper & Row, Publishers.

Braudel, Fernand. 1984. *The Perspective of the World.* New York: Harper & Row, Publishers.

Bricker, Jesse, Arthur B. Kennickell, Kevin B. Moore and John Sabelhaus. 2012. "Changes in U.S. Family Finances from 2007 to 2010: Evidence from the Survey of Consumer Finances" (Federal Reserve Bulletin, June 2012). Washington, DC: Federal Reserve. Retrieved January 15, 2013 (www.federalreserve.gov/pubs/bulletin/2012/pdf/scf12.pdf).

Dolan, Kerry A. 2012. "Methodology: How We Crunch the Numbers" (March 7, 2012). *Forbes.* Retrieved January 7, 2013 (www.forbes.com/sites/kerryadolan/2012/03/07/methodology-how-we-crunch-the-numbers/).

Eisenstadt, Stuart N. 1974. "Studies in Modernization and Sociological Theory." *History and Theory* 13: 225–52.

Emmanuel, Arghiri. 1972. *Unequal Exchange: A Study of the Imperialism of Trade.* New York: Monthly Review Press.

Firebaugh, Glenn. 2003. *The New Geography of Global Income Inequality.* Cambridge, MA: Harvard University Press.

Forbes. "The World's Billionaires 2011". 2017. *Forbes.Com.* https://www.forbes.com/lists/2011/10/billionaires_2011.html.

Forbes. "Forbes World's Billionaires 2012". 2017. *Forbes.Com.* https://www.forbes.com/sites/luisakroll/2012/03/07/forbes-worlds-billionaires-2012/#63c53bc92c9d.

Frank, Andre Gunder. 1966. "The Development of Underdevelopment." *Monthly Review* 18 (September): 17–31.

Freeland, Chrystia. 2012. *Plutocrats: The Rise of the New Global Super Rich and the Fall of Everyone Else.* New York: The Penguin Press.

Hoselitz, Bert F. 1960. *Sociological Factors in Economic Development*. New York: Free Press.

Inkeles, Alex and David H. Smith. 1974. *Becoming Modern: Individual Change in Six Developing Countries*. Cambridge, MA: Harvard University Press.

Korzeniewicz, Roberto Patricio and Timothy Patrick Moran. 2005. "Theorizing the Relationship between Inequality and Economic Growth." *Theory and Society* 34: 277–316.

Korzeniewicz, Roberto Patricio and Timothy Patrick Moran. 2009. *Unveiling Inequality*. New York: The Russell Sage Foundation.

Myrdal, Gunnar. 1964 [1957]. *Economic Theory and Under-Developed Regions*. London: Gerald Duckworth & Co., Ltd.

Neumayer, Eric. 2004. "The Super-Rich in Global Perspective: A Quantitative Analysis of the Forbes List of Billionaires." *Applied Economic Letters* 11 (13): 793–796.

Piketty, Thomas and Emmanuel Saez. 2012. "Top Incomes and the Great Recession: Recent Evolutions and Policy Implications." Paper presented at the 13th Jacques Polak Annual Research Conference Hosted by the International Monetary Fund, Washington, DC (November 8–9).

Prebisch, Raul. 1950. *The Economic Development of Latin America and Its Principal Problems*. New York: United Nations.

Rostow, Walt W. 1963. *The Stages of Economic Growth: A Non-Communist Manifesto*. Cambridge: Cambridge University Press.

Schumpeter, Joseph A. 1942. *Capitalism, Socialism and Democracy*. New York: Harper and Row.

Tomaskovic-Devey, Donald and Ken Hou Lin. 2011. "Income Dynamics, Economic Rents, and the Financialization of the US Economy." *American Sociological Review* 76 (4): 539–559.

Wallerstein, Immanuel. 1974. *The Modern World-System, Vol. 1*. New York: Academic Press.

Wallerstein, Immanuel. 1979. *The Capitalist World-Economy*. New York: Cambridge University Press.

Wallerstein, Immanuel. 1983. *Historical Capitalism*. London: Verso.

World Bank. 2013. "How We Classify Countries." Retrieved September 16, 2013 from http://data.worldbank.org/about/country-classification

Appendix A Industry Designations

Agriculture	Food crops or livestock; includes tobacco
Art	Art collecting/dealing
Chemicals	Production of industrial chemicals; includes fertilizers
Communication	Installation and maintenance of communications infrastructure
Construction	Construction and construction-related engineering
Consumer	Branding-centric design and production of mostly non-durable consumer goods (e.g., apparel)
Diversified	The individual's activities are sufficiently diverse as to not warrant a single designation
Energy	Production and distribution of electricity
Entertainment	Includes a broad range of products/services oriented towards entertaining the consumer—e.g., sports, gambling.
Extraction	Extraction and distribution of natural resources—oil, metals, lumber, etc. Does not include food stuffs (e.g., agriculture, fishing)
Finance	Allocation of financial resources, either on one's own behalf (e.g., investments, capital gains) or of others (e.g., hedge fund, service fees)
Health Care	Medical technologies and services; includes pharmaceuticals and medical insurance providers
High Tech	Design/production of devices using new technologies (e.g., computers)
Inherited	Wealth is inherited and relatively dormant
Manufacturing	Mass production of undifferentiated goods or on a contractual basis with the brand owner; production of heavy manufactures (e.g., cars)
Media	Information dissemination, principally through 'traditional' technologies, e.g., television, radio, newspaper.
Real Estate	Collecting rents from owned properties or purchasing and reselling properties for a profit
Retail	Intermediaries between producers and consumers
Service	All other services
Software	Services provided electronically/digitally through the execution of computer code; includes internet services
Transportation	Transportation-related infrastructure (e.g., airport) and transportation services (e.g., trucking)

PART III

DEVELOPMENTS ON AND FROM EUROPE'S EASTERN PERIPHERY

8

1918–1945–1989

POLITICAL SHIFTS IN EASTERN EUROPE AND THREE LOGICS OF CATCH-UP DEVELOPMENT IN POLAND

Dariusz Adamczyk

Eastern Europe, the space between Russia in the East and Germany in the West, underwent during the so-called short twentieth century three profound political-hegemonic shifts and, as a consequence, fundamental economic and social transformations: in the wake of World War I the collapse of the Habsburg monarchy, the dissolution of the Russian empire and the weakening of Germany; as a result of World War II and the collapse of the "Third Reich" the incorporation in the Soviet sphere of influence—and socialist World-System; and last but not least in 1989 after the disintegration of the Soviet Union, the subsequent enlargement of the EU and the rise of the so-called BRIC countries. These events have stimulated renewed discussion on the economic, political, social and cultural factors of catch-up development (Zeitschrift für Weltgeschichte, 2012).

In ideal-typical terms, two catch-up strategies could be distinguished: on the one hand, there is the liberal option, based upon free movements of goods, capital and persons, production for the world market and unlimited property rights. On the other hand, there is the neo-mercantilist option, based upon protectionism, import-substitution and production for the domestic market. Beyond, there were mixed forms of both (Gerschenkron, 1962; Abramovitz, 1986; Burkett, Hart-Landsberg, 2003). However, the situation seems to have been more complicated: first of all, we have to keep in mind that the history of Eastern Europe during the twentieth century suggests that catch-up development cannot be reduced on the question of how to generate industrial growth and how the poorer economies have to "catch-up" with the more developed countries. On the contrary, at least in the Polish case the consideration must include a number of other questions as well: how to recover society and economy after disastrous wars; how to create a domestic market in a state that became independent after more than 100 years' partitions; and finally, how to transform society and economy after the collapse of state socialism. Consequently, we should discuss not only how did specific catch-up strategies in Poland relate to the interaction of internal factors (like the absence of reforms, of capital, of innovation and of functioning markets) and of external determinants resulting from World-System dynamics, but also what ways of development during the twentieth century were characteristic in which specific historical phases? In this sense, "catching up" cannot be separated from the respective historical stage in which it took place and does not necessarily mean to reach the development and income level of better developed countries. It contains, however, strategies to overcome the absolute poverty and to guarantee a minimum of state and social order.

The Creation of Domestic Market After the Partitions

Let me start with the situation after World War I. Poland did not exist as a state for 123 years from the third partition in 1795 until 1918—divided between Germany, Austria-Hungary and Russia. As one consequence of the war and collapse or dissolution of these empires, Poland became an independent state.

From the very beginning the Polish elite was confronted with the question of how to overcome not only the implications of World War I, but also the longue durée-consequences of the partitions—among others, the fact that old markets and the old division of labor had ceased to exist. 1918 in Poland there were five currencies, three administrations and three law systems. Moreover, the Polish state comprised regions which presented very different levels of economic development and different social structures. For example, Polish areas which belonged to the Habsburg and Germany empires had status of inner periphery. In contrast to that, the Polish areas which constituted a part of the Russian empire were strong textile centers which during the nineteenth century produced for the huge Russian market (Adamczyk, 2001).

Therefore, as one of the first steps to unify the new Polish economy in November 1919 the government introduced a common external tariff. Shortly thereafter, internal tariffs and a system of widespread regulations of commodity and factor markets were reduced. Hence, the internal custom's frontier was removed in mid-1921, and by the end of 1921 most other regulations on the commodity markets disappeared. Moreover, by 1924 the Bank of Poland was created and the Polish currency implemented. In addition, the most obvious non-tariff barriers to trade and mobility within the new Polish state such as different currencies, different tax systems and a shortage of transport facilities were considerably reduced if not completely removed by 1926 (Trenkler, Wolf, 2005, 202–203; Wolf, 2005).

The German economic historian Nikolaus Wolf comments on the development of Polish industry as follows:

> There was a strongly significant and economically important forward linkage but also a significant and even larger effect of the interaction between skill-intense industries and a locations endowment with a skilled labour force, as well as an increasingly important role for innovative activity. Poland's industry adjusted to the dramatic border changes in the wake of the First World War in a manner which was surprisingly similar to the dynamics of the modern European Union.
>
> (Wolf, 2007, 39)

Thus, it seems a domestic market would have been strengthened in this time and contacts to foreign markets reduced as the following table of the trade relationships between Poland and Germany, the most important commercial partner of Poland, impressively demonstrates.

In this sense, catch-up development, understood as the creation of a unified domestic market in post-partitioned Poland, may have been successful.

Table 8.1 Poland's Trade with Germany (in Percent of Total Trade; following Wolf, 2007, 27)

	1923	1926	1928	1932	1935	1937
Imports body text	44	24	23	20	14	15
Exports	51	25	34	16	15	14

122   *Dariusz Adamczyk*

Nonetheless, the big projects such as the establishment of the Central Industrial District in the South-Eastern parts of Poland in the 1930s or the Port of Gdynia in the 1920s could absorb only a few unemployed, and particularly in the countryside with 70–75% of population, the level of unemployment was very high—much people there lived in extreme poverty, especially during the world economic crisis from 1929 onward (Kostrowicka, Landau, Tomaszewski, 1975, 360).

A significant contrast to West European core countries is illustrated by the next table.

Table 8.2 GNP of Poland per capita (in 1960 US Dollars) 1913–1938 (following Aldcroft and Morewood, 1995, 84)

	1913	*1929*	*1938*
Poland	301	350	372
England	996	1038	1181
Germany	757	770	1126
France	695	982	936
Belgium	894	1098	1015
Netherlands	754	1008	921

If we would conceive the catch-up politics only as an attempt to reach the level of Gross National Production in core states, then the development process in Poland obviously failed. Thus, the results of catching up seem to have been ambivalent.

After Apocalypse: State Socialism and Modernization

Failing as a state in World War II was due not to Poland's backward economic structure, but to a military superiority of Germany and the Soviet Union which in September 1939 divided Poland. As a consequence of World War II Poland was incorporated into the Soviet sphere of influence (Kersten, 1984). Two profound concomitants of this war were, first of all, a dramatic change in the population structure of Poland: almost 90% of Jewish citizens were exterminated by Germans, and shortly thereafter, several million Germans fled from the Red Army or were expelled by the communist government. The second significant change was the shift of state borders to the West: most of Silesia and Pomerania as well as the southern parts of Eastern Prussia became now Polish territory. On the other hand, Western Ukraine, Western Belarus and parts of Lithuania, which had belonged to Poland before the war, were annexed by the Soviet Union.

Figure 8.1 Shift of state borders after World War II
Source: en.wikipedia.org/wiki/Oder-Neisse_line

The Polish sociologist Andrzej Leder speaks in this context of "overdreamed" revolution which took place in the 1940s/1950s (Leder, 2014). In his opinion, ordinary Poles, mostly descended from peasants, have been the main beneficiaries of this revolution based upon the confiscation of post-Jewish and post-German property as well as the violent expropriation of the pre-war Polish landowner class. Thus, a dramatic social change followed and the foundations for the rise of the middle class were laid. If Leder is right, this transformation, cynically speaking, would have been the most radical form of catch-up development in Polish history of the twentieth century.

The incorporation of Poland into the Soviet sphere of influence was connected to the implementation of socialist industrialization. The striking

124 *Dariusz Adamczyk*

elements of state socialism were Marxist-Leninist ideology legitimating the one-party monopoly on power, domination of the economy by state and central planning as well command-administrative coordination (Kornai, 1992). All spheres of social activity were placed under the political and ideological control of the party. In the 1950s/1960s state socialism was based upon the industry of means of production and heavy industry. At the same time the production of consumer goods was very modest and, consequently, produced only a very modest wealth that could not meet more than the basic needs of population. Heavy industry did need huge investments which bound manpower, capital, raw materials and energy. Moreover, the heavy industry used the most part of mining and metallurgy production, of energy sector and of heavy manufacturing industry and was highly inefficient. This situation generated, in turn, absurd economic cycles and caused discontent within the population. In the mid-1960s two Polish intellectuals, Karol Modzelewski and Jacek Kuroń, discerned the economic, social and political drawback of state socialism in Poland. Furthermore, in 1956 and 1970 worker riots against the Polish Communist Party took place (Kuroń, Modzelewski, 1969).

The main goal of the Polish economic strategy from the late 1940s and 1950s onwards was to reduce the dependency on imports from the capitalistic world as much as possible and to take part in the socialistic division of labour. However, the government of Edward Gierek in the 1970s decided to change the politics of import substitution. A new goal was formulated: deep modernization of Polish industry by, at least partly, incorporation into a capitalistic division of labour. Gierek tried to create a new economic program, based on large-scale borrowing from banks in the West—mainly from West Germany and the US—to buy technology that would upgrade Poland's production of know-how goods which then would be sold on the world market and the credits repaid. This borrowing, estimated to around 10 billion US dollars, was used not only to modernize Polish industry, but also to import consumer goods to give the workers more incentive to work (Strobel, 1980). The shift of foreign trade is illustrated by the next table.

Table 8.3 Geography of Polish Foreign Trade 1970–1975 (in percent; following Kaliński, 1995, 171)

Countries	Imports 1970	Imports 1975	Exports 1970	Exports 1975
Socialistic	68.6	45.8	63.9	59.9
Core	25.8	49.3	28.4	31.5
Periphery ("Third World")	5.6	4.9	7.7	8.6
Total	100	100	100	100

Massive investments were made, expected to improve the standard of living of the various segments of society and establish an internationally competitive Polish industry and agriculture as well. For the first time many Poles could afford to buy cars, televisions and other consumer goods because the government made sure that the workers received proper wages. However, this catch-up strategy failed after some few years. Why?

The "New Development Strategy", based upon import-led growth, depended on the global economic conditions which changed dramatically after 1973/1974—among others, because of worldwide recession and increased oil prices (Adamczyk, 2012, 83; Komlosy, 2015). The oil crisis produced a sharp increase in the price of imported consumer goods and a rise in inflation which resulted in a recession in the West. Subsequently, demand for Polish exports, particularly coal, declined. Poland's foreign debt rose from US$ 23 billion at the end of 1980 to 26–28 US$ at the end of 1981 (Schröder, 1982, 127). Borrowing from the West had become increasingly difficult. On the other hand, the new factories built by Gierek's government proved extremely ineffective and mismanaged—foremost cost effectiveness and the growing demand for consumption goods were often ignored. As a consequence of misallocations in industry Poland had to import raw materials. In addition, we should keep in mind that several Polish products were of extremely poor quality and not competitive on the world market. A Polish intellectual Stefan Kisielewski depicted this system as a rule of amateurs (Kisielewski, 1978).

The failure of Gierek's politics led between 1976 and 1980 to an emergence of oppositional groups like the *Worker's Defence Committee* (KOR) and trade union *Solidarity*, and finally, to the collapse of state socialism (Mackenbach, 1982; Fenchel, Pietsch, 1982). Ironically, just the attempt to save socialism by, at least partly, integration into a capitalistic world system caused its fall (Pleskot, 2015).

Imitative Market Economy in the Wake of the European Union

Gierek's politics seem to have been a transitional period from state socialism, a catching up strategy based upon central planning, to a catch-up project based upon the opening to foreign markets that occurred after 1989. In global perspective 1989 has marked continuity with the 1970s, in the political and social one a sharp break with state socialism. Interestingly, the Polish political elite, no matter whether of the former Solidarity or of the former Communist Party, applied for Poland's accession into the European Union—not only because of expectations of getting money from Brussels, but also because of the sense of belonging to Europe—whatever this might mean—and obtaining validity and a say in EU structures. In the run-up

126 *Dariusz Adamczyk*

to the 2001 parliamentary elections leader and next Prime Minister Leszek Miller from the former Communist camp argued that his party "would preside over the most momentous event in the country's history—Poland's EU-accession—since Mieszko I converted to Christianity in 966." (Taras, 2003, 3). One year later after final negotiations between the Polish government and EU Leszek Miller announced:

> We have removed the heavy burden of the Yalta agreement and the postwar division of Europe. From Polish Solidarity, which won freedom and democracy for Central and Eastern Europe, we are approaching the true solidarity of Europe and of Europeans.
>
> (Taras, 2003, 3)

It is useless to speculate whether the accession into the EU was the most important event since Mieszko's conversion to Christianity in the tenth century, but anyway it was connected to a fundamental attempt to modernize the Polish economy, politics and society by imitation; that is to say the implementation of privatization, deregulation, liberalization and the transfer of political institutions from the EU (Norkus, 2012)—and not to forget, based upon cheap and skilled manpower. However, the financial expectations were of high importance. From 2007 to 2013 Poland has received 283.4 billion zloty (c. 67 billion Euro net)—nearly 18% of Gross National Product in 2008 (Polityka, 62; Główny Urząd Statystyczny). Between 2014 and 2020 344.4 billion zloty (c. 83 billion Euro) are expected to have been transferred from Brussels—83 billion Euro constitutes c. 20% of Polish Gross National Product in 2013 (Polityka, 62). No question: these money flows contributed to an increase of the economic growth—a considerable part has been invested in infrastructure. And yet more for figure fetishists: the cumulative growth between 2003 and 2013 can be estimated in Poland at 46%, thereof from the financial crisis in 2008 to 2013 at nearly 20%. In contrast, between 2003 and 2013 the percent rate of growth in Czech Republik was 23, in Hungary 13, and in Germany 14 (Polityka, 63). Another issue in this context is the question whether the politics of growth can be continued when the Brussels funds will expire after 2020 and whether the imitative catch-up strategy can be transformed into a more innovative development.

Has this mimetic catch-up strategy implemented after 1989 been successful? Some indicators suggest an affirmative response.

The development of Gross National Product demonstrates a modest increase—foremost since the financial crisis of 2008—but shows, on the other hand, that the gap to Germany has substantially been remaining the same for 100 years. In addition, the table also illustrates significant differences

Table 8.4 GNP per capita based on purchasing power parity 1997–2012

	1997	2000	2004	2005	2006	2007	2008	2012
EU-27	100	100	100	100	100	100	100	100
Poland	47	48	51	51	53	55	56	66
Germany	125	119	117	116	114	115	113	121
Czech.R.	73	69	75	77	79	81	82	79
Slovenia	77	79	85	87	88	92	92	82
Bulgaria	27	28	34	35	37	38	39	47

Source: Eurostat

between the new EU-members: on the one hand between Poland and the Czech Republic or Slovenia, and on the other between Poland and Bulgaria. Nevertheless, for more than two decades Germany has been Poland's by far most important trading partner.

We do also have to note several changes regarding Poland's position in the international division of labor. While in the early 1990s Polish industry made mostly semi-finished products and exported raw materials, in the last years we can observe an increased share of consumer goods and technology-intensive products in Poland's exports—above all in the car industry. Granted that most investments have originated from West European corporations. Nonetheless, a couple of domestic companies making technology goods such as the manufacturer of city buses *Solaris* with hybrid drive have successfully appeared on domestic and foreign markets—among others, in Hannover where the author of these words lives (Kowanda, 2015, 41).

Additionally, there is no doubt that we have to consider not only hard indicators like Gross National Product and position in the international division of labor, but also "soft" factors such as life expectancy, education level or democracy index. The life expectancy, for example, shows a substantial increase between 1990 and 2001.

In any case, imitative modernization and the transfer of economic and political institution as well as *acquis communautaire* from the EU were in Poland the key elements from the very beginning of transformation.

Table 8.5 Life Expectancy in Poland (following Skalski, 2003, 15)

	Male	Female
1990	66.5	75.5
1995	67.6	76.4
2001	70.2	78.2

128 *Dariusz Adamczyk*

Conclusions

In this paper I have tried to show how fundamental political shifts in the twentieth century did impact the strategies of catch-up development in Poland. First of all, Poland became in the wake of World War I an independent state, but consisted of different areas, different administrations, different law systems, different currencies, and last but not least different people with different mentalities. Despite these obstacles Poland did not fail as a state—even if several politicians in the East as well as in the West presented Poland as a "seasonal" state. The creation of a unified domestic market with unified currency was a great achievement of Polish governments between 1918 and 1926—particularly as Poland in this time fought a war against the Bolsheviki.

The attempts occurring from the 1940s/1950s onward show other logic of catch-up development. The establishment of state socialism was accompanied by the use of extreme violence and should be seen in the context of World War II—foremost the extermination of the Jews by Germans and, at the end of the war, the expulsion of German inhabitants from the former German territories which were annexed by the new Polish state. Additionally, state borders were shifted westwards and the strategy for socialist industrialization was implemented. It seems to have been the most radical transformation of Polish society which took place during the twentieth century.

In the 1970s Polish government headed by Edward Gierek started a next stage of catch-up development by partly integrating into the international division of labor. His politics quickly failed and contributed to a deep political, economic and social crisis that finally caused a system transformation from 1989 onward. Whether this market oriented catch-up strategy will remain successful cannot be said. The most important question in this context, in my opinion, is whether Poland's growth can be continued without funds from the EU and whether the imitative catch-up strategy can be transformed into a more innovative one.

References

Abramovitz, Moses. 1986. "Catching Up, Forging Ahead, and Falling behind." *Journal of Economic History*, 46 (2): 385–406.
Adamczyk, Dariusz. 2001. "Polens halbperiphere Stellung im internationalen System: eine Long-Run-Perspektive." *Zeitschrift für Weltgeschichte*, 2 (2): 79–91.
Adamczyk, Dariusz. 2012. "'Polen, nachholende' Entwicklung und die Rhythmen der Globalisierung im 20: Jahrhundert." *Zeitschrift für Weltgeschichte*, 13 (2): 75–90.
Aldcroft, Derek H., Steven Morewood. 1995. *Economic Change in Eastern Europe since 1918*. Aldershot: Edward Elgar Publishing.
Burkett, Paul, Martin Hart-Landsberg. 2003. "A Critique of 'Catch-Up' Theories of Development." *Journal of Contemporary Asia*, 33 (2): 147–171.

Political Shifts in Eastern Europe 129

Fenchel, Reinhard, Anna-Jutta Pietsch (eds). 1982. *Polen 1980–1982: Gesellschaft gegen den Staat*. Hannover: SOAK Verlag Hannover.

Gerschenkron, Alexander. 1962. *Economic Backwardness in Historical Perspective*. Cambridge: Harvard University.

Kaliński, Janusz. 1995. *Gospodarka Polski w latach 1944–1989: Przemiany strukturalne*. Warszawa.

Kersten, Krystyna. 1984. *Narodziny systemu władzy: Polska 1943–1948*. Poznań: SAWW.

Kisielewski, Stefan. 1978. *Polen: oder die Herrschaft der Dilettanten: Sozialismus und Wirtschaftspraxis*. Zürich: Verlag A. Fromm.

Komlosy, Andrea. 2015. "Systemtransformation als Krisenmanagement: Der RWG-Umbruch im globalen Kontext, 40 Jahre danach (1973–2003)." In Dariusz Adamczyk and Stephan Lehnstaedt (eds.), *Wirtschaftskrisen als Wendepunkte: Ursachen, Folgen und historische Einordnungen vom Mittelalter bis zur Gegenwart*. Osnabrück: fibre Verlag: 337–376.

Kornai, Janos. 1992. *The Socialist System: The Political Economy of Communism*. Princeton, NJ: Princeton University Press.

Kostrowicka, Irena, Zbigniew Landau, Jerzy Tomaszewski. 1975. *Historia gospodarcza Polski XIX i XX wieku*. Warszawa: Państwowe Wydawnictwo Naukowe.

Kowanda, Cezary. 2015. "Zmiany, zmiany, zmiany: Każdy chce więcej zarabiać, nawet wielki i bogaty." *Polityka*, April 8–14, 40–42.

Kuroń, Jacek, Karol Modzelewski. 1969. *Monopolsozialismus: Offener Brief an die Polnische Vereinigte Arbeiterpartei*. Hamburg: Hoffman und Campe (transl. and ed. by Helmut Wagner).

Leder, Andrzej. 2014. *Prześniona rewolucja: Ćwiczenie z logiki historycznej*. Warszawa: Wydawnictwo Krytyki Politycznej.

Mackenbach, Werner (eds.). 1982. *Das KOR und der 'polnische Sommer': Analysen, Dokumente, Artikel und Interviews 1976–1981*. Hamburg: Junius Verlag.

Norkus, Zenonas. 2012. *On Baltic Slovenia and Adriatic Lithuania: A Qualitative Comparative Analysis of Patterns in Post-Communist Transformation*. Vilnius: Apostrofa CEU PRESS.

Pleskot, Patryk. 2015. "Der kuriose Triumph des Marxismus? Zum internationalen Kontext der ökonomischen Krise in der Volksrepublik Polen als Ursache des demokratischen Systemwandels (1987–1989)." In Dariusz Adamczyk and Stephan Lehnstaedt (eds.), *Wirtschaftskrisen als Wendepunkte: Ursachen, Folgen und historische Einordnungen vom Mittelalter bis zur Gegenwart*. Osnabrück: fibre Verlag: 377–398.

Polityka. 2014. "*10 lat w Unii*." 28 April–6 Mai 2014.

Schröder, Klaus. 1982. "Die Verschuldung Polens im Westen." *Europa-Archiv*, 5: 117–126.

Skalski, Ernest. 2003. "*Biedni, ale równi*." Gazeta Wyborcza, 28 Juli.

Strobel, Georg W. 1980. "Die wirtschaftliche und soziale Entwicklung Polens: Auftrieb und neue Probleme in den siebziger Jahren." *Europa-Archiv*, 3: 65–80.

Taras, Ray. 2003. "Poland's Accession into the European Union: Parties, Policies and Paradoxes." *The Polish Review*, 48 (1): 3–19.

Trenkler, Carsten, Nikolaus Wolf. 2005. "The Polish Interwar Economy 1921–1937." *European Review of Economic History*, 9: 199–231.

130 *Dariusz Adamczyk*

Wolf, Nikolaus. 2005. "Path Development Border Effects: The Case of Polands Reunification (1918–1939)." *Explorations in Economic History*, 42: 414–438.

Wolf, Nikolaus. 2007. "Endowments vs. Market Potential: What Explains the Relocation of Industry after the Polish Reunification in 1918?" *Explorations in Economic History*, 44: 22–42.

9

DEBT-RIDDEN DEVELOPMENT ON EUROPE'S EASTERN PERIPHERY[1]

Tamás Gerőcs and András Pinkasz

In our paper we deal with Eastern European semi-peripheral dependent development which we put in the broader context of the historical evolution of the capitalist world-system. Our research question is how the changing structure of the international division of labor induces Eastern Europe's reindustrialization. Whether this structural change would open up spaces for those semi-peripheral societies within the hierarchical structures of the European division of labor. Or if such a change would in fact lead back to the historical dependencies that are characteristics of capitalism's uneven development. The broader motivation behind the research is to track spaces for manoeuvering within the structures of the global division of labor from the perspective of semi-peripheral dependent development. To operationalize this question we will need an elaborated definition of semi-peripheral dependent development.

132 *Tamás Gerőcs and András Pinkasz*

Contrary to the mainstream literature of transitology,[2] our method demonstrates that the mode of Eastern European reintegration into the capitalist world economy that started in the 1970s was fueled by structural changes in the world economy (Arrighi, 2000).

We aim to understand the uneven nature of the evolving interaction between the Comecon and the capitalist world-economy after the 70s that lead to both political and structural changes in Eastern Europe. To prove our case we will briefly demonstrate some differences within the Comecon. For example, how the legacy of their position within earlier structures of the capitalist division of labor and the different nature in which they started to interact as Comecon members with western partners varied.

In our research we will focus on the case of Hungary which had a somewhat specific position both within the Comecon and also in the integration process. The changes in the global economy after the 1970s lead to the evolution of the "new international division of labor" (see e.g. Fröbel et al., 1980) in which divergent industrial developments appear up to now. In our evaluation reindustrialization seems to indicate a new position for Eastern European societies.

Our hypothesis is that in the case of Hungary the country's so called bridge position between the Comecon and the world market explains the long process of integration that finally resulted in the specialization in the automotive industry. Therefore, we need to start our analysis in the early 70s when the Comecon market became strongly affected by the forces of global capitalism. In our explanation we will intentionally focus on two external dependencies: (1) external financial dependence which in the case of Hungary resulted in a rapid debt accumulation between 1973 and 2008, and (2) the changing structures of the international division of labor in which our research intends to analyze the newly emerging automotive industry. Analyzing the process from the outside of Eastern Europe, reindustrialization is the mere outcome of a more dialectical process that produces simultaneous deindustrialization in other locations within the global commodity chains (Hopkins and Wallerstein, 1986; Gereffi and Korzeniewicz, 1994). Thus, our concept will emphasize the process of industrial relocation which is part of the reconfiguration of the international division of labor.

Overall, the subsequent processes we want to understand are more global than transitology studies suggest. We will need to understand the broader context of international capital flows and the reconfiguration of the production and trade networks in order to conceptualize semi-periphery. In order to do so, we will focus on the intersection of the international division of labor and international finances in the uneven development of capitalism. Before going into deeper historical analysis, we give an initial definition of the semi-periphery.

Semi-Peripheral Dependent Development: A Concept

Besides detecting the historical legacy of Eastern European integration into the capitalist world economy, conceptualization of the semi-periphery is essential in our inquiry. We will place emphasis on two key elements in the evolution of capitalism that we think will help us in our inquiry. These are the degrees to which a state gains access to capital and technology in the global process of accumulation. Thus, semi-periphery is a structural position in the evolution of historical capitalism (see e.g. Chase-Dunn, 1998; Radice, 2009). It is a dependent form of interaction that leads to the relative scarcity of capital and technology. The roots of relative scarcity lie in the unfavorable condition of specialization within the international division of labor. World-system scholars call this the unequal development, or underdevelopment (Frank, 1966; Szentes, 1988).

Underdevelopment in this understanding is not the lack of integration in the global division of labor, as for example transitology suggests, or something which mainstream political economy calls lagging behind the advanced economies, but the actual result of the integration which develops hand in hand with advanced economies through complex mutual ties. The long-term consequences of dependent semi-peripheral development are the limited access to the country's own internal resources in the process of capital accumulation. As a result, there is a heavy dependence on external resources for both investment and consumption purposes (Arrighi et al., 2003; Amin, 1977). We are fully aware of the fact that definitions of semi-periphery can vary to a large degree and some less critical literature deploys a very different methodology to prove how successful "catching up" economies make capitalism appealing for semi-peripheral integration (see the different definitions: e.g. Worth and Moore, 2009).

On this level of abstraction some strong pieces of evidence for the cyclical imbalances can already be found in the external financial position of semi-peripheral economies (Amin, 1977, 181–197; Emmanuel, 1972, 167). In our understanding, such a position is one of the structural reasons partly responsible for debt accumulation and for the reproduction of dependencies. Hence, external resources are crucial in the development of semi-peripheral economies. With respect to scarcity of capital we will make a distinction between three forms of external finances in order to demonstrate that the very similar results of such a development are not coincidental but systemic. These three forms are the international loans, the foreign direct investment (FDI) and different sorts of transfers (e.g., EU-funds).

To understand the nature of external finances we shall not only treat it as a particular form of financial transaction but in a broader socio-political context. In our understanding the form of access to international capital is tied to a certain geopolitical situation. Complex geopolitical regimes change

134   *Tamás Gerőcs and András Pinkasz*

over time, however, according to the global logic of capital accumulation. One example is the collapse of the Bretton Woods system that led to the change of both the form of international capital and the role of the institutions that regulated capital (see on this: Arrighi and Silver 2003; Gowan, 1999).

Eastern Europe in the Capitalist Division of Labor

'Bridge Model' in the 1970s: Growing Role of International Loans

The emergence of the European division of labor in which Eastern Europe captured a distinctive position by the late 1990s is not comprehensible without taking into account the latest mode of their reintegration to the capitalist world-system, which in fact started with the global economic crisis in the 70s (Chase-Dunn, 1980). Initial attempts within the Comecon were made for the sake of economic self-reliance, a purpose served by policies of import-substitution industrialization (ISI) from the early 1950s to the 1970s. Nevertheless, Comecon countries were never fully self-sufficient as it was proved by André Gunder Frank and Immanuel Wallerstein in the late 70s (Frank, 1977; Wallerstein, 1976). ISI policies, for instance, which officially were designed to serve self-reliant modernization, simultaneously created a demand for western technology, the import of which was meant to contribute to the catching up strategy.[3] Ties to western economies were reinforced by the expanding loans from western creditors to debtor states in the East. In the stagflation of the 70s almost all the Comecon states benefited from the cheap credit that was made temporarily available by western commercial institutions (see Comisso and Tyson, 1986). From the 70s onwards, international loans became the instrument of integrating socialist semi-peripheral states into the capitalist division of labor. However, loans were available even before that and during the Cold War era this was the dominant form of external finances for most of the socialist and some of the non-socialist semi-peripheral states in their pursuit of modernization. Hungary was one of those socialist semi-peripheral states that due to its position in the international trade between Comecon and the west started to rely on international loans.

Hungary in the 1960s followed an economic model of "bridging" the channels of western goods and technologies to the users of ISI throughout the Comecon[4] (Vigvári, 1990, 2008; Szegő, 1989; Lóránt, 1990). The bridge-model meant a dialectical relationship between western capital (looking for new market opportunities) and the modernization efforts of Eastern European states. Hungary's contribution to this was that the country imported western technology (machineries and intermediaries) in exchange for hard currency in order to re-sale those processed products that contained western elements in the Comecon market. There it gained non-convertible currencies, most

Figure 9.1 Terms of trade, 1960 = 100

Source: Hungarian Central Statistical Office.

notably transferable-ruble. Although, in the history of Comecon-integration there were several reform attempts to create a convertible-currency, but these efforts could never materialize (Bideleux, 1996; Stone, 1996; Feitl, 2013).

The consequence of the existing international trade relationship and the failure of the Comecon-integration was that the country had to seek export opportunities in order to cover the costs of western import by hard currency (Bekker, 1995). There were a variety of sources for hard currency even from fellow Comecon members although it was seldom that they shared currency reserves. More typical was that the country could produce convertible currency via export to non-socialist (either core or peripheral) markets. The model was based on the assumption of favourable terms of trade towards both the Comecon and western-markets which seemed to have been the case until the mid-1970s (we show the changing pattern of the terms of trade between 1960 and 1993 in Figure 9.1).

The bridge-model also served the interest of the rest of the members of the Comecon, especially the Soviet Union's which faced difficulties in gaining western technology. It served western interests too, because of an evolving tendency of market saturation and the subsequent profit crisis in the 1960s which forced western corporations to seek new market opportunities (Gowan, 1999, 39–60). The productive sectors suffered from overproduction, therefore the companies' willingness to cooperate with Eastern European states grew substantially after western markets slipped into recession in the 1970s (Frank, 1977). The more general structural crisis was exacerbated by a series of oil price shocks. Peaking oil prices changed the conditions for profitability among several industries and had an impact on the global distribution of income.

In such a situation western companies came under pressure to renew their value chains through technology-intensive investments which they could only achieve by the end of the 1980s.

Meanwhile the energy crisis created a liquidity abundance in the 1970s to which scholars sometimes refer as the source of petrodollar illusion (see e.g., Ortiz, 2014). Petrodollars were produced because of the sharp increases in the price of oil. As western economies had stuck in the crises, investment opportunities became very scarce. Liquid capital found no easy way to be reproduced, thus accumulation was globally disrupted (Harvey, 1989). It was an illusion in a sense that the abundance of free liquidity proved to be only a temporary state of the markets that still suffered from the crisis of overproduction and the need for effective demand.

The illusion of liquidity abundance was translated in the form of easy access to cheap hard-currency denominated loans. The dominance of international loans as a form of external finance grew substantially between the 1970s and 1980s for Latin-American and Eastern European semi-peripheral states (Eichengreen, 1990). Their growing debt burden turned unsustainable when international liquidity was squeezed due to a combination of monetary and geopolitical changes. Western capital in the form of credit was abundant until the end of the 1970s when the United States entered the global capital market to compete for the dollars it needed for financing her own debts. The policy change was marked by a series of interest-rate rises by the Federal Reserve under the chairmanship of Paul Volcker. Capital suddenly became scarce for semi-peripheral states that were neither competitive in the world market, nor did they have easy access to finance their external needs. Not surprisingly vulnerable states all over the global semi-periphery turned into a very deep recession which was followed by financial meltdown and the subsequent series of defaults.

We have to see that these mechanisms have different effects on the Comecon members. Their reaction for instance towards openness or reliance on western markets differed to a very large extent (Tyson, 1986). Some countries managed to sustain their older form of investment-led policies while others were already in urgent need of correction by the late 1960s. For example, Czechoslovakia managed to tie itself more closely to the Comecon trade and developed its own technology-base. Czechoslovakian policies preferred not to open to western markets but to sustain the fading ties within the Comecon (Stevens, 1985). This was an orthodoxy in the eyes of leading Hungarian politicians who—instead of keeping the door of their economy closed—developed a one-way dependence (openness) on western-inputs for which they needed liberalization. It is remarkable that when capital became scarce, Hungary's dependence was rapidly translated into a coercive external force, the result of which was rapid debt accumulation.

In this paper we cannot elaborate further on how developmental models in the Comecon bifurcated due to this pressure. What we want to emphasize here is that Hungary was probably in one of the most vulnerable positions since its economy had already been exposed to western trade and capital-flows to a large extent due to the bridge-model. Terms of trade in Hungary, which was previously positive as the quintessential element for the bridge-position, also turned negative (as it is demonstrated in Figure 9.1). Deteriorations in the terms of trade both in socialist and non-socialist relations became the source of a growing financial burden (Allen, 1982). One source of the deterioration in the terms of trade was that the price of energy which the country imported from the Soviet Union and the prices of machineries and intermediaries that dominated western import rose sharply. Contrary to this trend, the relative price of the traditional Hungarian export products, such as consumption goods from light industries, fell in comparison to the price of import products.

Vigvári argues that Hungary was particularly badly hit because of the misconception of the bridge-position (Vigvári, 1990). The country could hardly manage its growing debt service and the above mentioned forces pushed it even closer to western markets. In 1982, three years after the Volcker shock, the country could no longer survive without IMF intervention. After the IMF-membership the state had to gradually abandon its original socialist modernization targets. As a consequence, the original ISI-effort was also shifted to an export-led developmental model (Comisso and Marer, 1986). The result of this shift was that the share of the non-socialist market destination (Figure 9.2) and the share of convertible currency trade in the total trade (Figure 9.3) significantly increased after 1985 (Nyers, 1993).

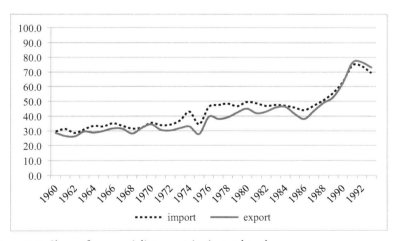

Figure 9.2 Share of non-socialist countries in total trade

Source: Hungarian Central Statistical Office.

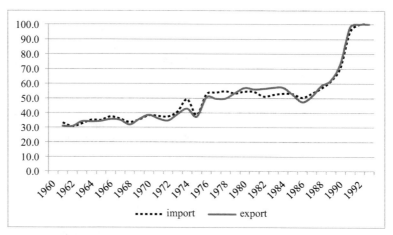

Figure 9.3 Share of convertible currencies in total trade

Source: Hungarian Central Statistical Office.

We can detect some consequences of this shift in several policy terrains. For our purpose the most important result of the change from ISI to an export-led model could be grasped in the sinking level of investment (Figure 9.4) which became spectacular from the late 70s—except for a short but mismanaged period in 1985 (Mong, 2012; Berend, 1996). The growing share of western trade

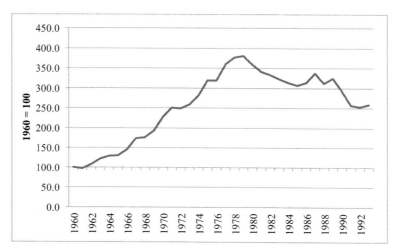

Figure 9.4 Real growth rate of gross capital formation, 1960 = 100

Source: Hungarian Central Statistical Office.

vis-á-vis Comecon trade had a lasting impact on the structure of the Hungarian economy. The unstoppable growth of the external debt level and the growing noise of those technocrats who argued for further liberalization and closer ties with western partners were the results of the shift. From the mid-1980s we see these technocrats all around in the Hungarian administration and by 1987 the highest ranks in the government were all occupied by a new generation of monetarists (Gagyi, 2015).

Hungarian Economic Transition in the 1990s: Growing Reliance on Foreign Direct Investment

Despite the fact that political and economic transitions are separate processes, they intertwine in the longer run. Economic transition from a centrally planned ISI-basis to a free market export-led economy started already in the mid-1980s in many Comecon countries with one of the highest speeds in Hungary. The process accelerated by the late 1980s in Hungary when dozens of reforms were introduced to attract foreign direct investment (Comisso and Marer, 1986; Berend, 1996; Kozma, 1996). It was followed by a landslide political change. By the time of the regime change the most important market reforms were in place, even privatization was kickstarted (Czaban and Henderson, 2003; Stark, 1996; Éber et al., 2014). Similarly to other Eastern European former socialist states, the transition period took less than a decade and by the late 1990s the reintegration was complete. Apart from international loans other forms of capital appeared in the external finances. In the period between the late 1980s and early 2000s, it was the foreign direct investors who appeared to be interested in the Hungarian market which they could reach during the period of the privatization (Lóránt, 2010).

Both the growing share of FDI in the external finances and the drop of the share of the Comecon market in the international trade (as Figures 9.5 and 9.6 illustrate) were part of a more general transformation in the economy. Comecon's accounting unit and means of payment was the transferable ruble which as a non-convertible currency meant protection to the companies that were not competitive enough to produce effectively to the global market. Socialist markets were thus secure outlets for Hungarian products as well. As Czaban and Henderson demonstrated when hard currencies became dominant but scarce in Comecon transactions, the protection of large state-owned Hungarian companies slowly terminated (Czaban and Henderson, 2003). By the early 1990s when state subsidies were suspended, companies even with relatively competitive technology and know-how endowments were hit by the sharp shrinkage of their natural markets (Stark, 1996).

Furthermore, the need for hard currency accelerated the process of opening the capital market. Before 1987, there were joint venture companies

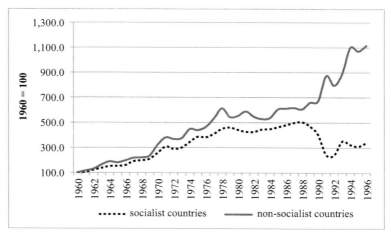

Figure 9.5 Real growth rate of import, 1960 = 100

Source: Hungarian Central Statistical Office.

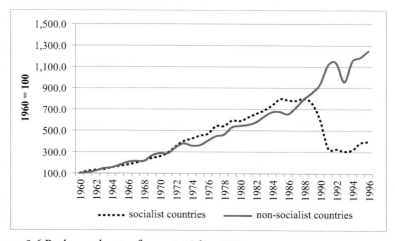

Figure 9.6 Real growth rate of export, 1960 = 100

Source: Hungarian Central Statistical Office.

in Hungary, but companies that had complete foreign ownership did not exist. However, from 1987 foreign direct investment as a form of external financing appeared in Hungary beside international loans as it is shown in Figure 9.7. Due to both external and internal factors it soon became the dominant form. On the one hand, it was the time when US-capital at the peak of global financialization left the United States to seek investments elsewhere.

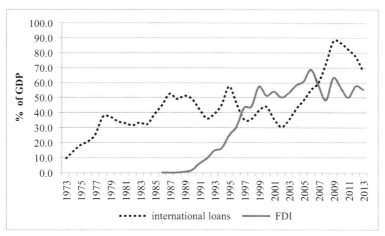

Figure 9.7 Net international investment position, % of GDP

Source: Hungarian National Bank; Eurostat.

A large part of this capital sought market opportunities in Europe while the European integration also proceeded. It was the time when Eastern Europe was finally adopted to the common European market institutions through free trade agreements. On the other hand, Hungary followed by other former socialist economies started to privatize their state owned companies and other facilities. This process can be described by uneven development. In a core-periphery relationship the price for imported capital depends on a "bargaining situation". During the period of privatization Eastern Europe's cumulative need for external finances was far greater than the investments of international capital in their economies. This fact created unfavorable conditions in the negotiations. The fact that there was far fewer capital available than those indebted economies would have needed created a competitive situation amongst them. Their bargaining position vis-á-vis capital was undermined during privatization.

This period, however, witnessed one of the biggest FDI booms in this region in the twentieth century. The consequences of the actual form of privatization made nevertheless a long-lasting impact on their economic transformation, however these were somewhat different among the respective economies. As one of the consequences in Hungary a dualistic structure emerged (Mészáros, 2004), in which the dominant market players such as transnational corporations (TNCs) conquered all strategic positions in the domestic economy, including banking, retail, energy, utilities, not to mention the export enclaves that they created. Dual structure is a reference to the domestic division of labor in which former local producers either became

142 *Tamás Gerőcs and András Pinkasz*

extinct or had to accept a very inferior supply position at the lower-edge in the global value chains. This type of specialization also contributed to enormous current account problems (Lóránt, 2013).

Despite the fact that incoming FDI could sustain Hungary's solvency for some time, it was no real remedy for the indebtedness in the longer run. The inflow of FDI has a very strong cyclical effect in a certain time-horizon (see the effects on Latin America: Hausmann and Fernández-Arias, 2000). Though it enters the economy by bringing in production, the income which is locally produced can easily be withdrawn in the form of profit or dividend. At the beginning of the cycle less income is produced than capital invested thus the sum of the balance is positive. But at the end of the cycle, the balance easily turns to be negative. Net export becomes crucial in this situation because if enough revenue is produced by exporters it can fill this gap. Revenues from export are limited though because a great part of the green-field investments specialize for the local market (the side effect of which was the extrusion of local producers) (Lóránt, 2010). Consequently, net export can fill this gap only in extreme situations when import demand is muted due to stringent fiscal restrictions whereas the export activity is relatively high.

In the 2000s, after the inflow of FDI slowed, the external imbalances reappeared in Hungary. Privatization ran out of steam and there was far less investment opportunity in the local economy. The income of the TNCs' started to exit Hungary in order to be re-invested somewhere else (Mihályi, 2014, 88–100). There was a deterioration in the current account (as import costs exceeded export revenues). Without a necessary equalization-mechanism, the growing gap in the current account was once again financed by an enormous inflow of loans. This resulted in the resumption of debt accumulation.

European Integration and the Role of Transfers in Hungary

Already by the time of EU-accession in 2004, Hungary witnessed a massive debt accumulation for several reasons. Privatization was complete by the time, while profits made by TNCs began to flee the economy to a growing extent which resulted in a growing gap in the current account. The process was exacerbated by the fact that the terms of trade surprisingly remained negative in Hungary though new industries were relocated to the country. Except for a very short period of a market collapse in the 1990s the trend of deterioration in the terms of trade has been uninterrupted since the 1970s which we think is the result of semi-peripheral reintegration to the capitalist world economy (see Figure 9.8).

During the interim period between the end of privatization and the access to EU funds, Hungary's total debt—with a growing share of private debt – grew threefold in less than a decade (2003–2008) (Figure 9.9).

Figure 9.8 Terms of trade, 1960 = 100
Source: Hungarian Central Statistical Office.

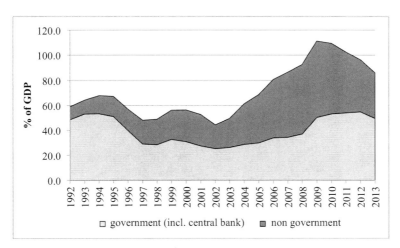

Figure 9.9 Gross external debt, % of GDP
Source: Hungarian National Bank; Eurostat.

After the EU-accession a new form of external finance gradually emerged. From a purely financial perspective, the function of the EU-funds has been the balancing out of the gap in the current account. EU transfers from the agricultural and regional funds sustain the solvency of the peripheral economy which is in a permanent need of external capital. Without a European

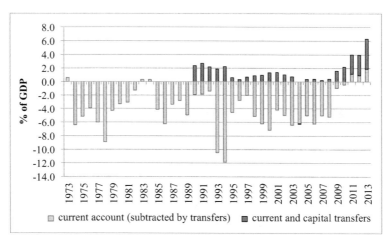

Figure 9.10 Net lending/borrowing, % of GDP
Source: Hungarian National Bank; Eurostat.

income redistribution, the whole economic integration could collapse as semi-peripheral states (or private entities) would immediately go bankrupt. Not to mention that this is exactly what happened during the crisis of the Eurozone with the existing mechanism.

In Figure 9.10 we show the function of the transfers. Without a substantial inflow, the current account could remain negative even if the net export is positive. Thus further indebtedness would be unstoppable without such a redistributive mechanism.

It is remarkable that EU-transfers help little to improve the competitiveness of semi-peripheral producers (that is, their access to capital or technology). Most of the transfers enter the infrastructure, the maintenance of which is important for global production but which the indebted member states could no longer provide on their own. The biggest domestic recipients of transfers are in the construction sector which produce non-tradable goods. The liquidity provided for local enterprises can be—in fact must be due to strict market regulation—spent on the European market. Consequently, the funds create a market-pool for the most advanced producers of technology in core countries while they reinforce the extrusion of local actors engaged in producing tradables. All in all, transfers from core to semi-peripheral economies contribute to keep the hierarchical structure of the given division of labor intact; as other sorts of transfers and aids do the same on a global scale (Amin, 1977, 181–208). Funds help little to improve the competitiveness of domestic firms against TNCs in the domestic market and state support is highly prohibited by EU regulation (see the case on Spain: López and Rodríguez, 2011).

Besides creating market pool for core producers, semi-peripheral societies that are an integral part of the given structure can provide cheap infrastructure and manpower for corporations engaged in world market competition. In some areas where global competition has become extremely fierce since the economic crisis hit in 2008 like in auto manufacturing, semi-peripheral locations have emerged as optimal sites for production (Sass and Szalavetz, 2014; Túry, 2014). Corporations in the automotive industry that are under pressure of lethal competition have been choosing Eastern European sites for producing their models on the lower edge of the value chains. In those segments of the value chains they need fewer innovations, but because the price of primary inputs—labor, energy and even tax rate—is lower, the necessary investments can still be concentrated (Barta, 2012, 54–58). Industrial relocation—accelerating most strikingly in consumer electronics and auto manufacturing—incorporates the processes of both reinsertion of the recipient economy to the global division of labor while in the meantime it provides capital (in the form of FDI) for its advancement (see the industrial upgrading in the Central European automotive industry: Pavlínek et al., 2009). The big question we want to answer is what kind of a developmental path such a reinsertion can bring to a semi-peripheral economy which is in a permanent need of external finance?

Reindustrializing Eastern Europe: A New Division of Labor in the EU's Periphery

Our methodology seeks to combine the analysis of specific forms of external finances with the analysis of the changing patterns in the international division of labor. The intersection of the two demonstrates how dependencies are reformulated along new modes of integration into the world economy. In order to exemplify the renewal of Eastern European semi-peripheral dependencies in the international division of labor, we will analyze the field of industrial relocation, paying close attention to German auto-manufacturers. We want to show that the mechanisms of external finances (see Chapter 2) are in fact connected to the process of industrial relocation. Without the former, the latter would not take the precise form that it takes.

Industrial relocation can be induced by many factors. What we see today as the relocation of manufacturing to semi-peripheral sites is not a new phenomenon. The pressure from overproduction and the subsequent profit-squeeze (Brenner, 2006, 161–186) induce reorganization in most cases. In the following we will concentrate on two determining global forces in regard to European car production: (1) the changing nature of market regulation from the protection of the Single European Market to trade liberalization in the Transatlantic region, and (2) the evolving technological revolution that seems

146   Tamás Gerőcs and András Pinkasz

to be going to shape the form and direction of car production, design and usage in the next couple of decades.

As several authors have shown, when overcapacity grows unbearable in the old production network, restructuring becomes necessary between the technology- and labor-intensive segments of the value chains (see for example: Gereffi et al., 2005; Bair, 2005; Smith et al., 2002). The lower edge of the chains is then mobilized under this severe pressure to be relocated to semi-peripheral sites in order to exploit the benefits of lower input costs (such as wages). While this may appease overproduction at a local level, this process nevertheless exacerbates overproduction globally.

As early as the late 1980s most of the Eastern European countries were welcoming those pioneering automotive manufacturers, mostly but not exclusively from Germany, that brought production to their economies. Most of these countries hoped that TNCs would contribute to upgrading their position within the global division of labor, including those, for example Hungary, that needed FDI to improve the country's devastating external financial position anyway. As we showed earlier the inflow of FDI not only does not translate to a break from historical dependencies, but the financial position can only improve temporarily due to the cyclical nature of this form of capital inflow. German car manufacturers entering the former socialist states were supported by the environmental regulations of the European Community due to the fact that car production in former socialist states could not comply with the European standards. During the transition, almost the entire Eastern European car market was replaced by western products in just a few years which meant a great opportunity for those Western producers which had long been suffering from global competition. The pioneers first used Eastern Europe for market consolidation with renewed sales. In order to succeed, the corporations were engaged in both brown field and green field investments.

Examples of brown field investments were the purchase of Czech automobile manufacturer Škoda by the German Volkswagen, or Romania's Dacia by the French Renault in the early 1990s. An example of green field: GM and Suzuki moved their production facilities to Hungary between 1991 and 1993 in order to better fulfill the local market demand. Despite local market saturation by the early 2000s, manufacturers did not stop the mobilization of their production, instead the process has accelerated. Contrary to most companies' motivations during the transition, most of the incoming manufacturers chose Eastern European destinations as part of their global optimization strategy. So while local markets had become less appealing because of the limitation of sales, several other factors became important in the relocation. Those were the geographical proximity, relatively developed infrastructure, high level of human capital with experience even in technology-endowed manufacturing and a cheap and flexible labor force, all attractive elements to those manufacturers that needed to reorient their former investment strategies in order to pursue consolidation under the depressing forces of global competition (Mahutga, 2014). In this way Eastern Europe started to play an increasingly important role in the consolidation of German automobile producers (Krzywdzinski, 2014).

In the meantime, their home market investments became more concentrated in technological innovation to renew product cycles which scholars call the second car revolution (Diez and Becker, 2010). These targeted research and design for electronic and hybrid-cars. This technological change affected the production and investment absorption capacity of the henceforth outdated internal-combustion engine models that still dominate the market up to now. Market experts predict that the outdated engines will dominate the commercial markets for the next two to three decades before they are completely replaced by the new models. The continuation of investment in outdated models means that with decreasing profitability over the longer-term, new calculations must be made on input costs.

These investments concentrate on the maturity stage of product life-cycle, instead of the introduction phase. In the maturity phase, investments become more cost-sensitive as outdated models slip towards the lower edge in the innovation chain. This process means that the outdated models are increasingly prone to geographical relocation to those areas where primary input costs are lower. On the contrary, the relative prices of the primary input are high in locations that specialize in cutting-edge technology.

Apart from the changes in the technology, there is also a long-term shift in the global market environment as new producers emerge to challenge the globally dominant players, such as the German car producers. Regulation in this regard is very important in shaping market environment, the creation of the Single European Market was one instrument for protecting the interest of German manufacturers in the global competition. It is still unclear how the Transatlantic Trade and Investment Partnership (TTIP) can change the market condition for European and American TNCs operating on a global scale. Some studies suggest,[5] though, that European manufacturers, especially in the automobile industry could be some of the biggest beneficiaries of the expansion of the free trade area (complementary to the United States financial sector that is also supposed to gain from liberalization).

At the time of writing, trade negotiations were still proceeding, thus the final outcome and long-term consequences could only be estimated on a very hypothetical level. What we wanted to emphasize here is that presuming European car manufacturers' interest and lobby power in the negotiations, market regulation within the EU would take a very new shape. One prediction is that the role of market protection in the Single European Area might be devalued due to decreased interest in the crisis-hit Southern and Eastern European region, especially if we take into account the growing share of export to outside of the EU. This is because, as we have already emphasized, the European market has been losing the pre-crisis appeal for globally operating European TNCs. Their interest in the negotiations is directed towards a more global free trade area in which consolidating their global position can be strengthened in an ever more competitive global environment. However, these plans of European companies to capitalize on the market penetration in the North Atlantic area, including Mexico does not render them antagonistic to European integration. Despite their lesser reliance on European market protection, relocation of production remains geographically limited with a strong regional focus.

The further integration of the European Union can still serve their interest with respect to the relocation of their production in the EU. The stability of the regional division of labor based on the structures of technology- and labor-intensive segments of the same value chain, organized regionally between Western and Eastern Europe needs the mechanism of income redistribution. As we showed in chapter 2 without such a mechanism, the hierarchical structure of the division of labor results in a growing gap in the semi-peripheral country's current account. Without the contribution of the European transfers such a stability of specialization of production could be endangered. Transfers appear to be in the need on both sides of the value chain that specialize on that higher and lower edges. For TNCs what is important is to be able to maintain the equilibrium between on the one hand being in need of EU transfers for infrastructure development, which lowers the costs of production for European companies seeking to take advantage of the abundant cheap labor, and on the other hand Eastern European states being stable enough so that there is no chance of structural collapse which would be risky for investment into production. For Eastern European states it is important to have access to liquidity in order to sustain solvency.

What we wanted to demonstrate in this paper through a historical analysis is that even though the forms of dependency can change over time, the global position of Eastern European economies within the international division of labor shows a surprising rigidity. To conclude, despite those changes in the external environment, the most important dependencies—such as the financial and technological ones—remain almost constant. To prove our case we detected the origin of the latest mode of integration since the 1970s in the capitalist world economy for Eastern European states. We believed that the origin of today's new phenomena of reindustrialization in the region lies in the more global reconfiguration of the international division of labor. Our question was if it is different this time with respect to economic advancement, thus the directions of such a change can mean a broader scope for semi-peripheral states to achieve their developmental goals. At the current state of our research the most likely scenario is that the specialization in the lower-edge of the European automotive manufacturing that is so much prone to technological competition together with the newest form of external finances work as new sources of dependency.

In this analysis we needed to understand the global context of these changes. One of the outer most context is the transatlantic regulation which is still on the verge of a radical shift. Transatlantic Trade and Investment Partnership will most probably have a decisive effect on the market regulation in Europe which was so crucial in the accommodation strategy of the automotive firms in the European core in the 1990s. The transatlantic free trade area will on the other hand give an opportunity for some of these manufacturers to widen the scope of resources when they decide their accommodation strategy. Further research is needed however to understand that within the context of the above described dependencies, what are the possibilities for semi-peripheral states in their economic?

Notes

1   Our research is part of a project within the Budapest-based Working Group for Public Sociology "Helyzet". Among others, the group analyzes semi-peripheral dependent development in interaction with the evolution of the capitalist division of labor.
2   See on transitology Sachs, 1989; Peck and Richardson, 1992.
3   On the working of ISI in Latin America see for instance Hirschman, 1968; Tavares, 1964.
4   Hungary's bridge position in the 1960s was not unique among Comecon members. See e.g. the case of Romania (Ban, 2012).
5   See e.g. studies from Bertelsmann-Ifo (Felbermayr et al., 2013) and the London-based Centre for Economic Policy Research (Francois et al., 2013) think-tanks.

References

Allen, Richard A. 1982. "The Evolution of the External Debt and Balance of Payments of Eastern Europe and the USSR since 1970." *BIS Working Papers*, 7.

Amin, Samir. 1977. *Unequal Development: An Essay on the Social Formations of Peripheral Capitalism*. New York: Monthly Review Press.

Arrighi, Giovanni. 2000. "Globalization, State Sovereignty and the 'Endless' Accumulation of Capital." In Don Kalb (ed.), *The Ends of Globalization: Bringing Society Back In*. Lanham, MD: Rowman & Littlefield. 125–150.

Arrighi, Giovanni and Beverly Silver. 2003. "Polanyi's 'Double Movement': The Belle Époques of U.S. and British World Hegemony Compared." *Politics and Society*, 31(2): 325–355.

Arrighi, Giovanni, Beverly J. Silver and Benjamin D. Brewer. 2003. "Industrial Convergence, Globalization, and the Persistence of the North-South Divide." *Studies in Comparative International Development*, 38(1): 3–31.

Bair, Jennifer. 2005. "Global Capitalism and Commidity Chains: Looking Back, Going Forward." *Competition and Change*, 9(2): 153–180.

150 Tamás Gerőcs and András Pinkasz

Ban, Cornel. 2012. "Sovereign Debt, Austerity, and Regime Change: The Case of Nicolae Ceausescu's Romania." *East European Politics and Societies*, 26(4): 743–776.

Barta, Györgyi. 2012. "Central and Eastern European Automotive Industry in European Context." In János Rechnitzer and Melinda Smahó (eds.), *Vehicle Industry and Competitiveness of Regions in Central and Eastern Europe*. Győr, Hungary: Universitas-Győr. 33–71.

Bekker, Zsuzsa. 1995. *Rendszerválság: Alkalmazkodási folyamatok a kelet-európai országokban 1970 és 1990 között*. Budapest: Aula.

Berend, Iván T. 1996. *Central and Eastern Europe, 1944–1993: Detour from the Periphery to the Periphery*. Cambridge: Cambridge University Press.

Bideleux, Robert. 1996. "The Comecon Experiment." In Robert Bideleux and Richard Taylor (eds.), *European Integration and Disintegration: East and West*. London and New York: Routledge. 174–204.

Brenner, Robert. 2006. *The Economics of Global Turbulence*. London: Verso.

Chase-Dunn, Christopher. 1980. "Socialist State in the Capitalist World Economy." *Social Problems*, 27(5): 505–525.

Chase-Dunn, Christopher. 1998. *Global Formation: Structures of the World-Economy (Updated Version)*. Lanham, MD: Rowan and Littlefield.

Comisso, Ellen and Paul Marer. 1986. "The Economics and Politics of Reform in Hungary." In Ellen Comisso and Laura D'Andrea Tyson (eds.), *Power, Purpose, and Collective Choice: Economic Strategy in Socialist States*. Ithaca, NY: Cornell University Press. 245–278.

Comisso, Ellen and Laura D'Andrea Tyson (eds.). 1986. *Power, Purpose and Collective Choice: Economic Strategy in Socialist States*. Ithaca, NY: Cornell University Press.

Czaban, Laszlo and Jeffrey Henderson. 2003. "Commodity Chains, Foreign Investment, and Labour Issues in Eastern Europe." *Global Networks*, 3(1): 171–196.

Diez, Willi and Dieter Becker. 2010. "Brand and Ownership Concentration in the European Automotive Industry: Possible Scenarios for 2025." URL: www.kpmg.com/TW/zh/IssuesAndInsights/Documents/IM/Brand-and-Ownership-Concentration-in-the-European-Automotive-Industry.pdf (accessed June 10, 2015).

Éber, Márk Áron, Ágnes Gagyi, Tamás Gerőcs, Csaba Jelinek and András Pinkasz. 2014. "1989: Szempontok a rendszerváltás globális politikai gazdaságtanához." *Fordulat*, 21: 10–63.

Eichengreen, Barry. 1990. "Trends and Cycles in Foreign Trade." *NBER Working Paper Series*, 3411.

Emmanuel, Arghiri. 1972. *Unequal Exchange: A Study of the Imperialism of Trade*. New York and London: Monthly Review Press.

Feitl, István. 2013. "Magyar elképzelések a Kölcsönös Gazdasági Segítség Tanácsának megreformálására (1967–1975)." *Századok*, 147(6): 1377–1422.

Felbermayr, Gabriel, Benedikt Heid and Sybille Lehwald. 2013. "Transatlantic Trade and Investment Partnership (TTIP): Who Benefits from a Free Trade Deal? Part 1: Macroeconomic Effects." Bertelsmann Stiftung's Global Economic Dynamics (GED) Program. URL: www.bfna.org/sites/default/files/TTIP-GED%20study%2017June%202013.pdf (accessed June 15, 2015).

Francois, Joseph, Miriam Manchin, Hanna Norberg, Olga Pindyuk and Patrick Tomberger. 2013. "Reducing Transatlantic Barriers to Trade and Investment: An

Debt-Ridden Development 151

Economic Assessment." Center for Economic Policy Research (CEPR). URL: http://trade.ec.europa.eu/doclib/docs/2013/march/tradoc_150737.pdf (accessed June 15, 2015).

Frank, André Gunder. 1966. *The Development of Underdevelopment.* New York: Monthly Review Press.

Frank, André Gunder. 1977. "Long Live Transideological Enterprise! Socialist Economies in the Capitalist International Division of Labor." *Review (Fernand Braudel Center),* 1(1): 91–140.

Fröbel, Folker, Jürgen Heinrichs and Otto Kreye. 1980. *The New International Division of Labour: Structural Unemployment in Industrialised Countries and Industrialisation in Developing Countries.* Cambridge: Cambridge University Press.

Gagyi, Ágnes. 2015. "Reform Economics at the Financial Research Institute in Late Socialist Hungary: A Case of Globally Embedded Knowledge Production." *Intersections: East European Journal of Society and Politics,* 1(2): 59–79.

Gereffi, Gary, John Humphrey and Timothy Sturgeon. 2005. "The Governance of Global Value Chains." *Review of International Political Economy,* 12(1): 78–104.

Gereffi, Gary and Miguel Korzeniewicz (eds.). 1994. *Commodity Chains and Global Capitalism.* Westport, CT: Praeger.

Gowan, Peter. 1999. *Global Gamble: Washington's Faustian Bid for World Dominance.* London: Verso.

Harvey, David. 1989. "From Fordism to Flexible Accumulation." In David Harvey (ed.), *The Condition of Postmodernity: An Inquiry into the Conditions of Cultural Change.* Oxford: Blackwell. 141–172.

Hausmann, Ricardo and Eduardo Fernández-Arias. 2000. "Foreign Direct Investment: Good Cholesterol?" *Inter-American Development Bank Working Paper,* 417.

Hirschman, Albert O. 1968. "The Political Economy of Import-Substituting Industrialization in Latin America." *The Quarterly Journal of Economics,* 82(1): 1–32.

Hopkins, Terence and Immanuel Wallerstein. 1986. "Commodity Chains in the World Economy Prior to 1800." *Review (Fernand Braudel Center),* 10(1): 157–170.

Kozma, Ferenc. 1996. *Külgazdasági stratégia.* Budapest: Aula.

Krzywdzinski, Martin. 2014. "How the EU's Eastern Enlargement Changed the German Productive Model: The Case of the Automotive Industry." *Revue de la regulation,* 15(1): 1–61.

López, Isidro and Emmanuel Rodríguez. 2011. "The Spanish Model." *New Left Review,* 69, May–June: 5–29.

Lóránt, Károly. 1990. "Adósságcsapda." In András Vigvári (ed.), *Adósság: Tanulmányok adósságunk múltjáról, jelenéről és jövőjéről.* Budapest: Szakszervezetek Gazdaság- és Társadalomkutató Intézete. 53–84.

Lóránt, Károly. 2010. Magyarország külső eladósodása és annak következményei. Manuscript.

Lóránt, Károly. 2013. Magyarország külgazdasági helyzete. Manuscript.

Mahutga, Matthew C. 2014. "Production Networks and the Global Manufacturing Economy." *Sociological Perspectives,* 57(2): 229–255.

Mészáros, Ádám. 2004. "A magyarországi közvetlen külföldi m ködőtőke-beruházások exportenklávé jellege." *Külgazdaság,* 48(4): 48–59.

Mihályi, Péter. 2014. *A magyar gazdaság útja az adósságválságba, 1945–2013.* Budapest: Corvina.

152 *Tamás Gerőcs and András Pinkasz*

Mong, Attila. 2012. *Kádár hitele: A magyar államadósság története, 1956–1990*. Budapest: Libri.

Nyers, Rezső, ifj. (ed.). 1993. *Külső eladósodás és adósságkezelés Magyarországon*. Magyar Nemzeti Bank.

Ortiz, Roberto José. 2014. "Agro-Industrialization, Petrodollar Illusions and the Transformation of the Capitalist World Economy in the 1970s: The Latin American Experience." *Critical Sociology*, published online: 599–621.

Pavlínek, Petr, Bolesław Domański and Robert Guzik. 2009. "Industrial Upgrading through Foreign Direct Investment in Central European Automotive." *European Urban and Regional Studies*, 16(1): 43–63.

Peck, Merton J. and Thomas J. Richardson (eds). 1992. *What Is to Be Done? Proposals for the Soviet Transition to the Market*. New Haven: Yale University Press.

Radice, Hugo. 2009. "Halfway to Paradise? Making Sense of Semi-Periphery." In Owen Worth and Phoebe Moore (eds.), *Globalization and the New Semi-Peripheries*. Basingstoke, UK and New York: Palgrave Macmillan. 25–40.

Sachs, Jeffrey. 1989. "My Plan for Poland." *The International Economy*, 3(6): 24–29.

Sass, Magdolna and Andrea Szalavetz. 2014. "R&D-Based Integration and Upgrading in Hungary." *Acta Oeconomica*, 64(S1): 153–180.

Smith, Adrien, Al Rainnie, Mick Dunford, Jane Hardy, Ray Hudson and David Sadler. 2002. "Networks of Value, Commodities and Regions: Reworking Division of Labour in Macro-Regional Economies." *Progress in Human Geography*, 26(1): 41–63.

Stark, David. 1996. "Recombinant Property in East European Capitalism." *American Journal of Sociology*, 101(4): 993–1027.

Stevens, John N. 1985. *Czechoslovakia at the Crossroads: The Economic Dilemmas of Communism in Postwar Czechoslovakia*. Boulder, CO: East European Monographs.

Stone, Randall W. 1996. *Satellites and Commissars: Strategy and Conflict in the Politics of Soviet-Bloc Trade*. Princeton: Princeton University Press.

Szegő, Andrea. 1989. "Világgazdasági függés, eladósodás, válság." *Eszmélet*, 1(1): 65–99.

Szentes, Tamás. 1988. *The Political Economy of Underdevelopment*. Budapest: Akadémiai Kiadó.

Tavares, Maria da Conceição. 1964. "The growth and decline of import substitution in Brazil." *Economic Bulletin for Latin America*, 9(1): 1–59.

Túry, Gábor. 2014. "Automotive Industry in the EU10 Economies: Developments in the Past Decade." In Andrea Éltető (ed.), *Mind the Gap*. Budapest: Centre for Economic and Regional Studies of the Hungarian Academy of Sciences Institute of World Economics. 94–119.

Tyson, Laura D'Andrea. 1986. "The Debt Crisis and Adjustment Responses in Eastern Europe: A Comparative Perspective." In Ellen Comisso and Laura D'Andrea Tyson (eds.), *Power, Purpose, and Collective Choice: Economic Strategy in Socialist States*. Ithaca, NY: Cornell University Press. 63–110.

Vigvári, András. 1990. "Eladósodás és adósságkezelés: Vázlat a magyar gazdaság közelmúltjának egy fontos kérdéséről." In András Vigvári (ed.), *Adósság: Tanulmányok adósságunk múltjáról, jelenéről és jövőjéről*. Budapest: Szakszervezetek Gazdaság- és Társadalomkutató Intézete. 7–52.

Vigvári, András. 2008. "Néhány adalék Magyarország külgazdasági sebezhetőségének okaihoz." *Eszmélet*, 20(80): 82–92.

Wallerstein, Immanuel. 1976. "Semi-Peripheral Countries and the Contemporary World Crisis." *Theory and Society*, 3(4): 461–483.

Worth, Owen and Phoebe Moore (eds.). 2009. *Globalization and the New Semi-Peripheries*. Basingstoke, UK and New York: Palgrave Macmillan.

10

NEW CONFIGURATIONS OF INEQUALITY AND GLAM-CAPITALISM STRUCTURES[1]

Dmitry Ivanov

Inequality is a traditional theme for the sociological community, but in recent years inequality became the key topic presented in titles of numerous books, articles and conferences. Current sociology's turn to inequalities has at least two reasons. The first is the sociological community's awareness of increasing levels of economic inequalities and rising social discrimination and exclusion. Sociologists relate the rising inequality to general dynamics of contemporary capitalism. Michael Burawoy in his presidential address to the XVIII World Congress of Sociology in Yokohama has expressed this approach toward inequality as crucial issue for social researchers and social movements challenged by dynamic capitalism (Burawoy, 2015). The second reason is sociologists' perception of inequality as multi-faced or multi-dimensional. Developing theories of inequality, sociologists now take into account not only economic differentiation but various ways to make distinctions and to establish unequal access to material, human and symbolic resources (Bourdieu, 1979; Sen, 1992; Therborn, 2006; Tilly, 1998). In the perspective of the multi-dimensional inequality concepts various social institutions, groupings, patterns of interaction, solidarities and conflicts can be interpreted and explained as ways to maintain inequalities or to overcome them.

Revealing multiple forms or dimensions of inequalities, sociological theories reduce them to a common view: "inequalities are differences which we consider unjust" (Therborn, 2006: 4). Sociologists can consider all inequalities unjust while economists and management gurus can justify some of them as productive and motivating, and conservative intellectuals can justify some inequalities as natural. Subjective moral and political judgments can be disputed but such controversies themselves specify those differences which are to be defined as inequalities. Inequalities are differences which alienate people from each other.

This article is to contribute into studies of relation between multi-dimensional inequality and recent dynamics of postindustrial capitalism. New configurations of inequality are characterized by the rising spatial and temporal structures of inequality related to the newest form of postindustrial socioeconomic order which we consider as glam-capitalism. Inequality here is defined as differences in access to socially significant resources (material, human, symbolic). Structures of inequality are patterns of that access differentiation.

New Spatial Structures of Inequality

Sociologists consider spatial aspects of social inequality mostly in the frameworks of the world-system theory and various theories of globalization. Unequal world is presented in terms of the GDP/the living standard gap between the "core" countries and countries belonging to "periphery" and "semi-periphery" of the global economy (Wallerstein, 2004; Babones, Zhang, 2008) or between two groups of nations identified as "global North" and "global South" (Arrighi, 2001; Kacowicz, 2007; Reuveny, Thompson, 2008). However, another configuration of spatial inequality emerges with globalization as socioeconomic differences do not coincide with national borders. Rather the wealth and power controls are concentrated in networks of super-urbanized areas playing role of "command centers" in transnational economy (Sassen, 2005).

The world has become super-urbanized as more than 50% of the world's population live in urban areas since 2010 (United Nations, 2014). In 1950, there were six cities with populations exceeding 5 million, by 2010 this number had risen to 60 and by 2014 to 71 (United Nations, 2014). In this super-urbanized world (Figure 10.1) inequalities should be considered not only in

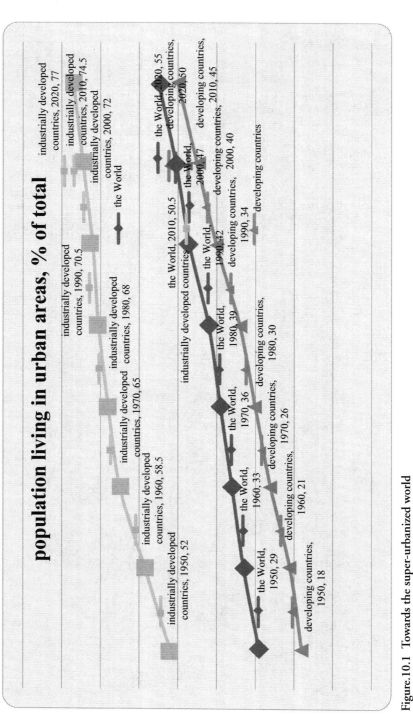

Figure.10.1 Towards the super-urbanized world

Source: United Nations Department of Economic and Social Affairs

Inequality and Glam-Capitalism   157

the context of gaps between urban and rural areas but also in the context of gaps between super-urban areas and the rest of the world. The super-urbanized areas outperform national economies and therefore open new dimensions of inequality. According to research data of the Brookings Institution, the largest 300 cities contain only 19% of the world's population but they generate 48% of the world's GDP (The Brookings Institution, 2012). More research conducted by the McKinsey Global Institute has revealed the top 600 cities by economic output concentrate 22% of global population and provide more than 50% of global GDP (McKinsey Global Institute, 2011).

The economic and social divide between the group of the largest cities and the rest of the world supports the idea that globalization has resulted not in the "world society" or "worldwide sociality" but rather in networked enclaves of globality. In such metropolitan areas as Los Angeles, New York, London, Tokyo, Hong Kong, Moscow, Seoul and other megacities interlinked by cross-border material, human and symbolic flows people experience globality as borderless, mobile and multicultural life. Therefore, "globalization" does not mean planetary spread of social structures but rather localized displacement of habitual social structures by intensive flows (Appadurai, 1990, Lash, Urry, 1994, Castells, 2000). It follows, that the distinction between "core" and "periphery" in the global socioeconomic order should be revised.

The spatial configuration of inequality in the super-urbanized world is characterized not only by concentration of wealth, power and cultural dominance in the enclaves of globality. Compared to their countries, metropolitan areas outperform in economic growth and at the same time they are more unequal in terms of Gini index (Table 10.1). The combination of relatively higher levels of both economic performance and income disparity shows that the networked enclaves of globality represent two faces of inequality defined as exclusion and unequal inclusion (Burawoy, 2015). The inhabitants of small

Table 10.1 National Gini vs Super-Urban Gini (Selected Countries and Cities)

Country/City	Gini index (year of estimation)
Russia	0.420 (2012)
Moscow	0.486 (2012)
St. Petersburg	0.443 (2012)
USA	0.469 (2010)
New York	0.499 (2010)
Los Angeles	0.489 (2010)
Japan	0.329 (2012)
Tokyo	0.375 (2011)
Osaka	0.400 (2011)

Sources: Euromonitor International, National Bureaus of Statistics

158 *Dmitry Ivanov*

cities and rural areas are disadvantaged because they are excluded from flows of resources circulating inside the network of large cities. Nevertheless, people involved in such flows are disadvantaged too as they are included as workforce for the newest form of capitalism arising in networked enclaves of globality.

Dynamics of Capitalism: From Logic of Virtualization to Logic of Glamour

By the end of the twentieth century postindustrial capitalism in networked super-urban areas has been transformed into glam-capitalism which is contrasting sharply with traditional social reality (Ivanov, 2008). Preconditions for the newest form of capitalism have been created by virtualization of social structures. Virtual reality is a good metaphor and adequate model for so called "new economy" of brands, networked enterprises, financial derivatives and consumer credits. Virtual reality is also an efficient tool to analyze politics based now on image making and media more than on traditional activities and organizations.

Virtualization in general is a replacement of physical reality by images simulating real objects' properties. Economic institutions and the whole society become a kind of virtual reality when people manipulate virtual objects (images) while institutional norms require us to do the real things. By the end of the twentieth century institutions of capitalism were virtualized as branding and public relations activities transferred competition from the material production domain to the virtual reality of communications where socially constructed "special qualities" of commodity or company affect consumers and investors more than real things and doings. As a result, basic components of contemporary economic system cease to be a familiar reality, and virtual products, virtual organizations and virtual money are increasingly created.

Virtualization of consumer goods and commodities is a process underlying the brands' expansion. In a market supersaturated with similar products the branding is an effective weapon to struggle for the consumer attention which is the scarcest resource of advanced economy. Brands created as images identified with some product or company are not only orientation tools for consumers at the marketplace. Images themselves have become the proper consumption objects for people who construct and maintain social and cultural identity buying and displaying branded things. Because of that at the edge of the twentieth century the branding was formed into a particular professional field and had become a common technology of the virtual value creation.

By the late 1990s markets had been saturated by brands, and intensive commodification of images has led to overbranding and triviality of virtualization strategy. Overproduction of virtuality has become obvious in crises which happened in 2000 and 2008. They revealed an exhaustion of the virtualization logic of "new economy". It requires another logic of competitive advantage creation. The competition among brand images is so intensive that in the struggle for the scarcest resource—targeted groups' attention, it becomes rational strategy to make images brighter and lighter. The goods/services should be aggressively beautiful to be intensively attractive for targeted groups. Such intensity can be maintained only for relatively short periods and because of that value creation process now is related more to trends, than to brands, not only in traditional fashion industry and show business but also in high-tech and financial industries. With the shift of competitiveness from brands to trends, the "new economy" is shifted from the logic of virtualization to the logic of glamour.

The glamour now is not only the lifestyle of "blondes" and "metrosexuals" schematized in the urban folklore or specific aesthetics realized in popular culture phenomena from Hollywood stars of the 1930s to the glam rock of the 1970s. In the 2000s marketing and management gurus considered it to be one of the "strategic cultural ideas" for revolutionizing branding (Grant, 2006, 226–227). Defining glamour as an idea in the consumerism complex, experts recognize its power at consumer goods markets but they miss other economic realizations of logic of glamour. Financial analytics since the mid-1990s use the term "glamour" to designate specific strategy of stock traders buying not worthy but rather trendy assets (Chan et al., 1995; Conrad et al. 2003). Multifaceted glamour appearing in different economic activities and discourses could not be reduced to lifestyle of specific consumer group, popculture aesthetics, or consumerist ideology. The glamour is common logic of various value creation processes and therefore it can be defined as the rationality of current capitalism (Ivanov, 2008). Glamour, which since the 1930s is in existence as a specific aesthetic form/lifestyle, has become now rationality of the newest version of capitalism.

As phenomena considered to be glamour can vary from a lifestyle to stock exchange trading, some general theory of glamour is needed to conceptualize all of them. The general theory of glamour may be summarized by a simple formula: *glamour = "Big Five" + "Top Ten"*.

As a lifestyle glamour is commonly identified with luxury brands, exotic places, erotic looks, something pink and somebody blond. This common truth about glamour is included in the general theory which however provides broader definitions of five components. The "Big Five" is a "matter" of glamour composed by such elements as follows:

- "*luxury*" that is recognized as an exclusive consumption beyond functionality of goods/services;
- "*exotics*" that is quotidian practices performed as events beyond ordinary life;

- "*erotic*" that is the pumping extra-sexuality beyond natural human sexual life;
- "*pinkness*" that is not only specific color but radical visual solution of problem;
- "*blondness*" that is not only the hair color but a generally managed look that can manage consciousness.

"Top Ten" is the form of the glamour existence. "Top Ten" is not a number but an organizing principle. All top-lists, nominations, ratings, hit-parades and so on, make every included object actual and significant. Glamour is consolidated in structuring the world order of 100 most valuable brands, 500 most successful companies, 400 richest people, 1000 great persons of the millennium, 10 most beautiful beaches, 5 must-have things etcetera. The world of glamour is created and structured by intensive communications turning subjectively composed "top tens" into objectified media reality.

The world of "Big Five" and "Top Ten" is constructed and expanded by not only visibly glamorous pop culture stars and consumers who tend to be "blondes" and "metrosexuals". Their practices of managed looks managing consciousness is only the most visible example of making the bright and light images valuable. The leading entrepreneurs and professionals of the "new economy" use the same "Big Five" and "Top Ten" as resource and technology and therefore make the glamour to be some kind of capital. They contribute into development and expansion of a new mode of production—glam-capitalism. Alongside with the "new economy" a "new politics" arises where the glamour is converted into political capital by candidates who construct their images in MTV-style. Replacing traditional political charisma by the image of cool, exotic, sexy and looking-younger leader, new campaign drivers like "Obama girls" performances, political blog "Glamocracy" and Paris Hilton's intervention contribute into development of the glam-democracy.

Even intellectual capital can be accumulated through the glamour. The glam-science is intensively developed by gurus of management and marketing who makes the "Big Five" the main subject-matter of research and uses the "Top Ten" as a method. The logic of glamour penetrates practically all domains of society. In the 1990s and 2000s the glamour has become the life-world for many businessmen, managers, politicians, scientists, artists developing their products and projects to enter top-lists generated by the "Forbes" and other creators of "Top Ten" structures.

Terms like "glamour", "Big Five" and "Top Ten" could seem to be too extravagant for scientific analysis. But it should be noted that this is not a problem for science in general. It is normal for physicists to operate with elementary particles defined by "color", "charm" and "beauty" (Poole, 1998, 395–398). And it is the glamour and its elements that can explain logically some tendencies and paradoxes of the postindustrial capitalism.

Inequality and Glam-Capitalism 161

Glam Industries

It is not only the high-tech goods production that has constituted the leading industries of recent two decades. With the shift from logic of virtualization to logic of glamour, components of glamour as an esthetic form or life style—luxury, erotic, exotics, "pinkness" and "blondness", become new drivers of the production and consumption growth. Glamour-intensive production of trends driven by the "Big Five" provides extraordinary growth rates even in the times of crisis. During the recent 15 years these glam-industries grew up twice as fast as the global economy as a whole. Industries which produce the "Big Five" become leaders alongside with high-tech industries. The success of the high-tech is explained traditionally by the implementation of scientific knowledge, but the success of luxury, hospitality, adult entertainment and beauty industries is a puzzle for that knowledge-based economy paradigm. The logic of glamour can be a common explanandum for glam-industries producing the "Big Five" and for high-tech industries which tend to adopt logic of glamour in production of life-style electronics.

The *luxury industry* manufactures exclusive consumption attributes using various functional things from watches and underwear to cars and yachts as "containers" or "platforms" to carry the luxury "substance". The term "luxury industry" sounds as an oxymoron because traditionally there was a gap between craftsmen making exclusive things for small number of rich clients and mass production of ordinary goods for the middle strata consumers. But in recent decades logics of exclusive authentic luxury and of mass market were combined and the previously restricted luxury market expanded dramatically. Now it is developed by growing number of professionals and organizations concentrated on creating possibilities of extraordinary consumption for millions of people. By 2000 the global market of luxury was estimated at $70 billion and in 2005 at $130 billion. That means average annual growth rate was about 14%. The global economic crisis affected in 2009 the sales of luxury industry but the industry's top players lost not too much: LVMH reported 0.8% decrease in sales, Richemont—4.5%, Burberry—1.4%. Some companies even continued to grow: Gucci Group reported 0.3% increase, Hermés +8.4%. In 2010 and 2011 luxury industry returned to double-digit rates of growth that is above the World (4–5%), USA (2–3%) and even China (8–9%). LVMH reported +19.2% and 16.4% revenue increase, Richemont +33.1% and 28.7%, Gucci Group +18.3% and 20.4%, Hermés +25.4% and 18.3%, Burberry +26.7% and 23.8%. In the period of 2010–2014 the global luxury market outperformed all national economies, growing annually by 9% in average.

Such impressive expansion is commonly explained geographically: the luxury industry spreads to emerging markets in Asia. But actually the growth is determined by the spreading across institutional and strata

162 *Dmitry Ivanov*

boundaries. The luxury industry is a *trans-industry* because its organizational structures penetrate traditional borders of different industries. The trans-industry consists of units manufacturing very different things but producing the same goods. For example, producers of cars, mobile phones and leather bags turn into units of the same trans-industry as, like Porsche, Vertu and Louis Vuitton, they use different raw materials, technologies and staff skills but common methods to "implant" luxury into glamour-intensive products. Spreading luxury from classics as jewelry, haute-couture clothes and sport cars towards endless range of goods produced ordinarily but branded and priced extraordinarily, the trans-industry penetrates boundaries of middle and lower strata making them emerging markets for less authentic but more glamorous luxury.

The *hospitality industry* also is a trans-industry integrating tourist agencies, restaurants, clubs, hotels and other enterprises which produce glamorous exotics as air-conditioned adventures. As people constructing their world of glamour are interested in extraordinary forms of quotidian practices the exotics for them can be provided in any place. It is not necessary to go abroad in search for experience of natural but rare landscapes and cultures. Expansion of the hospitality industry is driven by "thematic" hotels, restaurants, clubs, parks which provide different services but create value in the same way: "implanting" glamorous exotics in the interior design, food, entertainment programs and so on. Constructing accessible and comfortable destinations for the glamorous exotics seekers, the hospitality industry generates globally more than \$3 trillion of revenues and provides about 20% of jobs in the contemporary World.

The *sex industry* in recent decades has become much broader than the traditional sex-for-money market and now it pretends to be an "adult entertainment industry" selling experience of sexuality integrated into everyday life. The majority of the industry customers need not sex in itself but rather to be sexy. Sex for them is an impressive accessory of the cool person image. Such extra-sexuality can be "implanted" into diverse things and events and because of that the sex industry grows through expansion of the exposed and pumped sexuality provided in strip-shows and strip-dance classes, sex-shows and sex-shops, swing-clubs and pick-up master classes, phone sex and erotic video chat firms. Despite all diversity, the dominating business-model in current sex trans-industry is pornography. The global sales of pornographic materials grew in the early twenty-first century by 6% a year and reached \$97 billion in 2006 (Ropelato, 2007). The new driver of the growth is the Internet with above 4 million porn sites that is 12% of the total number of websites (Penn, Zalesne, 2007, 277). The Internet video sales rose from \$2.8 billion in 2006 to \$4.9 billion in 2009. Worldwide web provides easy access to porn studio products and to homemade content of so-called "amateurs"—individual entrepreneurs and enthusiasts of the pumping extra-sexuality. In the last five years, sales of porn magazines and DVDs declined, sales of pay websites grew slowly, but revenues from licensing sexy brands (like Playboy) and from advertising on the free content websites grew sustainably. The sex industry seems to adopt business-models developed by Google and Facebook making money on the context of advertising exposed to the Internet users.

The *trend industry* produces radical visual solutions that can provide any product with "fashionability" generating the trend as a momentum of product mass adoption. This industry unifies traditional fashion houses, trend bureaus like Trend Union or Worth Global Style Network (WGSN) and diversified design studios like Pininfarina or Porsche Design Group because their designers and trend-watchers working with various things elaborate only one ephemeral but valuable product—visual expression of the time ("zeitgeist"). Consumers living in the world of glamour are interested not in things or brand images in themselves but in their distinctive ability "to be trendy". To be trendy can be manifested by everything: apparel, accessories, cosmetics, gastronomy, entertainments, interiors, cars, gadgets etc. The added value created by designers and trend-watchers is the association of any industry product from textile to high-tech with some today's trend. Visual solutions—form, silhouette, color, texture, logo and so on, successfully applied to one market can be transferred to other markets to make ordinary goods much fancier and brighter. Dealing with customers from different markets, the trend industry operates as the glamorous trans-industry of the "pinkness" generating serious increase in sales. For example, in 2010 WGSN generated revenues of £40 m, up 5% on the previous year; the Porsche Design Group in 2011 posted a 30% increase in revenue to a total of €79.8 million.

The *beauty industry* unifies cosmetics producers, hair and nail salons, fitness and shaping clubs, spas, plastic surgery clinics and other enterprises which despite all differences in technologies produce the same "substance"—a managed look that can manage consciousness. In the world of glamour there is a strong correlation between attractive appearance and income (Economist, 2007, 50), and women and men living in this glam-capitalism world manage their looks intensively. As a result, the beauty industry is growing dramatically. By 2006 worldwide sales of beauty goods reached $280 billion and revenues from services provided by beauty industry professionals exceeded $100 billion level. The top players in the beauty goods market successfully overcame the downturn in 2009, and in 2010 such companies as L'Oreal and Estee Lauder grew by more than 10%. Maybe the most impressive statistics characterizing the beauty industry expansion are provided by American Society of Plastic Surgeons reporting the 444% increase in the number of cosmetic procedures for the period 1997–2007 (Penn, Zalesne, 2007, 243–244). Even global economic crisis could not stop this growth and in 2010 the increase in number of procedures was 5% and surgeons' revenues were above $10 billion (American Society of Plastic Surgeons, 2010).

164   *Dmitry Ivanov*

Glamorous trans-industries are rapidly institutionalized through the establishing of specific professional associations and conventions, magazines and graduate courses that are constructing a common identity for heterogeneous market segments and agents. Luxury, hospitality, sex, trend and beauty industries are only five examples of the instantaneous institutionalization of glamour-intensive production. The product becomes more glamour-intensive if the "Big Five" elements are combined. Such product can be presented in any market developed by professionals of glam-industries. Using logic of the "Big Five" as the combinatory one, managers and professionals can expand "implantation" of glamour and therefore create new markets and establish new trans-industries. The glam-capitalism trans-industries, using technologically different products as raw materials, create specific added value in common way. Glam-industries are structures penetrating institutional boundaries and boundaries of traditional social networks. Generating trends as flows of material, human and symbolic resources throughout the social institutions and networks, trans-industries of glam-capitalism are functioning as structures of specific type: *flow-structures*.

Glamour-Industrial Complex Structures

Glam-capitalism requires a new organizational form and a new logic of business. After industrialization with its focus on material production and after virtualization with its focus on branding the new logic is making and selling trends. To make trends and to become trends many companies transform their organization structures into a nexus which can be defined as glamour-industrial complex (hereinafter—GIC). The GIC is a structure involving the process of trend creation activities of: (1) company's product development and marketing staff, (2) professionals from trend bureaus and design studios, (3) creative consumers who can be characterized as trendoids. The GIS is a network structure but it differs from network structures of virtualization. The GIC is structured by the "Top Ten" principle. In contrast to virtualized structures, organization solutions and procedures, the structures of GIC are not aimed at creating the strong brand as a distinctive and stable identity. The aim is to become trendy even for very short time. Because of that the GIC operates as a *trans-structure* that is composed of workflows and communication flows penetrating habitual institutional boundaries. The GIC operates across symbolic and organizational boundaries of different brands and industries to develop *trans-brands*.

The standard of such trans-structures was elaborated in the late 1990s by Nokia arranging joint development of new mobile phones by ICT-professionals and fashion designers. In the first decade of the twenty-first century followers of the trend generated by Nokia created many GICs producing trans-brand products: glam-phones like "Motorola—Dolce&Gabbana" and "LG—Prada", glam-books like "Acer—Ferrari" and "Asus—Lamborghini" and even glam-cars like "Hyundai—Prada". The mentioned GICs exemplify symptomatic tendency of glam-capitalism: to sacrifice brand for trend.

The sacrificing of brand for trend is even more obvious in cases of fast capitalization of creative communications. Series of acquisitions in the early twenty-first century could demonstrate how much cash can be an equivalent of a pure trend value. In 1998 AOL bought instant messages service ICQ for $400 million; in 2005 Emap bought trend-watching website WGSN for £140 million, News Corporation acquired social networking website MySpace for $580 million, and eBay bought the Internet-based voice communication service Skype for $2.6 billion; in 2006 Google bought the video sharing website YouTube for $1.65 billion. The most prominent among such deals is the acquisition of mobile messenger WhatsApp by Facebook in 2014 for $19 billion. The assets bought by large corporations were not profitable businesses or unique technological platforms. Actually, the buyers paid for exclusive access to the trend—rapid growth of the users' community perceived as a market with great prospects.

The GIC can generate such immense market value because it involves activities of the company's customers into the processes of product development and promotion. Therefore, it employs traditional workers but exploits also creativity of consumers who tend to be in trend. Penetrating boundaries of social institutions and networks, structures of GIC are the flow-structure of creative consumption. Creativity and mobility of people involved in fast but short movements of business projects create temporary but intensive disparities between leaders of consumerism and outsiders as well as between trendsetters and latecomers.

The flow-structures of GIC, which look ephemeral from the traditional institutionalism point of view, demonstrate the differences among phases of the contemporary capitalism dynamics. Industrial economy is a set of institutions providing possibilities and regulations for capitalization of things. Industrial capitalism is based on the value of products. Virtualized economy is a set of networks for capitalization of images. The virtual capital is accumulated value of brands. The glamour economy is a complex of flow-structures, and capitalization of flows is possible because of value of trends.

Owners of trends incorporated in flow-structures of GICs and professional trend makers compose new status groups: glam-capitalists and glam-professionals, which represent new strata arising above traditional middle class. Despite all apology of glam-capitalists and glam-professionals as "creative class" (Florida, 2002), capitalization of trends is so profitable because of the copyright system that provides monopoly on mass production of practically costless copies however priced like an original. The creativity discourse is an ideology justifying the high level occupied by glam-capitalists and glam-professionals in contemporary stratification, and the copyright is a juridical tool to retain that level. With the glam-capitalism growing, glam-capitalists and glam-professionals become a relatively large category that transforms contemporary stratification.

Glam-Capitalism Impact on Inequality

At the century's edge the "onion-like" stratification with dominant middle strata is replaced by the "pear-like" bimodal stratification (Figure 10.2). The majority of small business holders, professionals and high-skilled workers traditionally composing the middle strata are now much below the mean income level. In economically advanced countries they become a new poverty strata. In contrast to the habitual poor, the new poverty strata households have all attributes of normal middle class: a job that provides enough money for current consumption, a house/apartment big enough for the family, savings for a car, vacations or education. But people feel themselves to be poor because in order to maintain a desirable level of consumption they have to get more

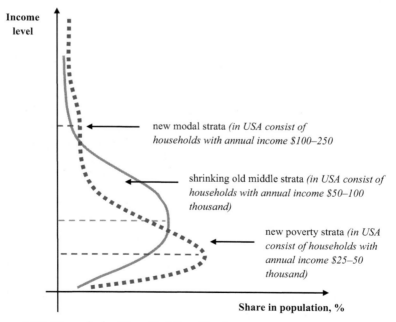

Figure 10.2 Towards the "Pear-like" Stratification

Source: the author's model based on data from www.census.gov

means—additional job and borrowings. The traditional middle strata are under pressure of additional jobs and loan payments because they try to follow the standard of wellbeing defined by the rising group of entrepreneurs and professionals who capitalize on glamour and elaborate new consumerism patterns more influential than old-fashioned social virtues.

The shift to the new stratification began in USA in the late twentieth century and during the first decade of the new century similar processes became evident in other developed countries. American researchers characterize the majority of the rich people as "shy millionaires" who have huge assets but prefer a relatively modest lifestyle. Only 30% of 9 million of American millionaires can be characterized as cool "deal masters" and "status chasers" (Penn, Zalesne, 2007, 221–223). But these 30% affect the whole stratification as the ambitious *"nouveaux riches"* entering the upper stratum remain the "hungry middles" in their consumption patterns. They spend extraordinary amounts of money on the ordinary set of the middle strata wellbeing components: residence, car, clothing, vacation, entertainment. As a result, they develop patterns of hyper-consumerism in the glamour style: "superhouse", "supercar", "megashopping", "megaparty" and so on. Such patterns are adopted by glamers—protagonists of the glamour as a lifestyle, which are numerous among households with incomes of $100–200 thousand which is approximately 3/4 of the highest quintile. New modal strata emerging in the highest quintile are displacing traditional middle strata as the source of social normativity. The catchy businesses and lifestyles of glam-capitalists and glam-professionals become new sources of mass-media coverage and provide followers and imitators from lower strata with value orientations and modes of behavior challenging traditional virtues of petty bourgeoisie.

Glam-capitalists and glam-professionals do not represent the ideal type of bourgeoisie depicted 100 years ago by Max Weber in *The Protestant Ethic and the Spirit of Capitalism*. Weber considered capitalist rationality as the "iron cage" of calculation, discipline and modesty that makes life the permanent work accumulating the wealth (Weber, 2003). The rationality of glam-capitalism is quite different. It appears not in such work ethic but in consumerism aesthetic. *Sweaty consumption* is the general activity under conditions of glam-capitalism. Glamers take everything just to consume. They consider all components of life as projects to be invested (financially, physically and emotionally) while returns grow rapidly. As the growth rate has reached a maximum they tend to cancel the project and to go to the next start-up. For example, glam-capitalists demonstrate such unusual and paradoxical logic as they sell businesses which are just started and growing. To develop business just to sell it is the project logic evidently adopted by founders of ICQ, Skype, WGSN, MySpace, YouTube, WhatsApp and many other start-ups.

Huge earnings and lack of social responsibility among glam-capitalists and glam-professionals at the time of economic crisis became a stake in public

168   *Dmitry Ivanov*

Table 10.2 Bimodal Stratification in Russia

	Russia (2012)	Moscow (2012)
Average monthly income per head, Russian rubles (US $1 = RUR30)	23,058	48,621
Share of income group in population, %		
above 45,000	10.6	35.3
27,000–45,000	17.1	21.7
19,000–27,000	16.7	14.1
10,000–19,000	30.9	18.3
below 10,000	24.7	10.6

Source: 'Rosstat'—Russian bureau of statistics (www.gks.ru)

debates. Uncontrolled financial operations, bonuses to top-managers and traders are proposed to be restricted and regulated. Projects of higher taxes on riches, luxury, short transactions and so on could not stop rising inequality but establish new social policy dependent on the "Big Five" and "Top Ten" taxation. Such laws could not restrict the glam-capitalism expansion, rather they could legitimate its impact on social structure.

The theoretical model of the shift from the "onion-like" stratification toward the "pear-like" bimodal stratification is supported by empirical data from different countries. In Russia, for example, statistical data on income distribution reveals the gap between two modal strata: the lower modal stratum with monthly income US $330–650 and the upper modal stratum with income above US $1000 (Table 10.2). It is obvious also that the bimodal configuration of income distribution among people correlates with the spatial configuration of inequality considered above. Moscow, the largest city attracting flows of material, human and symbolic resources is home for Russian glam-industries entrepreneurs and well-paid staff.

The new shape of stratification resulted from the rise of the glam-capitalism flow-structures. Structures of glam-capitalism are flow-structures because they coordinate participants (actors and actants, humans and things) through direction and intensity of moves penetrating barriers and boundaries established by traditional institutional structures and by network structures of recent decades. Flows of people, money, goods and information are structuring social life under glam-capitalism as they define intentions and outcomes of social activities. Involvement in flows is becoming a factor of social differentiation. People involved by their own intentions in the functioning of glam-industries and glamour-industrial complexes get access to more resources. Creative consumers get access to additional resources, despite glam-capitalists extract profits from consumers' enthusiastic participation in flow-structures. However, there are refugees, economic migrants and victims of human trafficking who lose their autonomy and become an objectified part of flow-structures when they try to get access to resources provided by the glam-capitalism in networked enclaves of globality.

Generating trends in the consumer markets, flow-structures of glam-capitalism cause effects of temporality or fluidity of social inequality. The rising significance of temporal organization of access to trendy goods allows a shift in focus of analysis from traditional quantitative gap between "having more" and "having less" toward the temporal lag between "having now" and "having later". Temporal inequality cannot be described in terms of discrimination on a "ladder" or exclusion from a "circle". Distinction has to be made between the outpacing and the outpaced by flow. Trendsetters make some objects valuable and leaders of consumerism pay for that object much more than masses of ordinary consumers who are waiting for reduced prices in season sales. All three groups of actors involved in consumption get the same goods but their access to the value is different in terms of time.

Temporal inequality adds one more dimension to contemporary configurations of inequality. Inequality now is not only a hierarchical order differentiating higher positions and lower ones, or an order of network differentiating core positions and peripheral ones. Inequality is also about differentiation of faster flows of resources and slower flows. Emerging flow-structures of glam-capitalism reshape configuration of social inequality traditionally based on institutional regulation of access to material, human and symbolic resources according to social status attained in frameworks of formal organizations. Now three types of inequality can be identified in current social practices of differentiation, discrimination, social conflicts and social policies:

1. *institutional inequality* based on social status that establishes correspondence between: class and property, income and stratum, symbolic capital and prestige of life style, personal rights and gender, civil rights and ethnicity and so on;
2. *networked inequality* based on cultural identity that provides distinction between those included in network who have privileges of membership and the excluded from network;
3. *flow inequality* based on spatial and temporal mobility/creativity that provides involvement in flows and corresponding advantages of place and moment.

The traditional forms of inequality are dominating even in new configurations, but the newest forms should be taken into account to explain multidimensional inequalities of our time.

170 *Dmitry Ivanov*

Note

1 This work has been supported by the Russian Science Foundation (grant number 14–18–00359).

References

American Society of Plastic Surgeons. 2010. "Report of the 2010 Plastic Surgery Statistics." https://d2wirczt3b6wjm.cloudfront.net/News/Statistics/2010/plastic-surgery-statistics-full-report-2010.pdf (accessed May 3, 2015).
Appadurai, Arjun. 1990. "Disjuncture and Difference in the Global Cultural Economy." In Featherstone, Mike (ed.), *Global Culture: Nationalism, Globalization, and Modernity*. London: SAGE Publications: 295–310.
Arrighi, Giovanni. 2001. "Global Capitalism and the Persistence of the North-South Divide." *Science & Society*. Vol. 65, No. 4: 469–476.
Babones, Salvatore, Xi Zhang. 2008. "Heterogeneity in the Global South in the Relationship between Income Inequality and Foreign Trade." *International Review of Modern Sociology*. Vol. 34, No. 1: 95–108.
Bourdieu, Pierre. 1979. *La distinction*. Paris: Ed. de Minuit.
The Brookings Institution. 2012. *Global Metromonitor: Slowdown, Recovery*. Washington, D.C.: Metropolitan Policy Program.
Burawoy, Michael. 2015. "Facing an Unequal World." *Current Sociology*. Vol. 63, No 1: 5–34.
Castells, Manuel. 2000. *The Rise of the Network Society*. 2nd ed. Malden, MA: Blackwell Publishing.
Chan, Louis K. C., Narasimhan Jegadeesh, Josef Lakonishok. 1995. "Evaluating the Performance of Value versus Glamour Stocks: The Impact of Selection Bias." *Journal of Financial Economics*, Vol. 38: 269–296.
Conrad, Jennifer, Michael Cooper, Gautam Kaul. 2003. "Value versus Glamour." *The Journal of Finance*, Vol. 58, No. 5: 1969–1996.
Dobbs, Richard, Sven Smit, Jaana Remes, James Manyika, Charles Roxburgh, Alejandra Restrepo, 2011. Urban World: Mapping the Economic Power of Cities. McKinsey Global Institute.
The Economist. 2007. December 22nd–29th: 50
Florida, Richard. 2002. *The Rise of the Creative Class*. New York: Basic Books.
Grant, John. 2006. *The Brand Innovation Manifesto*. Chichester: John Wiley & Sons Ltd.
Ivanov, Dmitry. 2008. *Glam-Capitalism*. St. Petersburg: Peterburgskoe Vostokovedenie (in Russian: Иванов Д.В. Глэм-капитализм. СПб.: Петербургское востоковедение, 2008).
Kacowicz, Arie. 2007. "Globalization, Poverty, and the North-South Divide." *International Studies Review*, Vol. 9, No. 4: 565–580.
Lash, Scott, John Urry. 1994. *Economies of Signs and Spaces*. London: SAGE Publications.
Penn, Mark J., E. Kinney Zalesne. 2007. *Microtrends*. London: Allen Lane

Poole, Charles. 1998. *The Physics Handbook: Fundamentals and Key Equations*. New York: John Wiley and Sons, Inc.

Reuveny, Rafael, William R. Thompson. 2008. "Uneven Economic Growth and the World Economy's North-South Stratification." *International Studies Quarterly*. Vol. 52, No 3: 579–605.

Ropelato, Jerry. 2007. "Internet Pornography Statistics." http:// internet-filter-review. toptenreviews.com/internet-pornography-statistics.html (accessed May 3, 2015).

Sassen, Saskia. 2005. "The Global City: Introducing a Concept." *Brown Journal of World Affairs*, Vol. 11, No 2: 27–43.

Sen, Amartya. 1992. *Inequality Reexamined*. Cambridge, MA: Harvard University Press.

Therborn, Göran (ed.). 2006. *Inequalities of the World*. London: Verso.

Tilly, Charles. 1998. *Durable Inequality*. Berkeley: University of California Press.

United Nations. 2014. *World Urbanization Prospects*. New York: UN DESA.

Wallerstein, Immanuel. 2004. *World-System Analysis: An Introduction*. Durham: Duke University Press.

Weber, Max. 2003. *The Protestant Ethic and the Spirit of Capitalism*. Mineola, NY: Dover Publications.

PART IV

FUTURE PROSPECTS

11

PROSPECTS FOR THE WORLD LEFT

Immanuel Wallerstein

There have always been historical systems in which some relatively small group exploited the others. The exploited always fought back as best they could. The modern world-system, which came into existence in the long sixteenth century in the form of a capitalist world-economy, has been extremely effective in extracting surplus-value from the large majority of the populations within it. It did this by adding to the standard systemic features of hierarchy and exploitation the new characteristic of polarization.

The result has been an ever-increasing degree of exploitation by what we now call the 1% of the others (these days called the 99%). Within the modern world-system, resistance initially took the form primarily of either spontaneous uprisings or escape into zones in which it was harder for the 1% to reach and impose its authority. However, the increasing mechanization and concentration of productive enterprises within the modern world-system led, as we know, to an ever-increasing degree of urbanization. The urbanization of the modern world-system in turn opened new ways for the working classes to challenge the modes of extraction by the dominant forces.

176   *Immanuel Wallerstein*

The French Revolution further changed the structure of the modern world-system by unleashing two new concepts, whose impact was to transform the modern world-system. These concepts were the "normality of change" as opposed to its exceptional and limited reality, and the "sovereignty of the people" as opposed to that of the ruler or the aristocracy. This pair of concepts was the basis of something new, a geoculture that spread throughout the historical system and legitimated radical "change" of the system by the "people." It was in response to this danger to the dominant forces that the three modern ideologies—conservatism, liberalism and radicalism—emerged.

Each of the ideologies represented a program of political action. Conservatism was the first and most immediate response, notably in the writings of Edmund Burke and Joseph de Maistre. The core of the conservative ideology was to deny the prudence, even the possibility, of substantial change. Conservatives reasserted the priority of the judgments of traditional elites, locally situated and supported by religious institutions.

Liberalism arose as an alternative mode of containing the danger. Liberals argued that reactionary conservatism, which inevitably involved suppressive force, was self-defeating in the medium run, pushing the oppressed to rebel openly. Instead, liberals said, elites should embrace the inevitability of some change and defer nominally to the sovereignty of the people, but insist that social transformation was a complicated and dangerous process that could only be done well and prudently by specialists whom all others should allow to make the crucial decisions. Liberals thus envisaged a slow, and limited, process of societal transformation.

Radicalism was the last ideology to emerge. It began as a small annex to liberalism. Radicals argued that relying on specialists would lead to no more than a slightly revised social structure. Instead, they said, the lower strata should pursue transformation of the system as rapidly as possible, guided by a democratic ethos and an egalitarian ideal.

The world-revolution of 1848 marked a turning-point in the relations of the three ideologies—rightwing conservatism, centrist liberalism and leftwing radicalism. It began with a social uprising in Paris in February, in which the radical left seemed momentarily to seize state power. This uprising was unexpected by most persons—a happy surprise for the working classes, a serious danger from the point of view of the elites. It so frightened both conservatives and liberals that they buried their voluble differences that had loomed so large up to then and formed a political alliance to suppress the social revolution. The process in France essentially took three years, culminating in the creation of the Second Empire under Napoleon III.

Nor was the social revolution all that was happening. The same year, 1848, was the moment of nationalist uprisings in much of Europe—notably in Hungary, Poland, the Italies and the Germanies. The historians have dubbed these uprisings "the springtime of the nations." Just like the social revolution in Paris, these various nationalist uprisings were suppressed within a few years—at least for the moment, but a long moment.

This pair of happenings in 1848—social revolution in France and nationalist revolutions in many countries—forced a reconsideration of basic strategy by the tenants of each of the three ideologies. The conservatives noticed that the one major country in which nothing seemed to happen in 1848 was Great Britain. That seemed very curious since throughout the first half of the nineteenth century, radical forces had seemed to be the most extensive, active and well-organized in Great Britain. Yet it was the one major country in which calm reigned amidst the pan-European storm of 1848.

What the conservatives then realized, and historians later confirmed, was that the British Tories had discovered a mode of containing radicalism far more effective than forceful suppression. The British Tories had been making constant concessions to the demands for social and institutional change. These concessions actually were relatively minor, but their repeated occurrence seemed to suffice to persuade the more radical forces that change was in fact taking place. After 1848, the British example persuaded conservatives elsewhere, especially in continental Europe, that perhaps they should revise their tactics. This revised analysis brought conservatives nearer to the position of the centrist liberals, and took the label of "enlightened conservatism."

Meanwhile, the radicals were equally unsettled by what happened. The principal tactics radicals had employed up to 1848 had been either spontaneous uprisings or utopian withdrawal. In 1848 radicals observed that their spontaneous uprisings were easily put down. And their utopian withdrawals turned out to be unsustainable. The lesson they drew was the necessity of replacing spontaneity with "organizing" the revolution—a program that involved more temporal patience as well as the creation of a bureaucratic structure. This shift of tactics brought radicals closer to the position of the centrist liberals, the radical bureaucrats now assuming the role of the specialists who would guide transformation.

Finally, the liberals too drew a major lesson from the world-revolution of 1848. They began to emphasize their centrist position, as opposed to their previously primary role of confronting conservatives. They began to see the necessity of tactics that would pull both conservatives and radicals into their orbit, turning them into mere variants of centrist liberalism. In this effort, they turned out to be hugely successful for a very long time—indeed until the much later world-revolution of 1968.

It was in the second half of the nineteenth century that we see the organizational emergence of what we consider to be antisystemic movements. There were two main varieties—social movements and nationalist movements—as well as less strong varieties such as women's movements and ethno/racial/religious movements. These movements were all antisystemic in one simple sense: They were struggling against the established power structures in an effort to

178 *Immanuel Wallerstein*

bring into existence a more democratic, more egalitarian historical system than the existing one.

These movements were however deeply divided in terms of their analysis of how to define the groups that were most oppressed, and what were the priorities of achieving the objectives of one kind of movement relative to other kinds of movements. These debates between the various movements have persisted right up to today.

One fundamental debate was how to think about the role of the states in the achievement of a different kind of historical system. There were those who argued that states were structures established by the elites of the system, mechanisms by which the elites controlled the others. States were therefore an enemy, to be shunned, and against which the movements must ceaselessly struggle. The principal tactic therefore must be to educate and transform the psychology of those who were oppressed, to turn them into permanent militants who would embody and transmit to others the values of a democratic, egalitarian world.

Against this view were arrayed those who agreed that the state was the instrument of the ruling elites, and for this very reason could not be ignored. Unless the movements seized power in the states, the ruling classes would use their strength—military and police strength, economic strength and cultural strength—to crush the antisystemic movements. This group insisted that, precisely in order to transform the historical system, movements had first to achieve control of the state. We came to call this the "two-step strategy"—first obtain state power, then transform the world.

The second argument was between the social movements and the nationalist movements. The former insisted that the modern world-system was a capitalist system and that therefore the basic struggle was a class struggle within each country between the owners of capital (the "bourgeoisie") and those who had only their own labor power to sell (the "proletariat"). It was between these two groups that the democratic and egalitarian gulf was enormous and ever-increasing. It followed that the natural "historical actor" of transformation was the proletariat.

The nationalist movements assessed the world differently. They saw a world in which states were controlled either by an internal dominant ethnic group or by external forces. They argued that the most oppressed persons were the "peoples" who were denied their democratic rights and consequently were living in an ever-increasingly inegalitarian historical system. It followed that the natural "historical actors" were the oppressed nations. Only when these oppressed nations came to power in their own state could there be expectations of a more democratic, more egalitarian historical system.

These two splits—that between those who abjured state power versus those who sought to obtain it as the first step; and that between those who saw the proletariat versus those who saw the oppressed nations as the natural

Prospects for the World Left 179

historical actors—were not the only matters under debate. Both the social movements and the nationalist movements insisted on the importance of "vertical" structures. That is, they both insisted that the road to success in obtaining state power was to have only one antisystemic structure in any state (actual state for the social movements, virtual state for the nationalist movements). They said that unless all other kind of antisystemic movements subordinated themselves to the single "principal" movement, the objective could not be achieved.

For example, take the women's or feminist movements. These movements insisted on the inegalitarian and undemocratic relationship of men and women throughout history and particularly in the modern world-system. They argued that the struggle against what was termed "patriarchy" was at least as important as any other struggle and was their primary concern as movements. Against this view, both the social and the nationalist movements argued that asserting an independent role for feminist movements weakened their cause, which took priority, and was "objectively" counter-revolutionary.

The "vertical" movements insisted that there could be women's auxiliaries of the social or of the nationalist movements, but that the realization of the feminist demands could only occur as a consequence of the realization of the demands of the "principal" historical actor (the proletariat or the oppressed nation). In effect, the vertical movements counseled deferral of the struggles of the feminist movements.

The same logic would be used against other kinds of movements—such as trade-union movements or movements of so-called "minorities" as socially-defined (whether by race, ethnicity, religion, or language). All these movements had to accept subordination to the principal movement and deferral of their demands. They could only be adjuncts of the principal movements, or else they were considered to be counter-revolutionary.

When these various movements first came to be large enough to be politically noticeable (circa the 1870s), the most important reality about all of them was that they were perhaps noticeable but in fact organizationally and politically quite weak. The idea that they could actually achieve state power seemed a matter of faith, unsustained by a sober assessment of the real *rapport de forces* in the modern world-system.

While their political power did increase slowly from then on, they still seemed relatively weak as late as 1945. It is therefore somewhat astonishing that in the period 1945–1970 the vertical antisystemic movements actually did achieve the first of the two steps. They did indeed come to state power, almost everywhere. This sudden shift in the political arena of the modern world-system warrants a careful explanation.

The end of World War II marked the onset of two important cyclical shifts in the history of the modern world-system. It marked both the beginning of a Kondratieff A-phase and the moment of undisputed hegemony in the

180 *Immanuel Wallerstein*

world-system of the United States. The success of the antisystemic movements cannot be understood without placing it in this context. It is most revealing to start with U.S. hegemony, which can be considered a quasi-monopoly of geopolitical power.

Hegemonic cycles are very long occurrences. But the high point, true hegemony, is actually rather brief. There have in fact only been three such high points in the history of the modern world-system—the United Provinces in the mid-seventeenth century, the United Kingdom in the mid-nineteenth century, and the United States in the mid-twentieth century. Each lasted perhaps for 25–50 years or so. The phase prior to the achievement of full hegemony has been each time a "thirty years' war" between a land-based power and a sea/air-based power. The "thirty years' war" in the most recent case was that between Germany and the United States from 1914–1945, and ended as we know, in the total defeat of Germany.

Hegemony is built on the existence of an enormous economic advantage, combined with political, cultural and military strength. As of 1945, the United States was able to assemble all this to its advantage. In 1945, the United States was the only important industrial power in the entire world that had escaped major destruction of its plants. Indeed, on the contrary, wartime production had made their productive enterprises more extensive and efficient than ever. At this time U.S. production was so efficient that it could sell its leading products in other countries at prices lower than these countries could produce these products themselves, despite the costs involved in transportation. These U.S.-based quasi-monopolies were guaranteed by the active role of the state in protecting and enhancing their exclusive privileges.

The result was the largest (by far) expansion of the world production of surplus-value in the 500-year-long history of the modern world-system. While the United States was the principal beneficiary—its state, its enterprises, its residents—the worldwide rise in production produced benefits to most countries, if to a far lesser degree than to the United States.

The problem with quasi-monopolies in leading products is that they are self-liquidating over time, for several reasons. The first is that the high rate of capital accumulation made these quasi-monopolies a very tempting target for penetration by other producers who sought to enter the world market. These other producers stole or bought technical knowledge and used their influence on other governments to counter the protectionist policies of the government primarily protecting the quasi-monopolies.

Furthermore, the U.S. government actively aided west European and Japanese economic reconstruction in order to provide customers for U.S. production as well as to maintain the political loyalty of these de facto satellite regimes. In addition, as long as the quasi-monopolies were in effective operation, the leading enterprises feared most of all any stoppage of production, since stoppages involved irrecoverable losses. Hence it made short-term

Prospects for the World Left   181

economic sense to make wage concessions to their workers rather than risk strikes. But of course over time this raised the cost of production and lessened the advantage vis-à-vis potential competitors.

By the 1960s, the improved economic position of western Europe and Japan could be observed in the dramatic inversion in one key leading industry, automobiles. Whereas in 1950 U.S. manufacturers could undersell competitors in their home markets, by the mid-1960s the reverse was true. West European and Japanese automobile producers began to penetrate the U.S. domestic market.

For all these reasons, others over time did in fact succeed in penetrating the world market, thereby increasing competition. This no doubt benefited some consumers, but at the same time it reduced the level of profitability of the erstwhile quasi-monopolies. U.S. producers had to give thought to how they could minimize the losses they were incurring in the rate of capital accumulation.

It was not helpful to U.S. capitalists that, as their quasi-monopoly of production was disappearing, so was the quasi-monopoly of U.S. geopolitical strength, which was beginning its inevitable decline. To understand how this happened, we have to see how it was established in the first place circa 1945. We have already mentioned the superiority in productive efficiency and the fact that this advantage underlay its political and cultural dominance.

There was however one last element in securing full hegemony, which was the military sphere. The fact that prior to 1939, the United States had *not* invested heavily in military technology and manpower had been one of the key elements in enabling them to achieve productive dominance. World War II changed that allocation of state revenues. The United States developed atomic weapons and displayed their power by using them against Japan. However, sentiment within the United States was heavily in favor of reducing the size of the armed forces.

The problem for the United States was that a hegemonic power cannot abstain from military commitment. It comes with the position. And in 1945 there was one other power that had a very strong military, the U.S.S.R., and unlike the United States it showed no signs of rushing to dismantle it. It was clear that, if the United States was to exercise hegemony, it had to make some deal with the Soviet Union.

They did make such a deal, and we have dubbed it "Yalta." This refers not really to the actual decisions of this meeting in February 1945 of what were then called the Big Three—the United States, Great Britain and the Soviet Union. "Yalta" was rather a set of unsigned tacit arrangements to which the United States and the Soviet Union were committed and which were maintained in place for quite some time.

There were in fact three such tacit arrangements. The first was that there would be a division of the world in terms of zones of influence and control.

The line would be drawn more or less where the two armies ended up in 1945, a division in the middle of Germany going from north to south, and the 38th Parallel in Korea. In effect, the Soviet Union would have primacy in about one-third of the globe and the United States in the other two-thirds. The deal was that neither side would try to change these frontiers by the use of military force.

The second part of the deal had to do with economic reconstruction. As we noted, U.S. producers needed customers. The Marshall Plan and similar arrangements with Japan provided these customers. The tacit U.S.-Soviet agreement was that the United States would provide such economic assistance to countries in its zone but not to any country in the Soviet zone, where the Soviet Union could arrange matters as it saw fit.

Finally, the third part of the deal was the so-called Cold War. The Cold War refers to the mutual denunciation of both sides, each proclaiming its virtues and its inevitable long-term ideological victory as well as the evil machinations of the other side. The deal was that this was not to be taken seriously, or rather that the function of the mutual denunciations was meant in no way to countermand the first part of the deal—the de facto freezing of frontiers indefinitely. The actual objective of Cold War rhetoric was not to transform the other side but to maintain the loyalty of the satellites on each side.

Although the first part of the deal lasted until the collapse of the Soviet Union, and the second part until at least the 1970s, the cozy arrangement began to be eroded by several factors. The de facto international status quo was not at all to the liking of a number of countries in what we then called the Third World. The first major dissident was the Chinese Communist Party (CCP), which straightforwardly rejected Stalin's advice to come to a power-sharing deal with the Kuomintang. Instead, the CCP's army entered Shanghai, and it proclaimed the People's Republic of China.

This dissidence was followed by the insistence of the Viet Minh to achieve control over all of Vietnam, the insistence of the Algerian *Front de Libération Nationale* to obtain total independence, and the insistence of the Cubans to arm themselves against U.S. intrusion. In each of these cases, it was the Third World power that was forcing the hand of the Soviet Union and not the other way around. On the other hand, the Soviet Union and the United States successfully sought to ensure that there was no use of nuclear weapons, which would have violated the pledge of mutual restraint.

The Vietnam War, in which the United States committed its troops actively, weakened U.S. hegemony in several ways. The United States paid a high economic price for the war. And it turned U.S. public opinion against involvement there (and subsequently elsewhere—the so-called Vietnam syndrome). Furthermore, the United States lost the war, which strengthened the views of others around the world that U.S. military power was less effective than it had seemed to be—incarnated in the concept of the "paper tiger."

Prospects for the World Left 183

It is in this context that the world-revolution of 1968 took place. It was a world-revolution in the simple sense that it occurred over most of the world, in each of what were at the time considered three separate "worlds." And it was a world-revolution in the remarkable repetitions of two main themes almost everywhere, of course garbed in different local languages.

The first main theme was the rejection of U.S. hegemony ("imperialism") by the revolutionaries, with however an important twist. These revolutionaries equally condemned the "collusion" of the Soviet Union with U.S. imperialism, which was how they interpreted the tacit Yalta accords. In effect, they were rejecting the ideological themes of the Cold War and minimizing the difference between the two so-called superpowers.

The second main theme was the denunciation of the Old Left (that is, Communist and Social-Democratic parties and the national liberation movements) on the grounds that these movements were not in reality antisystemic but were also collusive with the system.

They pointed to the historic two-step strategy and said that the Old Left movements had in fact achieved the first step—state power—but has not in any serious way changed the world. Economic inequalities were still enormous and growing, internally and internationally. The states were not more democratic, possibly even less so. And class distinctions had not disappeared, merely renamed, the bourgeoisie becoming the *Nomenklatura*, or some equivalent term. The revolutionaries rejected therefore the Old Left movements as part of the problem, not part of the solution.

While it is true that the revolutionaries were not able to remain in a position of real political strength very long and were suppressed as movements, just like those in 1848, their efforts did have one absolutely major consequence. The world-revolution of 1968 transformed the geoculture. The dominance of centrist liberalism over the two other ideologies came to an end. Centrist liberalism did not disappear; it was simply reduced to being once again only one of three. The radical left and the conservative right re-emerged as fully autonomous actors on the world scene.

What happened next to the movements was largely the consequence of the global economic stagnation of the Kondratieff downturn. The attempts to create new movements of the global left—the various Maoisms, the so-called New Left Green movements, the neo-insurrectionist movements—all turned out to have fleeting support in the face of the economic difficulties that had suddenly become so central to people's lives, again almost everywhere.

Meanwhile, the United States was undertaking a major shift of strategy in order to slow down the rate of its decline. To do this, the United States launched a threefold set of projects. The first had to do with its relation to its erstwhile principal satellites, western Europe and Japan. It offered a new arrangement to the now economically much more powerful and therefore politically more restless regimes. The United States would redefine their role,

184 *Immanuel Wallerstein*

turning them into "partners" in the geopolitical arena. Institutions were created to implement this new relationship, such as the Trilateral Commission, the G-7 and the World Economic Forum at Davos. The United States offer was that the partners might engage in geopolitical moves of which the United States disapproved—for example, West Germany's *Ostpolitik*, the building of the oil pipeline between the Soviet Union and western Europe, a different policy towards Cuba. The proviso was that this policy independence would be limited and did not go too far.

The second reorientation was the abandonment of the advocacy of developmentalism. In the 1950s and 1960s, everyone (the West, the Soviet bloc and the Third World) seemed to endorse the concept of national "development"—by which was meant essentially increased urbanization, the growth of an educated stratum, protection of infant industries, and the construction of state institutions and bureaucracies. Suddenly, the global language radically changed. Production for export was to replace protection of infant industries. State enterprises were to be privatized. State expenditures on education and health were to be radically reduced. And above all, capital was to be permitted to flow freely across frontiers. This set of prescriptions received the name of the Washington Consensus, about which Mrs. Thatcher famously proclaimed: "There Is No Alternative" or TINA. The mandate was enforced primarily by the International Monetary Fund (IMF), which refused to give states the loans they badly needed because of the economic downturn unless they agreed to observe these new rules.

The third part of the new strategy was to erect a new world order that ended what is called nuclear proliferation. Essentially, the United States had to accept the reality that the five permanent members of the U.N. Security Council all had nuclear weapons, but they wished the list to stop there. It made this offer to all other counties. A treaty would provide that the five nuclear powers would seek both to the reduce their nuclear weapons and offer aid to the other signatories in the obtaining of nuclear power for peaceful uses to all the rest of the world, provided the others abandoned all pretention to obtaining nuclear weapons. As we know, four countries refused to sign the treaty—Israel, India, Pakistan and South Africa. But many others acceded and ended their programs.

In fact this threefold redefinition of U.S. strategy, followed essentially by all U.S. presidents from Nixon to Clinton, was partially successful. It did slow down decline without stopping it entirely. The newly-regenerated conservative right, now being called neo-liberals, found this new geopolitical framework very conducive to the rapid growth of their movements. World discourse moved rightwards steadily. Regimes that didn't adjust to this new discourse fell from power. Finally, what had been symbolically defined as the symbol of successful Old Left politics and considered (by both partisans and opponents) to be unchangeable—the Soviet Union—collapsed from within.

Prospects for the World Left 185

This collapse was hailed in the Western world as their victory in the Cold War. This interpretation forgot that the whole point of the Cold War had not been to "win" it but to maintain it as a pillar of the world-system. It turned out in fact that the collapse of the Soviet Union would both accelerate the decline of U.S. hegemony and undermine the movements of the neo-liberal right.

The crucial geopolitical event was the first Gulf War (1990–1991), which commenced with the invasion of Kuwait by Saddam Hussein's Iraq. Iraq had for almost a century contested the creation of Kuwait as a separate state by the British. However, it never was in a position to do much about it. During the period in which the Baath party had been in power, the Iraqi regime was supported by the Soviet Union. It had however also been supported by the United States during the 1980s when the United States encouraged it to engage in the futile war with Iran.

As of 1990, the situation from the Iraqi point of view was dismal. They had paid an enormous price for the destructive war and now owed considerable sums to creditors, one of the largest of which was Kuwait. In addition, they believed Kuwait was appropriating Iraqi oil through slant drilling. But most importantly, the collapse of the Soviet Union, then in process, removed the constraints that Iraq would have felt during the Cold War. It seemed a propitious moment to liquidate Iraqi debts and undo the long-resented "loss" of Kuwait to Iraq.

We know what happened. The United States, after initial hesitation, mobilized the troops necessary to push the Iraqis out of Kuwait. This very action, however, revealed U.S. geopolitical weakness in two ways. First, the United States was unable to bear the costs of its own participation and was subsidized at a 90% level by four other countries—Kuwait, Saudi Arabia, Germany and Japan. And second, U.S. President George H.W. Bush was faced with the question of whether victorious U.S. troops would proceed to Baghdad or not. He prudently decided that this would be politically and militarily unwise. U.S. action in Iraq thereafter was limited to the imposition of various sanctions. Saddam Hussein remained in power.

Meanwhile, the dismantlement of the Soviet Union and the possibility for all its ex-satellites to pursue independent policies led to a rapid adoption by all of them of neo-liberal policies. However, within a few years, the negative effects of these neo-liberal policies on the real standard of living of the lower strata provoked a reaction wherein erstwhile Communist parties (now renamed) returned to power to pursue a mildly social-democratic program. At the same time, rightist nationalist parties began to gain strength as well. The magic realization of a "Western" style of government with a "Western" level of real economic uplift turned out to be very difficult to realize, and many of these governments became quite unstable.

It is at that point that the antisystemic movements began to revive. The initial reaction to the collapse of the Soviet Union had been an emotional

186 *Immanuel Wallerstein*

shock and even depression for left movements everywhere, even those that had been long very critical of the Soviet experience. After however a few years of this morose perspective, new light appeared on the horizon for the global left. Some movements refused the sense of inevitability of a triumphal right discourse. There could be a renewed global left discourse.

Thus far, we have been discussing the impact on antisystemic movements of the global stagnation that the Kondratieff B-phase involves. However, there was a further factor, which is the result not of cyclical shifts in the world-economy but of the long-term secular trends. In the ongoing life of historical systems, each cyclical downturn returns not to the previous low point but always to a point somewhat higher. Think of it as two steps upward, one step backward on percentage curves that move towards the asymptote of 100%. Over the long term, the secular trends must then reach a point where it is difficult to advance further. At this point the system has moved far from equilibrium. We can call this point the beginning of the structural crisis of the historical system.

The short explanation of why historical capitalism has reached its structural crisis is the steady increase over time of the three fundamental costs of production: personnel, inputs and taxation. Producers make their profits by keeping the total of these costs below the prices at which they are able to sell their products. As these costs rise over time, they reach levels at which the willingness of prospective buyers to purchase the goods is reached, at which point it is no longer possible to accumulate capital via production.

The three costs are each complex, since each is composed of several different subcosts. Personnel costs have always been the one that is most transparent. And among these costs, that of unskilled labor has been the one most discussed. Historically, costs of unskilled labor have risen as workers in Kondratieff A-phases found some way to engage in syndical action. The response of producers in Kondratieff B-phases has been the runaway factory, moving production to areas of "historically lower wages." This curious phrase actually refers to the ability of entrepreneurs to attract laborers from rural areas less tied into the world labor market who would work for lower real wages because these lower real wages offered higher real income than their previous work. After a number of years, these workers became more accustomed to their new environments and learned how to engage in syndical action. At this point, producers would begin to flee to still other areas. This solution for the entrepreneurs depended on the availability of these rural workers. The supply has now begun to be exhausted, as can be measured by the considerable deruralization of the world-system today.

The cost of unskilled labor has only been one part of personnel costs. A second part has been the relentlessly increasing costs of intermediate personnel, which were needed both organizationally to meet the complexities of larger corporate structures and politically to serve as a barrier to the syndical demands of unskilled labor.

Prospects for the World Left   187

The solution to increasing costs of unskilled labor has been to eliminate them almost totally from the work force through mechanization. In recent years this has also come to be the solution to increasing costs of intermediate personnel, whose tasks are also being taken over by mechanization. It is actually in the third personnel cost, that of top managers, that the biggest increase in personnel costs has occurred. Those in managerial positions have been able to use their positions as gatekeepers to exact enormous rents, which are extracted from the profits of investors (the shareholders). The bottom line is that today personnel costs are extremely high compared with past costs and constantly increasing.

The story is similar in the cost of inputs. Producers have tried to keep these costs low by externalizing three major types of expenditures: getting rid of toxic waste, renewing raw materials and building infrastructure. They were able for some 500 years to deal with toxic waste simply by dumping it into public space. But the world has nearly run out of public space, which has led to a worldwide environmentalist movement pressure to clean up the toxicity. This could only be done by the states, which involved the need for higher taxes. It also led the states to seek to force producers to internalize the costs, which has cut into profitability. The exhaustion of public space is analogous to the exhaustion of rural zones largely uninvolved in the market economy.

Similarly, the renewal of raw materials was not a problem until the combination of 500 years of usage that was not renewed and an expanded world population led rather suddenly to worldwide acute shortages of energy, water, forestation and basic foods (fish and meat). The shortages have led in turn to acute political struggles over distribution both within and between countries.

Finally, infrastructure is a crucial element in commercial outlets for production. However, here again producers historically have paid only very partially for their use of the infrastructure, foisting the costs on others, especially the states. Given the ever-rising costs of repairing and extending the infrastructure, the states have found themselves unable to bear the costs, which has led to a serious deterioration worldwide of necessary aids to transport and communications.

Finally, taxes have been steadily rising as well, despite what seems to be constant and enormous tax evasion. First of all, there are multiple kinds of governmental taxes—not only the national taxes that are widely noted but all kinds of local and intermediate structure taxes. These are used, when all is said and done, not merely to pay for the bureaucracy but also to meet the ever-increasing demands of the antisystemic movements for educational and health services and the provision of lifetime income guarantees such as pensions and unemployment insurance, which collectively constitute the "welfare state." Despite all the reductions of welfare state provisions that have been forced upon the states, the reality is that these expenditures continue to be significantly larger worldwide than they were in the past.

188   *Immanuel Wallerstein*

Nor does governmental taxation exhaust the story. We are daily bombarded with reports of corruption not only in relatively poor countries but even more in relatively rich ones, where there is more money to steal. From the point of view of the entrepreneur, the costs of corruption are every bit as much a tax as those imposed by governments. Finally, the constantly expanding reality of mafia-type operations resulting from the other constraints (especially the shortages) imposes real taxes on the entrepreneur.

As the costs of production have steadily risen (in the pattern of two steps forward, one step backward), the ability to raise the prices of products have been seriously limited by the vastly increased polarization of world income and wealth. Effective demand has fallen as persons have been eliminated from the work force. And as the possibilities of capital accumulation diminish, there has been increasing fear about survival and therefore willingness of both individual consumers and entrepreneurial producers to risk expenditures, which further reduces effective demand. Hence, the world-system arrives at its structural crisis, in which neither the underclasses nor the capitalist entrepreneurs find acceptable returns within the modern world-system. Their attention to turns to the alternatives available.

Once we are into a structural crisis, the system becomes chaotic. That is, the curves begin to fluctuate wildly. The system can no longer function in its traditional manner. It bifurcates, which means two things. One, the system is absolutely certain to go out of existence entirely, but it is intrinsically impossible to know what the successor system or systems will be. One can only outline in general terms what are the two alternative ways in which the chaotic situation can be resolved into a new systemic order.

Two, the bifurcation leads to a great political struggle concerning which of the two alternative possibilities the totality of participants in the system will "choose." That is to say, while we cannot predict the outcome, we can affect it. In terms of the role of the antisystemic movements, the turning-point occurred on Jan. 1, 1995, when the Zapatistas (the EZLN in its Spanish initials) rose up in Chiapas and proclaimed the autonomy of the indigenous peoples. Why however on Jan. 1, 1995? Because it was the day on which the North American Free Trade Association (NAFTA) came into operation. By choosing that day, the EZLN was sending the following message to Mexico and the world. The dramatic renewal of the 500-year-old demand of the peoples of Chiapas for self-government was being aimed both at opposing imperialism throughout the world and at Mexico's government for its participation in NAFTA as well as for its oppression of the peoples of Chiapas.

The EZLN emphasized that they had no interest in seizing power in the Mexican state. Quite the contrary! They wished to withdraw from the state and both construct and reconstruct the local ways of life. The EZLN was quite realistic. They realized they were not strong enough militarily to wage a war. Therefore, when sympathetic forces within Mexico pushed for a truce between the Mexican government and the EZLN, they fully agreed. To be sure, the Mexican government has never lived up to the truce agreement, but it has been constrained in how far it could go because of the support the EZLN was able to muster.

This support was the result of the second major theme the EZLN pursued. It asserted its own support for all movements of every kind everywhere that were in pursuit of greater democracy and equality. And the EZLN convened so-called intergalactic encounters in Chiapas to which they invited the entire global left. The EZLN also refused sectarian exclusions in these meetings—the pattern of the Old Left. They preached instead inclusiveness and mutual tolerance among the movements of the global left.

The revival of the global left received its second strong reinforcement in 1999. One of the principal objectives of the global right had been to institutionalize the Washington Consensus by adopting within the framework of the World Trade Organization (WTO) a treaty that guaranteed what were called intellectual property rights in all signatory countries. This would have effectively barred these countries from producing their own less expensive products for their own use and for sale to other countries—for example, in pharmaceuticals.

There were two remarkable aspects to Seattle. First of all, there was a major protest movement surrounding the meeting, which was composed of three forces that had hitherto never joined forces: the labor movement (and specifically the AFL-CIO), environmentalists and anarchists. In addition, the members of these groups who were present were largely U.S. persons, giving the lie to the argument that only in the Global South could one mobilize opposition to neo-liberalism.

The second remarkable aspect is that the protests succeeded. They enabled some sympathetic delegations within the WTO meeting to hold out against adopting the new treaty. The WTO meeting disbursed without a treaty. It was a failure. And ever since, any attempt to adopt the treaty has been blocked. The WTO became irrelevant. Furthermore, the Seattle protests led to widespread copying of the protest technique at international meetings of all kinds, to the point that conveners of such meetings began to schedule them for remote locations where they had a better possibility of blocking the presence and size of such protest movements.

This then brings us to the third major development in the second wind of antisystemic movements—after Chiapas and Seattle came Porto Alegre and the World Social Forum (WSF) of 2001. The initial call for the 2001 meeting was a joint effort of a network of seven Brazilian organizations (many of left Catholic inspiration but also the principal trade-union) and the ATTAC movement in France. They chose the name of World Social Forum in opposition to the World Economic Forum (WEF) that had been meeting at Davos for some 30 years and was a major locus of mutual discussion and planning of the world's elites. They decided to meet at the same time as the Davos meetings to emphasize the contrast and they chose Porto Alegre as the site of the 2001 meeting to underline the political importance of the Global South.

The organizers made the crucial decision that the meeting was open to all those who were against imperialism and neo-liberalism. They also made the more controversial decision of excluding political parties and insurrectionary movements. Finally, they decided not to have officers, elections, or resolutions. This was in order to frame a "horizontalist" approach to organizing the world's antisystemic forces, as opposed to the "verticalist" and therefore exclusionary approach of the Old Left movements. To summarize all this, they chose as the motto of the meeting the now famous slogan, "Another world is possible."

Porto Alegre was unexpectedly a major success. The conveners had hoped to attract 5,000 people and they attracted 10,000. To be sure, the initial participants were heavily from Brazil and close-by countries and from France and Italy. But they immediately did two things. They decided to continue with the Porto Alegre meetings, seeking to expand the participation geographically. And they created an international council, more or less by co-option, to oversee the organization of future meetings. In the years that followed, the WSF met in different parts of the Global South and with an enormous increase of the number of participants. In this sense, it has been a continuing success.

However, as the first decade of the twenty-first century went by, the dilemmas of the WSF came to the fore. They can best be understood in the context of the evolution of the world-system itself. There were two major elements in this evolution. The first was the bubble crisis in the U.S. housing market in 2007–2008, which led commentators around the world to recognize the existence of some kind of "crisis" in the world-system. The second was the economic and geopolitical rise of the "emerging" economies—in particular but not only the so-called BRICS (or Brazil, Russia, India, China and South Africa).

Together, the two issues led to a public debate about the enormous wealth gap and about the future of the geopolitical dominance of the Global North—and to great uncertainty among commentators about how to assess these events. Were we to think of it as fundamental change or as a passing bump on the world-economic and geopolitical scene? The antisystemic movements and their partisans have been equally ambivalent about how to assess the debate about inequality and the rise of the "emerging" nations. It has also led to an acute debate within the WSF about its successes and failures.

The antisystemic movements now face a number of serious dilemmas. The first is whether or not to recognize the existence of a structural crisis of historical capitalism. The second is about what should be the priorities of their short-term and middle-term activities. The most noticeable thing about antisystemic movements in the second decade of the twenty-first century is the degree to which the debates that embroiled them in the last third of the twentieth century, once exorcised in the world-revolution of 1968, have returned to plague them, virtually unchanged.

There were three debates that we outlined earlier. The first concerned the role of the states in the achievement of a different kind of historical system. The second was that between social movements and nationalist movements about the leading historical actor in the struggle for a more just historical order. The third was between the verticalists who insisted that multiple oppressed groups had to subordinate their demands to the priorities of the principal historical actor and the horizontalists who insisted that the demands of all oppressed groups were equally important and equally urgent, and should not be deferred.

Well, here we are again! Inside the WSF and in the larger global justice movement, there are those who shun in every way state power and those who insist that obtaining state power is an essential prerequisite. There are those who insist on the priority of the class struggle (1% vs. 99%) and those who insist on the priority of the nationalist struggle (South vs. North). And there are those who are verticalist, insisting on joint political action whether within the WSF or the wider global justice movement, and those who are horizontalist, insisting on not neglecting the truly forgotten groups, the lowest global strata.

These debates have been most visible in Latin America because it has become a prime locus of global developments on all these fronts most vividly. For various reasons (including the decline of U.S. geopolitical power), there have come to power in the twenty-first century a large number of governments that are on the left or at least left of center. There has also been a movement, led in different ways both by Venezuela and by Brazil, to create South American and Latin American structures (UNASUR and CELAC) that excluded the United States and Canada. There have also been steps towards creating regional economic zones and structures (Mercosur, Bancosur).

At the same time, these governments of the left, center-left and of course the few on the political right) have all pursued developmentalist policies, which involve extractive policies that violate the traditional zones of indigenous peoples. These latter groups have accused the left governments of being as bad in this respect as their rightwing predecessors. The left governments in turn have accused the indigenous movements of acting objectively and deliberately in accord with rightwing internal groups and the United States geopolitically.

The net result is a divided Global Left in the political struggle over the new systemic order it is trying to build by tilting the bifurcation in the direction of a relatively democratic, relatively egalitarian world-system (or world-systems). Of course, the Global Right is also engaged in an internal debate about tactics, but that is of little comfort to the Global Left.

192   *Immanuel Wallerstein*

One way to analyze the options for the Global Left is to put them in a time frame that distinguishes short-term priorities and middle-term priorities. All of us live in the short-term. We need to feed ourselves, house ourselves, sustain our health and just survive. No movement can hope to attract support if it doesn't recognize this urgent need for everyone. It follows, in my view, that all movements must do everything they can to alleviate immediate distress. I call this action to "minimize the pain." This requires all sorts of short-term compromises, but it is essential. At the same time, one must be very clear that minimizing the pain in no way transforms the system. This was the classic social-democratic illusion. It merely minimizes the pain.

The French Revolution bequeathed us with a concept intended to be the great equalizer. Did it bequeath us all with a poison pill that may destroy the global left and therefore the great equalizer? An intellectual, moral and political reunification of the global left is very urgent. It will require a good deal more of a sense of give and take than the principal actors have been showing. Still, there is no serious alternative.

In the middle-run (that is, the next 20–40 years), the debate is fundamental and total. There is no compromise. One side or the other will win. I call this the battle between the spirit of Davos and the spirit of Porto Alegre. The spirit of Davos calls for a new non-capitalist system that retains its worst features—hierarchy, exploitation and polarization. They could well install a world-system that is worse than our present one. The spirit of Porto Alegre seeks a system that is relatively democratic and relatively egalitarian. I say "relatively" because a totally flat world will never exist, but we can do much, much better than we have done heretofore. There is, in this sense, *possible* progress.

We do not know who will win in this struggle. What we do know is that, in a chaotic world, every nano-action at every nano-moment on every nano-issue affects the outcome. That is why I continue to end discussion of these issues with the metaphor of the butterfly. We learned in the last half-century that every fluttering of a butterfly's wings changes the world climate. In this transition to a new world order, we are all little butterflies and therefore the chances of tilting the bifurcation in our direction depends on us. The odds are 50-50. It follows that our efforts as activists are not merely useful; they are the essential element in our struggle for a better world.

CONTRIBUTORS

Dariusz Adamczyk is a researcher at the German Historical Institute in Warsaw on a project granted by the Deutsche Forschungsgemeinschaft and teaches history of Eastern Europe at Leibniz University of Hannover. He is author of the book *Silber und Macht. Fernhandel, Tribute und die piastische Herrschaftsbildung in nordosteuropäischer Perspektive (800-1100)* (Wiesbaden 2014) and co-editor (together with Stephan Lehnstaedt) of *Wirtschaftskrisen als Wendepunkte. Ursachen, Folgen und historische Einordnungen vom Mittelalter bis zur Gegenwart* (Osnabrück 2015) and (together with Norbert Kersken) of *Fernhändler, Dynasten, Kleriker. Die piastische Herrschaft in sozialen und kontinentalen Beziehungsgeflechten vom 10. bis zum frühen 13. Jahrhundert* (Wiesbaden 2015).

Vilna Bashi Treitler is a sociologist and visual artist who chairs the Department of Black Studies at the University of California, Santa Barbara. Her work centers on race and ethnicity, international migration and inequality. She recently co-edited (with Manuela Boatcă) a monograph issue of *Current Sociology* entitled "Dynamics of Inequality in Global Perspective", and she is at work on a new book on race theory.

Manuela Boatcă is professor of sociology and Head of School of the Global Studies Programme at the Albert-Ludwigs-University Freiburg, Germany. She is author of *Global Inequalities beyond Occidentalism* (Ashgate 2015) and co-editor (with E. Gutiérrez Rodríguez and S. Costa) of *Decolonizing European Sociology. Transdisciplinary Approaches* (Ashgate 2010) and of *Handbuch Entwicklungsforschung* (*Handbook of Development Sociology* with K. Fischer and G. Hauck) (Springer 2015).

Hartmut Elsenhans was a professor of International Relations. His last post was at Leipzig University, Germany. He specialized in development economics, development administration, North-South relations, decolonisation, history and economics of globalization and the capitalist world system. He follows a Keynesian approach of political economy. He taught and published

194   *Contributors*

in India, Pakistan, Bangladesh, Sri Lanka, China, Korea, Taiwan, Vietnam, Turkey, Egypt, Jordan, Tunisia, Algeria, France, Spain, Italy, Norway, Czech Republic, Canada, Mexico, Brazil, United States, Senegal, Portugal, Austria. He completed extensive field research in France, Algeria, Bangladesh, India, Senegal, Mali, Vietnam.

Antonio Gelis-Filho, bachelor at law (University of São Paulo), obtained his PhD in Management at FGV-EAESP in São Paulo, Brazil, where he teaches now in business management and public management programs, both at the undergraduate and graduate levels. His research interests include world-systems analysis, geopolitical aspects of business strategy and comparative law.

Tamás Gerőcs is a political economist at the Institute of World Economics, Hungarian Academy of Sciences. He graduated from the Corvinus University of Budapest (BUC) in 2008. His major degree was International Relations, his minor was Investment and Network Analysis. Tamás is currently doing his PhD at BUC. His research field of interest is Eastern European semi-peripheries with a special regard for economic transformation in Hungary and in other post-socialist countries, theoretical questions in semi-peripheral dependent development with respect to external financial and trade dependencies. He is a member of the Working Group for Public Sociology "Helyzet".

Dmitry Ivanov is professor of sociology at St. Petersburg State University, Russia. His research interests include current sociological theory, social change and new forms of inequality. He is the author of several books published in Russian including *Virtualization of Society* (2000) and *Clam-Capitalism* (2008). His recent international publications are "New Forms of Inequality and Structures of Glam-capitalism" in *Social Evolution & History* 2016. T. 15. № 2 and "The 2017 Problem: A Next Revolutionary Situation" in *The Arab Revolution of 2011: A Comparative Perspective*, ed. by S. Arjomand (State University of New York Press 2015).

Andrea Komlosy is professor at the Institute for Economic and Social History, University of Vienna, Austria, where she is coordinating the Global History and Global Studies programs. She has published on labor, migration, borders and uneven development on a regional, a European and a global scale, recently: "Work and Labour Relations", in: Kocka Jürgen/van der Linden Marcel (eds.), *Capitalism: The Re-Emergence of a Historical Concept* (Bloomsbury 2016); *Centers and Peripheries revisited, Review* Fernand Braudel Center Special Issue XXXVI, 3–4 (2013), ed. by Andrea Komlosy and Klemens Kaps; *Work: The Last 1000 Years* (Verso 2017).

Juho T. Korhonen is a PhD candidate in sociology at Brown University. His research focuses on historical transformations of political entities from empire to nation-state, socialism to post-socialism and from welfare to post-welfare state.

Roberto Patricio Korzeniewicz is professor and chair of sociology at the University of Maryland, College Park (U.S.). His book *Unveiling Inequality* (NY, 2009), co-written with Timothy P. Moran, won the 2010 Best Book Award of the Political Economy of the World-System section of the American Sociological Association. His current research focuses on global patterns of income inequality, social stratification and mobility and on historical and current patterns of political change in Latin America.

Hans-Heinrich Nolte, professor emeritus, Leibniz-Universität Hannover, Germany. New Publications: *Weltgeschichte des 20. Jahrhunderts, Wien 2009* (Böhlau); *Geschichte Russlands, Stuttgart 2012* (Reclam 18960); "The Tsar gave the Order and the Boiars Assented" in *The Medieval History Journal* (Delhi 2016), pp. 229–252; Kurze Geschichte der Imperien (Böhlau 2017).

Zenonas Norkus is professor at the Department of Sociology, Faculty of Philosophy, Vilnius University, Lithuania. His recent book publications include *On Baltic Slovenia and Adriatic Lithuania. A Qualitative Comparative Analysis of Patterns in Post-Communist Transformation* (Apostrofa/CEU Press 2012), *Two Twenty-Year Periods of Independence: Capitalism, Class and Democracy in the First and Second Republics of Lithuania from the Point of View of Comparative Historical Sociology* (in Lithuanian, Aukso žuvys 2014), *An Unproclaimed Empire. The Grand Duchy of Lithuania: From the Viewpoint of Comparative Historical Sociology of Empires* (Routledge 2017, in press).

András Pinkasz is an economist and historian of science. He is a PhD student at the Budapest University of Technology and Economics, since 2016 he has been working as an economic statistician in the Hungarian Central Statistical Office. His recent research interest is the political economy of the world system, economic and social history in Eastern Europe, and how globalization challenges the traditional structures of economic statistics. He is a member of the Working Group for Public Sociology "Helyzet", and the editor of the Hungarian journal *Fordulat*.

David A. Smith is a Professor of Sociology at UC-Irvine. He was Editor of the major sociology journal, *Social Problems*, was Co-Editor of *Contemporary Sociology*, currently is Editor of *International Journal of Comparative Sociology*, and was recently President of the Society for the Study of Social Problems

(2015–2016). His central scholarly interest is in the political economy of the world system, with expertise in Third World development, global urbanization, global commodity chains and social change in East Asia.

Immanuel Wallerstein has been a senior research scholar at Yale University since 2000, having taught previously at many distinguished universities. Among his many books, he is the author of the magisterial four-volume work, *The Modern World System*. Volume IV is recently published.

POLITICAL ECONOMY OF THE WORLD-SYSTEM ANNUALS SERIES

Immanuel Wallerstein, Series Editor

Globalization, Hegemony & Power: Antisystemic Movements and the Global System
Edited by Thomas Reifer (2004)

Allies as Rivals: The U.S., Europe, and Japan in a Changing World-System
Edited by Faruk Tabak (2005)

Hegemonic Decline: Present and Past
Edited by Jonathan Friedman, Christopher Chase-Dunn (2005)

Latino/as in the World-System: Decolonization Struggles in the 21st Century U.S. Empire
Edited by Ramon Grosfoguel, Nelson Maldonado-Torres, Jose David Saldivar (2005)

Islam and the Orientalist World-System
Edited by Khaldoun Samman, Mazhar Al-Zo'by (2008)

Asia and the Transformation of the World-System
Edited by Ganesh K. Trichur (2009)

Mass Migration in the World-System: Past, Present, and Future
Edited by Terry-Ann Jones, Eric Mielants (2010)

198 *Political Economy of the World-System Annuals Series*

Global Crises and the Challenges of the 21st Century
Edited by Thomas Reifer (2012)

Overcoming Global Inequalities
Edited by Immanuel Wallerstein, Christopher Chase-Dunn, Christian Suter (2014)

Social Movements and World-System Transformation
Edited by Jackie Smith, Michael Goodhart, Patrick Manning, John Markoff (2016)

The World-System as Unit of Analysis
Edited by Roberto Patricio Korzeniewicz (2017)

Global Inequalities in World-Systems Perspective
Edited by Manuela Boatcă, Andrea Komlosy, Hans-Heinrich (2017)

INDEX

abandonat, the: Brazil's middle class as 39–42; defined 33–4; origins of 34; scenarios for the evolution of 42–3; why study 36; world-system and geoculture and 36–9
Acemoglu, Daron 95, 96
Acer 165
Agamben, Giorgio 60
agonistics of potentiality 51–3, 60; statehood and 57–60
Alves, Giovanni 40–1
American Society of Plastic Surgeons 163
American Sociological Association xiii
American Sociological Review 11
Amsler, Sarah 54, 57
antisystemic movements 177–9; the Cold War and 182–5; costs of production and 186–8; denunciation of the Old Left and US hegemony 183–4; global South and global North in 189–90; political struggles and turning point in 1995 188–9; US hegemony and 179–81; World Social Forum 189–91; Yalta accords and 181–2
AOL 165
Arrighi, Giovanni 7–8, 15, 42, 80; on the Capitalist World-System (CWS) 85–6; on Creative Destruction 97
Asus 165
attributional measures 6–8

Babones, Salvatore xv, 80
Bank of Poland 121
beauty industry 163, 164
Beckfield, Jason 12, 15
Bergesen, Albert 57
Berlin Wall, fall of 40
billionaires during the Great Recession 98–100, 101–2, 111–13; by economic activity and country 105–11; geographical distribution reconfiguration 102–4, 112–13; rates of convergence and 104–5
Blau, Peter M. 79
Boswell, Terry 58
Braudel, Fernand 33–4, 39, 95
Brazil 191; from "abandoned" to "desperate" middle classes in 39–40; billionaires of 110, 112; mongrel complex in 38–9; semiperiphery in turmoil in 40–2
BRICS, rise of 190
bridge model of international loans 134–9
Brookings Institution 157
Burawoy, Michael 154
Burberry 161
Burke, Edmund 176
Bush, George H. W. 185

Canada 191
capitalism 19–20; abandonat and (*see* abandonat, the); and Brazil's middle class 39–40; costs of production and structural crisis in 186–8; division of labor in Eastern

Europe 134–45; dynamics from logic of virtualization to logic of glamour 158–60; inequality impact of glam- 166–9; middle class and 34; not characterized by capital accumulation 20–1; stable hierarchies due to absence of exploitation in 24–5; statehood and 57–60; tendency to remove unequal technical capabilities within multinational 21–4

Capitalist World-Economy, The 4

Capitalist World-System (CWS) 36, 78–9, 81; core 86, 88; implications for further research and forecast for 91; mega-class structure 88; middle positions 87; mobility in 90–1; new and old activities in 86–7; periphery 86; theoretical rationale for changing N of classes in 82–4

Carroll, William 60

Chase-Dunn, Chris 4, 5, 15, 60; on attributional measures 6–7

China 108–11, 112; Chinese Communist Party (CCP) 182

Clark, Rob 12, 15

classes 79–80; closure process 85; elite 33–4; findings of empirical research on 80–2; low 33–4, 38; middle 33–4, 38–40, 65; struggles and exploitation 175, 191; theoretical rationale for changing N of capitalist world system 82–4; usurpation 85

Clinton, Bill 184

closure 85

Cold War 182–5

coloniality of power xiv, 56

Comecon: bridge model and international loans 134–9; foreign direct investment 139–42

Connolly, William 58

conservatism 176, 183

consumer goods, virtualization of 158–60

contestation, modes of 52

convergence 104–5

core: countries 4, 5, 7; in CWS 86, 88; increased pluralization of varieties of liberalism in 52–3; migration from periphery to 68–9

creative destruction 94–5, 112–13; background and theoretical framework 95–8; defined 95–6; and impact of the Great Recession by economic activity 105; innovation and 96–7; *see also* Great Recession

Cuba 184

Czechoslovakia 136, 146

Dacia 146

Davis, Byron L. 81

de-industrialization 6

dependency theory 82, 89

Dependent Development 5

dependent uncertainty 58

developmentalism 184

division of labor, new industrial 5

Dolce&Gabbana 165

Drangel, Jessica 7–8, 15, 80; on the Capitalist World-System (CWS) 85–6

Duncan, Otis Dudley 79

Eastern Europe, post-socialist 50, 119–20; capitalist division of labor in 134–45; creation of domestic market in 120–2; imitative market economy in the wake of the European Union 125–7; integration and role of transfers 142–5; reindustrializing of 145–9; semi-peripheral dependent development 131–4; state socialism and modernization in 122–5

eBay 165

Economist, The 35

elite 33–4; exploitation of others by 175, 191

Emap 165

energy crisis, 1970s 136

Estee Lauder 163

ethnographic interviewing 66

European Union xiv
European universalism 37
Evans, Peter 9
exploitation 175

Facebook 163, 165
Federal Reserve 136
feminist movement 179
Ferrari 165
fetishism 37
Firebaugh, Glenn 96
flow inequality 169
Forbes 98–100, 101
foreign direct investment (FDI) in Hungary 133, 139–42
Frank, Andre Gunder 19, 134
Freeland, Chrystia 102
French Revolution 175–6, 192

General Motors 146
geoculture and world-system 36–9
geography of the Great Recession 102–4
geopolitics 183–5
Georgia 50, 55
Germany 21–3, 108, 119, 128, 180; Gulf War and 185; Oder-Neisse line 182; Poland modernization and 123–4; reindustrialization of 145–9; trade with Poland 121–2
Gezi protests 41
Gierek, Edward 124, 125, 128
Gini index 157–8
glam-capitalism and inequality 166–9
glamour: -industrial complex structures 164–6; industries 161–4; logic of 158–60
global assemblyline 5
globalization 6
Global Left 191–2
global North 155, 190
Global Right 191–2
global South 155, 189–90
Google 163, 165
Great Britain as part of the Big Three 181
Great Recession, the 98, 111–13; billionaires by economic activity

and country during 105–11; different rates of convergence in 104–5; findings 100–11; geography of 102–4; as global financial crisis 100–1; impact by economy activity 105; impact on billionaires 98–100, 101–2
Gross Domestic Product (GDP) 100–1; during the global financial crisis 100–1; super-urbanized areas and 157
Gross National Income 100, 103–4
grounded theory 66
Gucci Group 161
Gulf War, 1990-1991 185

hegemonic crises 21
hegemony 180–2, 183
Hermés 161
hierarchy, world-system 13–15
Hong Kong 110, 112
hospitality industry 162, 164
Hungary 132; bridge loans and 134–9; in capitalist division of labor 134–45; economic transition in the 1990s and growing reliance on foreign direct investment 133, 139–42; European integration and role of transfers in 142–5; reindustrialization of 145–9
Hussein, Saddam 185
Hyundai 165

ICQ 165, 167
immigrants *see* migration
India 112
Indonesia 108, 112
inequality: defined 64–6; flow 169; how networks respond to 67–74; impact of glam-capitalism on 166–9; institutional 169; migration as response to global 63–4; networked 169; new spatial structures of 155–8; sociological turn to 154–5; temporal 169
innovation 96–7
institutional inequality 169

202 Index

intellectual property rights 189
International Monetary Fund (IMF)
  137, 184
Interpretation of Dreams 37
Iraq 185
ISIL 34
Italy 110

Japan 108, 181; Gulf War and 185

Kentor, Jeffrey 8
Keynesian economics 19
Kick, Edward 8, 9, 10, 12, 81
Kisielewski, Stefan 125
knowledge production 50, 53–4, 60;
  Georgian field of 55; in post-Soviet
  periphery 57
Komlosy, Andrea xv
Kondratieff A-phase 179–80, 186
Kondratieff B-phase 186
Kondratieff waves theory 79, 83–7, 90
Korea 182
Koselleck, Reinhart 52
Kuwait 185
Kyrgyzstan 50, 55

Lakatos, Imre 80
Lamborghini 165
Leder, Andrzej 123
left neoliberalism 40
Lemert, Charles 49–50
Lenin, Vladimir 90
LG 165
liberalism 176, 183
loans, international 134–9
logic of glamour 158–60
logic of virtualization 158–60
L'Oreal 163
Louis Vuitton 162
low classes 33–4, 38
luxury industry 159–60, 161–2, 164
LVMH 161

McKinsey Global Institute 157
Mahutga, Matthew 11, 12, 81, 88, 91
Maistre, Joseph de 176
Marshall Plan 182

Marx, Karl: on classes 80; on fetishism
  37; on owners versus non-owners
  of means of production 82
Marxism 19, 20; classes and 82; post-
  socialism predicament and 54–5
Mexico 188–9
middle classes 33–4, 166–7; from
  "abandoned" to "desperate" in
  Brazil 39–40; geoculture and 38,
  39; as local-level phenomenon 65
migration xiv, 74; to escape political
  and economic stagnation 65–6;
  forging socioeconomic footholds
  in destinations through 69–71;
  for getting out of the periphery
  and into the political-econonomic
  core 68–9; and how networks
  respond to inequality 67–74, 75n2;
  as international process 64–5;
  managing social integration after
  71–4; network structures 66–7;
  racism and 71–3; reputations
  and 73–4; as response to global
  inequality 63–4
minority movements 179
modernization: state socialism and
  122–5; theory 82
mongrel complex 38
Motorola 165
MySpace 165, 167

nationalist movements 177, 178
National Quota Act 71
Negri, Antonio 60
Nemeth, Roger 8, 10, 81
neoliberalism 190; left 40
neo-Marxian approach to classes 79–80,
  83
neo-Weberian approach to classes
  79–80, 83; ideas for 84–91
neo-Zapatistas (EZLN), Mexico 188–9
networked inequality 169
network structures 66–7, 74, 75n2;
  response to inequality 67–74,
  75n2; *see also* migration
New Left Green movement 183
new proletariat 41

News Corporation 165
Nixon, Richard 184
Nokia 164–5
Nora, Pierre 58
North American Free Trade Association (NAFTA) 188–9
nuclear proliferation 184
Nyerere, Julius 56

Old Left 183, 184, 189, 190
onion-like stratification 166–8

Pamuk, Orhan 38–9
Parkin, Frank 85
Pax Occidentalis 43
pear-like bimodal stratification 168–9
perimeter of core countries 7
perimeter of periphery 8
periphery countries 4, 8, 11–12; increased pluralization of varieties of liberalism in 52–3; migration to political-economic core from 68–9; reindustrialization of 145–9; Soviet (*see* Eastern Europe, post-socialist)
Poland 128; creation of domestic market in 120–2; imitative market economy in the wake of the European Union 125–7; state socialism and modernization in 122–5
political economy of the world-system (PEWS) 3, 6, 65; network analysis applied to 9, 13; *see also* world-system perspective
Porsche 162
Porto Alegre 189, 190, 192
postmodernism 57
post-socialist predicament 53–7; *see also* Eastern Europe, post-socialist
Prada 165
Prell, Christine 12
Prew, Paul 12
productivity increases 25
Protestant Ethic and the Spirit of Capitalism, The 167
psychoanalysis 37

racism 71–3
radicalism 176, 183
rapport de forces 179
reindustrialization of Eastern Europe 145–9
relational measures 9–13
Renault 146
reputations 73–4
Review (Fernand Braudel Center) 7
revolt of the precariat 40
Richemont 161
Robinson, James 18, 95, 96
Rodrigues, Nelson 38–9
Rojas, Carlos Antonio Aquirre 59
Russia 119; abandonat of 41, 42–3; billionaires of 108–11, 112

Saad-Filho, Alfredo 40
Sapinski, Jean Philippe 60
Saudi Arabia 185
Schumpeter, Joseph 94–8
semicore 88
semiperiphery 88–9; class analysis in 82; countries 4, 8; dependent development in Eastern Europe 131–4; mongrel complex and 38–9; theory of 85; in turmoil in Brazil and beyond 40–2
sex industry 162–3, 164
Silent House, The 38
Singer, André 41
Skoda 146
Skype 165, 167
Smith, David A. 8, 12, 15, 81, 88, 91
Snyder, David 8, 9, 10, 12, 81
Social Forces 11
social integration of migrants 71–4
socialism 50–1, 119; modernization and state 122–5; post-socialist predicament and 53–7
social movements 177–8
Solidarity 125
South Korea 108–10
Soviet Union, the: Cold War 182–3; collapse of 54, 119, 184–6; Gulf War and 185; as part of the Big

204   Index

Three 181–2; periphery countries 50; post-socialism predicament 53–7; Vietnam War and 182; *see also* Eastern Europe, post-socialist; Hungary; Poland
spatial aspects of inequality 155–8
spokes 69–70
stable hierarchies due to absence of exploitation 24–5
Stalin, Josef 182
state-building 51
statehood 57–60
state socialism and modernization in Poland 122–5
strong periphery 88–9
super-urbanized areas 155–7
Suzuki 146
sweaty consumption 167

Taiwan 108–10, 112
Tanzania 50, 55–6
temporal inequality 169
Thatcher, Margaret 184
TimeSpace 49–50, 51
trade-union movements 179
Transatlantic Trade and Investment Partnership (TTIP) 147–9
trans-brands 164–5
trans-industries 162, 164
transnational corporations (TNCs) 141–2, 147–8
trans-structures 164
trend industry 163, 164
Trend Union 163
Trilateral Commission 184
Trotsky, Lev 37
Turkey 42–3

uncertain worlds 49, 53
United States, the 108–11; Cold War 182–3; Gulf War and 185; hegemony 180–2, 183; Marshall Plan 182; as part of the Big Three 181; post-war strategy 182–4; Vietnam War and 182
urbanization 155–7
US Immigration Act of 1924 71

usurpation 85
utopistics 54

Van Rossem, R. 11
Venezuela 191
Vertu 162
Viana, Silvia 41
Vietnam War 182
Vigvári, András 136
virtualization, logic of 158–60
Volcker, Paul 136, 137
Volkswagen 146

Wallerstein, Immanuel xiv–xv, 7, 14, 43, 59, 80; on the Cold War 182–5; on Comecon countries' self-sufficiency 134; on costs of production and structural crisis in capitalism 186–8; on geoculture 36–7; on integrated production processes 75n1; on liberalism, conservatism, and radicalism 176–7; on nationalist movements 177, 178; on nuclear proliferation 184; research programme anomalies 80–2; on shift in world-systems after World War II 179–82; on social movements 177–8; on transformational TimeSpace 49, 51; on transformations of world-systems 176–92; on unequalising tendencies of capitalism 18–19; on utopistics 54; on world-system zones 4, 5
weak periphery 88, 90
Weber, Max 167
Wenman, Mark 60
WGSN 167
WhatsApp 165, 167
Why Nations Fail: The Origins of Power, Prosperity, and Poverty 95
Wolf, Nikolaus 121
women's movement 179
Wood, Tony 41
Worker's Defence Committee (KOR) 125
World Bank 50, 100

World Economic Forum (WEF), Davos 184, 189–90, 192
World Social Forum (WSF) 189–91
world-system perspective: agonistics of potentiality in 51–3, 60; alternative approaches and specific measures 6–13; attributional measures 6–8; Cold War and 182–5; concept of core/semi-periphery/periphery hierarchy 4; end of World War II shift in 179–82; exploitation in 175; findings of empirical research 80–2; geoculture and 36–9; geopolitics and 183–5; hierarchies measurement 13–15; 19th and 20th century transformation of 176–8; nuclear proliferation in 184; operationalizing positions in 5; postmodernism in 57; rapport de forces in 179; relational measures 9–13; shifts in xiii–xiv; statehood and 57–60; zones 4

world-systems analysis (WSA) 18–20, 28–30; capitalism not characterized by capital accumulation and 20–1; futile hope of relying exclusively on the state for catching up and 26–8; stable hierarchies due to absence of exploitation and 24–5; tendency to remove unequal technical capabilities within multi-nation capitalist system and 21–4
World Trade Center 34
World Trade Organization (WTO) 189
Worth Global Style Network (WGSN) 163
Wright, Eric O. 82
Wundt, Wilhelm 37

Yalta accords 181–3
Yörük, Erdem 41
YouTube 165, 167
Yüksel, Murat 41

zones, world-system 4